An ANZAC on the
Western Front

First published as
The Gallant Company: An Australian Soldier's Story of 1915–18
by Angus & Robertson Limited, Sydney, 1933.

An ANZAC on the Western Front

The Personal Reflections of an Australian Infantryman from 1916 to 1918

HAROLD ROY WILLIAMS

With a Foreword by
Lieutenant-General Sir Talbot Hobbs
KCB, KCMG, VD

Presented and edited by
Martin Mace and John Grehan

Pen & Sword
MILITARY

First published in Great Britain in 2012 by
PEN & SWORD MILITARY
An imprint of
Pen & Sword Books Ltd
47 Church Street
Barnsley
South Yorkshire
S70 2AS

ISBN 978-1-84884-767-5

Typeset by Concept, Huddersfield, West Yorkshire.
Printed and bound in England by CPI Group (UK) Ltd, Croydon, CR0 4YY.

Pen & Sword Books Ltd incorporates the Imprints of Pen & Sword Aviation,
Pen & Sword Family History, Pen & Sword Maritime, Pen & Sword Military,
Pen & Sword Discovery, Wharncliffe Local History, Wharncliffe True Crime,
Wharncliffe Transport, Pen & Sword Select, Pen & Sword Military Classics,
Leo Cooper, The Praetorian Press, Remember When, Seaforth Publishing and
Frontline Publishing.

For a complete list of Pen & Sword titles please contact
PEN & SWORD BOOKS LIMITED
47 Church Street, Barnsley, South Yorkshire, S70 2AS, England
E-mail: enquiries@pen-and-sword.co.uk
Website: www.pen-and-sword.co.uk

Contents

List of Plates

Hall, with battlefield debris removed from the site of the Fromelles (Pheasant Wood) Military Cemetery.

17. A military issue pocket watch, dated 1916 and stamped with the number 61900, pictured soon after being uncovered from the site of the mass burial pits at Fromelles.

18. The same watch having been opened during the subsequent conservation process.

19. A 'Rising Sun' collar badge uncovered during the excavations at Fromelles.

20. An aerial view showing the construction of Fromelles (Pheasant Wood) Military Cemetery underway in late 2009, early 2010.

21. A view of Fromelles (Pheasant Wood) Military Cemetery.

22. The completed Fromelles (Pheasant Wood) Military Cemetery pictured in July 2010 being prepared for the burial service of the final soldier recovered from the site of the original German mass burial pits at Pheasant Wood, Fromelles.

23. The consequences of the Battle of Fromelles can be seen at V.C. Corner Australian Cemetery and Memorial.

24. The Australian Memorial Park is about 200 yards from the V.C. Corner Cemetery and Memorial, on the same road (Rue Delval) in the direction of the village of Fromelles.

25. Australian soldiers with a German A7V tank, nicknamed *Elfriede*, that was captured in the fighting near Villers-Bretonneux in April 1918.

26. The Battle of Amiens. This painting by Australian official war artist Will Longstaff depicts the view towards the west, looking back towards Amiens.

27. German prisoners captured during the Battle of Amiens, 8 August 1918.

28. All that remains of the Amiens Gun – the barrel – on display at the Australian War Memorial in January 2009.

29. The ruins of the church in Villers-Bretonneux after the town was recaptured by Allied troops in April 1918.

30. Australian soldiers on the quayside at Cape Town during a break in their return journey to Australia in the winter of 1918/1919.

Author and Editor's Notes

On active service I kept a diary. On my return to Australia many letters which I had written during the war came again into my possession. From these resources I have compiled this story of wartime life in the Australian Imperial Force.

My gratitude is due for much kindly advice from Dr Gordon Tait, and Major W.J.R. Scott, D.S.O., and for valuable assistance in revising the manuscript to Mr F.M. Cutlack.

H.R. Williams

We have endeavoured to leave Harold Williams' fascinating and valuable account intact and, as far as possible, unaltered, restricting our involvement purely to the addition of a few notes and explanations where applicable.

However, in a very few instances it has been considered prudent to alter some of the terminology used by the author to words or terms that are more appropriate for a modern readership.

Martin Mace and John Grehan
Storrington, 2012

Foreword

I have been requested to write a foreword to a new war book, written by Lieutenant H.R. Williams, formerly a sergeant and later a subaltern in the 56th Battalion, A.I.F.

By force of circumstances I write this at sea *en route* to South Africa and Europe, and I am denied the assistance of my war notes and diary, from which I should like to have refreshed my memory, for some comment upon incidents and events. This excellent story recalls most vividly some of the stirring exploits of a 'gallant company.' Indeed, the title suggests – as probably the author intended – a wider association of great hearts than that alone of 'A' Company 56th Battalion, or even of the 5th Australian Division alone, in which it was a renowned unit.

Mr Williams's book is the best soldier's story I have yet read in Australia. It is written from within the battalion of course, and yet is so general and so lifelike in fidelity to his scenes, that it would illustrate any Australian infantryman's story, in whatever unit he served in France, his memories of life behind the lines and in England as well as of experiences in action. The incidents are not exaggerated, with regard to either the horrors of the war, or the magnificent gallantry, determination, and endurance of the Australian soldier. I fear that many Australians in their desire to forget the war, or their disgust perhaps for some of the so-called war books that have been published, do not yet fully know or appreciate the part Australian soldiers played in that terrible struggle for freedom and humanity. Mr Williams's story now gives them in a concise but most interesting and readable form a great deal of the war record of the A.I.F., and no true Australian can read it without his blood tingling with intense pride in the achievements, the endurance, and the reputation of his countrymen.

As Commander for nearly two years of the 5th Australian Division, I cannot find words adequate to express my admiration and gratitude for their wonderful cheerfulness, loyalty, courage, and devotion to duty, no matter what the risk or the cost. Nothing could daunt or discourage them, and they refused to consider the possibility of failure or defeat.

I especially commend to the people of Australia, and particularly the young men and women of to-day, the last seven paragraphs of the last chapter of this book. There they will find not only something well worth reading and learning, but also something to live up to.

I most sincerely congratulate the author on his story, and earnestly hope it will receive the public appreciation which it undoubtedly deserves.

Lieutenant-General Sir Talbot Hobbs, K.C.B., K.C.M.G., V.D.
Late G.O.C. Fifth Australian Infantry Division
At sea, 1933.

Introduction

WAR WITHOUT END

'The ordeal of the night was plainly visible on all faces, ghastly white showing through masks of grim and dried sweat, eyes glassy, protruding, and full of horror seen only upon men who have lived through a heavy bombardment.' So wrote Harold Roy Williams of his time in the trenches at Fromelles in July 1916 with the Australian 56th Battalion.

Located on the Aubers Ridge, to the south of Armentières, lies the small French village of Fromelles. The battle fought here was the Australian Imperial Force's first major engagement of the First World War on the Western Front.[1] Its objective was to help the British forces that had failed to break through the German positions on the Somme. It was Williams' baptism of fire. It was a bloodbath.

Events started to go wrong almost from the outset. At 11.00 hours on 19 July 1916, as the men of the Australian 5th and British 61st Divisions made their way up to their jumping-off points, the British artillery put down a bombardment on the German front line.[2] It brought a swift response from the enemy.

The German counter-bombardment wrecked havoc on the Allied lines. Soldiers pressing forward through communication trenches were confronted by the injured heading back, desperately trying to reach first aid posts. The route, either way, was already littered with the dead.

On leaving their front line trenches and heading out into No Man's Land, the soldiers were met by an intense barrage of German machine-gun fire. Those that made it across found the enemy's barbed wire intact. A German counter-attack during the night and early hours of the 20th added to the carnage and confusion in the fields in front of Fromelles. By the end of the attack, the very few Allied units that managed to break into the first and second German lines were eventually surrounded, cut off, killed or taken prisoner. No ground had been permanently taken.

One survivor, W.H. 'Jimmy' Downing, later recalled that the 'air was thick with bullets, swishing in a flat, criss-crossed lattice of death. Hundreds were mown down in the flicker of an eyelid, like great rows of teeth knocked from a comb.'

After a night and a day of fighting, some 1,500 British and 5,533 Australian soldiers had been killed, wounded or taken prisoner. The 5th Division, of which the 56th Battalion was a part, was effectively incapacitated for many months afterwards. The Battle of Fromelles is described as the worst ever twenty-four hour period in the history of the Australian Army.

When the Germans were approached to allow the wounded to be recovered from No Man's Land they refused and the Australians had to watch the heart-rending scene just yards in front of them: 'They called out unceasingly for help and water. The sun and flies persecuted them. Those of them who were able to crawl were sniped at by the Germans. One man almost in front of our bay crawled inch by inch towards us, drawing a badly wounded pal with him. He got within a few yards of our parapet when he was fired upon by a German sniper.'

After Fromelles, Williams was thrown into the bloody, muddy struggle of the Somme. He describes the horrors of the battlefield in shocking clarity and the conditions the troops had to endure are revealed in disturbing detail.

Surviving such ordeals would seem to be a blessing but it only meant being available for the next deployment – and more fighting. After a period of leave and a spell on an officers' training course in Britain, following his acceptance of a commission Harold Williams was back at the front.

Soon he was to endure one of the most frightful experiences of the conflict on the Western Front – a gas attack. Despite the training there was little that could be done when gas shells exploded and Williams was badly affected. The doctor told him he should be evacuated but Williams, even though he had lost his voice, refused to leave his men.

Williams' subsequent postings read like a tour of the Western Front battlefields. There was the mud and squalor of the Ypres Salient, after which, back in France, the Australians faced the might of the great German Spring Offensive of 1918. Then came the Battle of Amiens – frequently described as the most decisive battle against the Germans on the Western Front.

When the Germans were pushed back, the Australian 5th Division advanced upon Péronne. Williams described the Australian attack: 'Men collapsed in waves; their comrades hurried past them, with their faces set and the bright steel of their bayonets showing through the murk of the morning of death. None stopped to help those who were stricken down ... any man who went down in this shell-blasted area stood a good chance of being blown to pieces as he lay, so combed was the earth by the density of the German barrage.'

It was here that Williams' luck ran out. Few men could be exposed to so much fighting and escape unharmed. During the advance upon Péronne he felt a painful jar in his left hand and a stinging pain in the upper part of his left thigh. 'Looking at my hand, I saw that I had been struck at the base of two fingers, which felt as if they were broken. I could feel the blood running down my thigh and, as I looked, the leg of my breeches became saturated red.' Williams' war was over. Little more than two months later the Germans surrendered.

In addition to his graphic portrayal of the trench warfare Williams makes a number of profound observations. As an example of this is the following comment he made about the effects of shelling upon soldiers: 'Put men out into holes in the ground where they could see the shells bursting around them and could hear plainly the rattle of the machine-guns, inure them to exposure of weather and battle, and they would fight whenever occasion arose. Take those same men and put them in a dugout (even if composed of only a sheet or two of galvanised iron and a waterproof sheet), and let them stew in their fears for several days, and they would soon get windy ... In the midst of danger and death the man who will force himself to look the unpleasantness straight in the face will retain his courage, but he who tries to cover up his eyes will probably become a gibbering coward. Nothing in war is so cruel, so terrible, so ghastly, as shattered nerves working on the imagination.'

Harold Williams endured it all and lived to tell the tale. Unlike many diarists and commentators of the First World War, Williams presented his story of events in a stark and factual manner, and this adds to its value as an accurate portrayal of the events in which he was directly involved. Indeed he was very alert to the danger of over elaboration, but he could not refrain from making the following observation: 'No one wishes to glorify war, but any man who saw it at first hand for any length of time realized that through all the horror, filth, and suffering there shone something inspiring, stimulating, sacred. This was the heroism, the selflessness of the men who fought for their country and died for their country.'

Williams ends his story on a sober note. Though his account was written, and published, long before the Second World War he could see what the future held. He had fought and survived the most terrible conflict then known to mankind. So atrocious had been the 'Great' War that men had called it the 'war to end war'. Yet Williams was not so deceived.

'The last war did not end war,' he wrote. 'Germany armed and schooled her people for many years towards one end – the conquest of other nations. In self-defence those other nations had to fight.' Another generation would have to continue that fight and war, as Williams fully understood, would know no end.

* * *

An ANZAC on the Western Front is without question one of the most powerfully-written and moving memoirs to have emerged from the First World War and we are fortunate that it will be once again available for the present generations to read and wonder upon.

The discovery of a mass grave of 250 bodies at Fromelles in May 2008 has thrust Williams' first battle into the news once again. Considerable efforts have been, and still are, undertaken to identify the casualties.

A new Commonwealth War Graves Commission cemetery was constructed to accommodate the bodies – the first since the Second World War – and is called the Fromelles (Pheasant Wood) Military Cemetery. The investigation work on the remaining bodies continues, demonstrating just how strong the link between the past and the present still is – a link that is strengthened by accounts such as this.

Notes

1. Although other divisions from 1 ANZAC had been deployed to the Somme, they had not yet been committed.
2. The German front at Fromelles in the summer of 1916 was held by the 6th Bavarian Reserve Division.

Chapter 1

From Liverpool to Cairo

Enlistment – The transport *Argyllshire* – Egypt – The beggars –
Zietoun Camp – Scenes in Cairo – The training battalion at Heliopolis –
'D' Company – 'The Tigers' and the Cairo picket –
Formation of 56th Battalion.
(1 November 1915 to 31 October 1916)

I enlisted on Sunday morning, 18 July 1915.[1] Until the landing of the
Australian troops on Gallipoli the war seemed a remote happening outside
the sphere of my life. But the tale of the landing brought it home to me as
something material and intimate; the names of men I had known swelled
the casualty lists.

Enlisting with me were four pals, Ben Brodie, Jimmy Sowter, Harry
Lucas and Fred Fyall. We four volunteered for the Infantry, this being the
arm which figured largely in the Press reports of the fighting. We began
training at Liverpool camp on 2 August. One looks back on what was
called training there with faint amusement. Still, those were days when
men were shipped overseas as fast as transports became available, and the
facilities for turning out well-trained troops from Liverpool camp simply
did not exist.

We spent several weeks there, and then the training company formed
the 5th Reinforcements of the 20th Battalion – O.C., Lieutenant (Joe)
Campling,[2] and Lieutenant O'Halloran second in command – and we
marched out for embarkation in the transport *Argyllshire* at Woolloomoo-
loo on 30 September. My pal Ben, who was staying behind to go through
an officers' school, carried some of my kit out for me. Day was just
breaking when we moved out of camp. Ben gripped my hand very tightly.
'Look after yourself, Dick, I will soon be over there with you.' Many things
happened before we met again.

The sea passage to Egypt was without special incident. Boxing-matches
were made parades to prevent our body muscles from softening, and
against the feet-relaxing effect of deck shoes we had to spend some hours
each day in wearing our military boots. Excitement mounted as we neared
Egypt, and we anchored in the Bay of Suez early on 30 October.

1

We were astir at daybreak. It was a queer feeling to gaze at the brown barren shore with great hungry treeless hills rising up from the bay. The water shimmered in the heat and the light was so strong that one almost imagined that the hills could be touched by leaning over the rail of the ship. The distance from shore was not realized until a train looking like a toy could be seen moving away from what appeared to be a wharf.

So this was the long-talked of Egypt! It filled one with a kind of awe, as though the body of dead and gone yesterday were laid out for view. It seemed to jeer at our most dearly prized achievements, firm in the knowledge that it would see the passing of the great nations of today, as of all that had been famous in the centuries gone by.

We had been warned to keep the bum-boats away from the ship, and when one came alongside selling newspapers it was driven off with a deck-hose. As the day wore on, the real thieving pedlars hung round in their boats, holding up to the men's gaze all sorts of nicknacks to try to induce trade. One old sinner was lured alongside by Joe and well hosed down – by the O.C. himself. The bum-boat beat a hasty retreat, and from a safe distance its owner traced our pedigrees back to the Stone Age; according to the occupant not one of them was even respectable. Between these diversions and the work of handing in and checking ship's stores and a general clean-up on board we spent the day.

Next morning at 9 a.m. we were alongside the wharf. As batches of troops were disembarked they were formed up and marched to the waiting trains. Seemingly all the native population was on the wharf to gather *baksheesh*. The Egyptian police (looking as hot as hell in their uniforms) had a real gala day caning small urchins and adult cadgers who had the audacity to approach the side of the ship. Most of the beggars managed to get a suit of dungarees. All the old clothes which they collected were donned immediately. One filthy-looking beggar paraded in three pairs of trousers and a red shirt that was worn very full, the tail of which flogged the back of his knees with every stride. We yelled with laughter when this enterprising fellow was chased and well caned by a nimble policeman.

My detachment filed down the gangway late in the afternoon. We entrained in third-class carriages, the roughest in appearance I have ever seen. The seats were of unrelieved wood; the windows were without glass and looked as if they had been hewn out with a tomahawk. The smell of unwashed persons hung about heavily.

Before we started the swarm of beggars moved from the ship side to the train imploring *baksheesh*. Some of the filthy children strengthened their appeal by saying: 'No favver, no muvver, poor little bastard, gibbit *baksheesh*.' One unfortunate little chap was horribly deformed, a deal filthier than the rest, and got over the ground on all fours like an animal. He scored well from the troops, notwithstanding that a band of small

2

urchins warned us that he was 'a bloody German'. As we steamed out the more able-bodied ran alongside the train, so long as they thought there was a chance of having something useful thrown to them.

The train soon ran out into the barren, brown desert. For miles the only sign of life would be a small encampment of Indian cavalry, patrolling the line. Occasionally we would pass areas that were part of an irrigation scheme, where green foliage contrasted strongly with the gauntness of the desert. Eventually after nightfall we reached a town of some size, known as Zagazig.[3] Here the carriages were besieged by more locals selling fruit, 'Eggs a cook,' 'Cakes a Cairo,' sherbet, cigarettes.

Of course, a lot of our chaps would buy. One gave a hawker a sovereign; the trader went to get change, and must have found it difficult – he had not returned when the train pulled out. One enterprising youth staggered into our carriage with a huge melon. Some of our crowd bought it at a job price. The melon was cut and proved to be of the pie variety.

Each of the purchasers armed themselves with a piece and did not have long to wait for their revenge. A massive local, with the front of his robe bulging with oranges, bustled into the carriage crying 'Oringes, two for a 'arf'. He was allowed to get well into the centre of the carriage before the bombardment opened upon him. He tried to bolt through, but was collared low, upset, his legs held high in the air so that his oranges ran out of his blouse, and then bundled out on the platform into a wailing mass of humanity.

Our train pulled into a siding about 11 p.m. We scrambled into our equipment, and fell in under floodlights. We marched off under the direction of guides along a good road, on both sides of which were military depots and headquarters. Where the road branched to the left was a large guard tent with the flaps folded up, from the darkness of which Australian voices hailed us asking whence we had come. After exchanging a few pleasantries with these voices we found ourselves before our quarters, large huts made of reed matting. We were in Zietoun Camp, outside Cairo.

Zeitoun was a large camp of Australian and New Zealand troops of all arms. Some were housed in low huts composed of reed matting, but many in the regulation bell tents. On the opposite side of the road from us were artillery, Light Horse, and A.S.C. detachments. The majority of the men in the infantry camp were reinforcements, with a number of details, men from the battalions just discharged from hospital, clink, etc., and awaiting drafts back to their units. Mess huts with long tables and forms had been erected. To the rear of these were the rough cook-houses, and at intervals further back, were shower-baths, and long washing-places. Much further to the rear again were the latrines and incinerators. The cook-houses had iron roofs but no sides, and the food was cooked in open dixies over

3

shallow fire trenches. This was a very bad arrangement, on account of the sand which found its way into the food during the process of cooking.

Our first work was that of erecting tents for ourselves – with a promise of leave to Cairo in the afternoon. A friend from the 14th Battalion offered to show us the sights of Cairo. We caught a train from the near-by station and were in the city in fifteen minutes. From the station we came out into a large square with flower-beds; on the city side many fine buildings could be seen. Hardly had we appeared in the square when from a cafe across the way a flying cloud of 'Boot-clean' boys made for us, carrying their tools of trade and yelling at the top of their voices.

A very small urchin was well out in front, with black robe ballooning behind him, his face and hands red with the mixture that passed for tan boot-polish in his trade, and a once-upon-a-time white skull-cap pulled tightly over his head. He was the first to reach us and panted out: 'Clean your boots for 'alf a disaster, Mr Mackenzie.' He waited for no reply but dived on the nearest boot and brushed the dust of the desert off in a twinkling. No doubt he would have completed the job, only our guide beat him and the rest of the crowd away with his cane. Every Britisher was addressed by some Scotch surname, usually Mackenzie.

Our first purchases were canes. Every soldier carried one mainly for the purpose of beating away persistent street sellers. All these pests had evidently graduated in a school of salesmanship which turned out one-trip sellers – if they made a sale the purchaser was robbed so brazenly that the seller dared not come back again.

At the railway end of the Wazir was a donkey stand, and here, flushed with alleged whisky and other things, were some of our company who had dodged the morning fatigue, riding races along the street on hired donkeys propelled by the waddy of Abdul, their master. Leaving this festive exercise, we entered the Wazir, and saw the ruins of several houses which had been burned by the members of a New South Wales Brigade in a great riot some time previously.

The street was rather narrow with high, Moorish buildings on both sides, and had many evil-smelling lanes running off it. Our guide led us to the largest house in the street, where in a large room a penny-in-the-slot piano shrieked tunes to a great muster of soldiers: Australians, New Zealanders, Jocks, and Tommies. The crowd was laced with women of many nationalities – coal-black Nubians, slim copper-coloured Arabs, a few Frenchwomen, fair-headed Russians, but low-browed, black-headed Greeks predominated.

We left this den and entered a small lane, not more than six feet wide, where we sank to our ankles in black, stinking mud. Here we found butchers' shops with the carcasses of sheep and goats exposed to dust and black with flies. Through these revolting purlieus we were led to the scene

4

of a cancan dance performed for our amazed education at the price of half a piastre a head. We concluded our first afternoon in Cairo in the shade of a cafe, sucking iced Pilsner through a straw, and finished up with a visit to the reading-rooms, wash-house, and restaurants conducted by the Y.M.C.A. in the Esbekia Gardens.

Drill began next day. We marched out into the desert and a not very brilliant-looking Tommy instructor supervised us in bayonet-fighting. He was weedy, with a large helmet, drill tunic, shorts and a pair of legs like a meatless Friday. After the grotesque position we had been taught as 'On Guard' at Liverpool camp, this chap's upright boxer-like stand seemed to be ideal. It was whispered round that he had been in the retreat from Mons; we gazed at him in silent awe. For a week the routine continued. We were exercised in the desert during the morning; parade finished at noon; and afternoon drill did not start until 2.30 in order to avoid the noonday sun.

Then on 14 November came news that we were to move. That afternoon we marched a couple of miles to our new camp at Heliopolis. We were, we thought, a stage nearer to Gallipoli, whither had gone several detachments from our lines.

At Heliopolis we formed 'D' Company, in a training battalion composed of the 4th Reinforcements of the 17th, 18th, 19th Battalions, and 5th Reinforcements of the 20th. In many respects our new camp was superior to Zietoun which was only a staging-camp for all arms. But evidently the evacuation of the Peninsula had even then been decided upon, although we did not suspect it. Separate training battalions were being formed of the reinforcements of each brigade.

Inside the tent on the right was our star comedian, Alfie. Next was his friend Jacko, with a perpetual smile and a mouthful of gold teeth. Then a quiet, decent, heavily-built fellow named Wally. A small, quaintly-spoken Welshman, who was of course called Taffy. Harry Binskin, father of five children, with the spirit of patriotism strong in him, who afterwards was one of those heroes, a battalion stretcher-bearer, for many months in France. Then my pal Harry, small in stature, but possessing the gameness of two men. Another pal, Fred, small, flaxen-headed, with an outsize in pipes and plenty of talk, known as the 'Tomtit.' Andrews, a country lad, and his mate Avis, two very fine fellows. Then Jimmy Sowter, my pal from start to finish, who would give you his shirt. I knew no truer mate in the hard days that were to come.

For the months we lived together there was never a quarrel, nor any of the bickering that makes life so miserable. Fate dealt cruelly with some of the members of that happy tent.

Alfie was wounded early in the piece, and was returned to Australia. Jacko, with his ready smile, was blinded by a shell-flash, whilst serving with the artillery, and the last I heard of him was from St Dunstan's Hospital in London. Harry Gaskill was killed near Fleurbaix, when the Germans battered the front line into dust and raided the 20th Battalion, early in 1916. Fred got his issue in the costly blunder of Fromelles. Harry returned invalided from Egypt to Australia, re-enlisted, and was wounded at Bullecourt. Andrews was killed at Pozières, and Avis lost a leg. Binskin was still carrying on early in 1918, but I do not know what happened to him. I heard that Wally was killed on the Somme in 1916. Jimmy was badly wounded at Flers, returned to the battalion, got a commission, and was still on deck when the war finished. Of Taffy's fate I do not know; he went to another battalion.

Our first parade here revealed to us a Tommy major, who had taken charge of our training battalion. He was a man of medium height, and immense girth, so cumbersome that his walk was a waddle. He was dressed in a khaki-drill tunic, and jodhpurs (breeches that balloon at the hips, and fit skin tight round the calves and ankles). He was a Regular and was said to have been in the retreat from Mons. He must have had a good start the night before, in a railway train. His adjutant was a small, weedy soldier in green-toned khaki, who carried an outsize in sticks, and had a habit of plucking at the peak of his cap, and then smelling his fingers. We had several instructors. These were also Regulars, all Mons men. They murdered their h's, insisted much on brass-work, and dearly loved to rub into us our lack of soldierly qualities.

Within twenty-four hours of the reinforcement camps being formed near Heliopolis the town was crowded with that scum of humanity which always clung to the outskirts of our camps in Egypt to batten on the soldiers' money. One vile-looking, cross-eyed individual appeared leading a filthy monkey about the streets. It danced to the beat of a stick on the ground and the crooning of a can-can tune by its master.

The day came when this individual encountered the opposition of two young natives with two much smaller monkeys. The older man was very jealous of this; things were brought to a head when the large monkey attacked one of the smaller animals in the opposition entertainment. This was followed by an assault by its master upon one of the youngsters. Some of the Australians separated the warring monkeys and, dragging the heavyweight Egyptian off his opponent, listened to their arguments for some time. Finally, taking the matter in hand, we moved the disputants to the end of the street. Here in a large sandpit it was decided to let the three men fight the matter out under Rafferty rules.

We decided that the heavyweight cross-eyed one should fight the two young fellows; a large Australian, taking off his tunic, made himself referee. In the orthodox manner of the boxing ring, he introduced the big fellow as 'Abdul Cross-Eyes, Heavyweight Champion of Heliopolis;' one of the youths as the 'Featherweight Champion of the Wazir;' and the other as the 'Lightweight Champion of the Esbekia Gardens.'

The spectators gathered round the lip of the pit. When all was ready the referee said, 'Let 'em go!' and scrambled out of the pit. There commenced a fight which, if it had been filmed, would have made someone a fortune. The heavyweight attacked. Many feet before he reached the nearest of his opponents, he beat the air with his arms. Roaring at the top of his voice, the lightweight took to flight.

While the big fellow was in hot pursuit, the featherweight leaped on his back, and started to beat him on the crown of the head with a downward smack of his open hand. This gave encouragement to the fleeing light-weight champion. He turned, managed to get a hold of the heavyweight's blouse, and hanging on with both hands, frantically kicked the cross-eyed one in the shins with his bare feet.

The big fellow screamed, and tried to dislodge the opponent perched on his back. At last he fell and the two youngsters sat on top of him and used their hands, feet, and teeth. It was a whirl of dust and a tangle of straining, sweating, and screaming natives.

The lookers-on howled with laughter, and urged the combatants on with cries of 'Good boy, Abdul!' 'Hang on to him, Mohammed!' and so on. Finally the heavyweight champion lay still in the bottom of the pit sobbing. The referee thereupon stopped the combat, crowned the two youths as the winners and, bestowing a kick upon the stern of the sobbing giant, told him to take his lousy monkey and 'imshi.' From our experience of the Greeks and Armenians in Cairo we began to sympathize with the Turks. The low drinking-dens where soldiers were sold alleged whisky – the contents disclosed under analysis could hardly be believed – were invariably conducted by Greeks. We had in our company a number of young bloods from Balmain and Rozelle who, from their first days in Liverpool camp, had christened themselves 'The Tigers,' thirsting for the enemy's blood.

On 21 November the company was called upon to send an escort to Babel Hamid Barracks in Cairo to bring back the Tigers under arrest. Late in the afternoon escort and prisoners reported back to camp. The Tigers bore the marks of having been engaged in a fierce combat. Their faces were cut, dry blood caked their uniforms, and they were smeared with tar from the roadway.

They had a terrific tale to tell. They had gone into Cairo with their pay, and indulged in some of the alleged whisky. This dope had turned them into lunatics. They had got into a brawl in the big cafe near the railway station, and had kicked the orchestra – bagpipes and drums – from the rostrum. The military picket was summoned and the Tigers adjourned to the roadway to await its arrival, singing ribald songs and yelling the war-cries of their favourite football team back in Sydney.

The picket, drawn from some English battalion, arrived in charge of a lieutenant with two Red Caps. They greatly outnumbered the Tigers, but these were in that fighting state of drunkenness that reeked not of odds opposed to them. When the picket endeavoured to arrest them, the war started. Such a Donnybrook had seldom been seen even in Cairo. The Tigers with their backs to the wall fought like men possessed. Many were the opponents that bit the dust under the flails of their fists; but numbers prevailed in the end, and the Tigers submitted when they were strewn along the roadway with men sitting on them to keep them down while handcuffs were put on their wrists. Now they were battle-scarred, and suffering from the effects of their beating and the awful dope they had drunk.

At orderly room next morning Lieutenant Joe Campling pleaded for them in such a manner that they were let down lightly, and for this the Tigers were so grateful that with Joe they ever afterwards conducted themselves like pet lambs.

Suddenly, on 19 December, as we lined up on the dixies for breakfast, we received news that flabbergasted us. Anzac had been evacuated. The news travelled around like wildfire. We wondered how it would be received in Australia. Although men from the Peninsula had told us that operations in that theatre of war had reached a stalemate, still, the news stunned us. We knew that reinforcement camps in Egypt were packed with men eager to do their bit; and we often wondered why we were not sent across. Now it was all plain to us. The only cheering part of the news was that the evacuation had been carried out without the loss of a man.

By early January we were heartily sick of the training battalion and wanted to be sent to our own unit. We were still only reinforcements, and on that account were somewhat looked down upon by the men of the battalions. Word had got around that a new Division was forming in Australia and that units were to be made up of the abundance of rein-forcements in Egypt. None of us wanted to be in these.

Our training consisted of much route marching and practising in attack. We would move out in column of route; from this deploy into artillery formations at the double; into a series of waves which advanced in short rushes to build up a firing-line; and finally to the assault, a long line of glistening bayonets and shouting, charging men.

These movements, carried out constantly in battle order over the soft sand, brought us into a state of great physical fitness. The open-air life, plain food, regular exercise, and camaraderie in the ranks made us all strong, healthy, laughing, young animals. The army was beginning to teach us how much good there is in the companionship of our fellow-men, and to know one another with an intimacy impossible in civilian life.

We had not long to wait for the change we desired. On 22 January a large detachment from our company in the training battalion was sent to join the 20th Battalion.[4] Seven out of our tent went. The list of names was made up in the Orderly Room, and neither Jimmy's, Fred's, nor mine was included.

Most of the Tigers went, and they were nearly all killed in the attack on Pozières Ridge. A few more days of uncertainty remained among those left behind, and then came the news that we were to form part of a new battalion, the 56th, in the 14th Infantry Brigade, 5th Australian Division.[5] In this new importance we entrained for Tel-el-Kebir, a camp lying out in the desert in part of the Egyptian battlefield of 1882, and on the railway between Cairo and Suez.

Notes

1. A 26-year-old Warehouseman when he volunteered, Harold William's date of enlistment from the Nominal Roll is 3 August 1915. He signed his Attestation papers the following day. Volunteers were questioned at their place of enlistment in order to complete these documents which included information such as the recruit's name and address, next-of-kin, date and place of birth, occupation, previous military service, and distinguishing physical characteristics. Recruits were asked to sign their Attestation papers, indicating their willingness to serve overseas. His papers describe Williams as being 5' 6" tall, of dark complexion, having black hair and brown eyes.
2. Lieutenant A.E. 'Joe' Campling certified Williams' Attestation papers at Liverpool on 9 September 1915.
3. Situated in the eastern part of the Nile delta and an important centre of the corn and cotton trade, the town of Zagazig is in Lower Egypt. It is some forty-seven miles north-north-east of Cairo.
4. The 20th Battalion Australian Imperial Force was raised at Liverpool in New South Wales in March 1915. A number of the battalion's original recruits had already served with the Australian Naval and Military Expeditionary Force in the operations to capture German New Guinea in 1914. The 20th left Australia in late June, trained in Egypt from late July until mid-August, and on 22 August landed at ANZAC Cove. Following the end of the Gallipoli campaign, the 20th returned to Egypt. Having been transferred from there to France, the 20th entered the trenches of the Western Front for the first time in April 1916. The following month it became the first Australian battalion to be raided by the Germans.
5. The 56th Battalion is officially listed as being raised in Egypt on 14 February 1916, as part of a 'doubling' in size of the AIF. Half of its recruits were Gallipoli veterans from the 4th Battalion, whilst the remainder were nearly all fresh reinforcements from Australia. Reflecting the composition of the 4th, the 56th was predominantly composed of men from New South Wales.

Chapter 2

Tel-el-Kebir and the Desert March

'A' Company, 56th Battalion – Tent mates – Captain Fanning –
Training on the desert – The march from Tel-el-Kebir to Ferry's Post.
(16 February to 29 March 1916)

We found ourselves in 'A' Company of the 56th Battalion. Our nucleus of war-tried officers, N.C.O.s, and men, was drawn from the 4th Battalion, 1st Australian Division. Practically all the officers and N.C.O.s of this nucleus were original Anzacs.[1] I never had the honour to serve in the 1st Australian Division, but I should like to pay a tribute to those leaders that were now to mould us into fighting troops. These officers and N.C.O.s from the 4th Battalion were fine soldiers; they knew their jobs, did them thoroughly, and gradually instilled into untried men that confidence which they themselves had gained in the bloody welter of the Peninsula.

In my tent were several who had come to the training company at Heliopolis. There was 'Long Jack' Edgar, a tall 6 feet 3 inches bushman, thin as a whipping-post, weighing about 10 stone, long legs and arms, a face burned to blackness with the sun of far west of New South Wales. His eyes were deep sunk, his skin like parchment, his teeth worn down by many pipes. He was cool-headed, resourceful, and had one of those sunny natures that can laugh and joke best at a time when one would get sore eyes looking for a silver lining in the black clouds of trouble. From head to toe Long Jack was an Australian. He throve on endless smoking and tea strong enough to poison a goanna. He was still a front line soldier when the war finished.

Next was Barney, a thickset, sturdily-built chap who in face and build so much resembled me that we were taken for brothers. Bob S—— also hailed from the Western Plains. His skin was so sun-tanned as to make his blue eyes the most prominent feature in his face. He was a very pleasant chap.

Then there were men who had come from the 4th Battalion – 'Snowy,' Alex O'Rourke, Tibby, and 'Grenna'. Snowy, who had been at the battle of Lone Pine, was the only member of the tent who had seen war.[2] Alex O'Rourke was built like a gorilla. He stood about 5 feet 7 inches and

10

weighed 13 or 14 stone; massive chest, thick neck, short sturdy legs, arms bulging with muscle and reaching below his knees, a round face distinguished by the high cheekbones of his Irish forefathers, strong teeth, and a close-cropped head of straw-coloured hair. He possessed the strength of an ox and the sunny nature of a boy. He was bush-bred with very little schooling, and had toiled hard since early youth. Before enlisting he had been a timber-sawyer. His coolness, courage, and great strength were to be the means of succouring many a stricken man in France.

Some of the most treasured memories that I retain of the A.I.F. centre around big, good-hearted Alex O'Rourke; Tibby was O'Rourke's pal. Grenna was a thin-built, black-haired little chap with very dark eyes shining from a face as small as a child's. He was always smoking an outsize in pipes, and was most argumentative. He came in for a good deal of banter in the tent, and was once goaded into saying that he had 'as much guts as any man present'. This statement was received with loud cheers from the crowd, but Grenna proved his boast before many months had gone by.

Breakfast over, on our first day in the new camp, we were paraded by Lieutenant Campling and handed over to a captain. We marched out a little way into the desert, formed line, and stood at the slope, while the captain walked slowly along the line and seemed to peer into each face. In a slow drawl he gave the command 'Order Arms', and then stood us at ease. Then he called Campling aside.

Already the personality of this captain impressed us. He stood about 5 feet 10 inches in height, and was of very active build; his tunic of the best cloth, buff riding-breeches, puttees rolled in the cross, hair as black as midnight, clean shaven, white teeth, head with the poise of a game cock, large blue eyes and heavy black eye-brows. He wore his hat turned down and set at a rakish angle that somehow indicated the character of the wearer. Such is my memory of Captain Fred Fanning on the first day I saw him at Tel-el-Kebir. When the war has become almost forgotten in the mist of passing years the memory will still be vividly with me of this striking personality and great leader of men.

None of us ever forgot the education he imparted to us and the manner of it. He had a picturesque vocabulary; he knew the sort of training the 4th Battalion had gone through when the 1st Division was being made ready for Gallipoli; and he meant his company in the 56th Battalion to learn in the same style with the same thoroughness. His first parades, the performance of even the simplest movements, shook all our confidence in our military abilities.

One of the earliest things he did was to show us how field-equipment should be worn. Our web equipment was a well thought-out system for giving the infantryman in handy form cartridges, water, food, bayonet, entrenching-tool, pack and rifle. We drilled in what was called battle order, the pack being discarded. Captain Fanning made us strip our equipment to the belt. Then the latter was fixed in such a. manner that the weight thereof was placed where it could most easily be carried – above the hips – and so tightly that it did away with that swaying of gear which took so much out of men on a long march. The new method was a wonderful improvement on the slipshod fashion we had used. It was characteristic of Captain Fanning that this item, overlooked in our previous training, should be one of his first lessons.

His personality gripped us. He made us jump to his commands as nobody had done before. We feared him, but even his dress had some romantic touch about it that fascinated us. I imagined him to have been in some other life a pirate chief. I have referred to the manner in which he wore his turned-down hat, cocked at a rakish angle. Our hats had to be adjusted likewise to make us look like men, he said.

Fanning's company sergeant-major was a snowy-headed Scotchman named Dykes. He spoke with a strong flavour of porridge and burrs. But he was right on the ground floor in knowing his work. He had served in the Imperial Army before coming to Australia, had enlisted in 1914, was at the landing on Gallipoli, and had been badly wounded in the attack on Lone Pine. In him very strong was that military spirit which most Scotch-men seem to take in with their mother's milk. He rose to commissioned rank, and died in front of Flers in 1916.[3]

A few days after the battalion was formed, Lieutenant Joe Campling left us to join the 20th Battalion. He came along the lines to say goodbye to the men of his old company, and we felt very sorry to see him go. Joe was a 'roarer', but very popular. He was outspoken, filled the bill as a man's man, and was of the type that made some of the best leaders in the A.I.F. He was killed near Bois Grenier in France, in the 20th Battalion, early in 1916.[4]

Campling's batman left our tent, and in his place moved in Peter Hughes. Born in London of Irish parents, Peter had been a rover. He stood fully 6 feet, was red-faced, slightly stooped, and one of those loosely-built men who can call up astounding reserves of strength; well-read, worldly wise, witty, and possessing a knack of summing-up men and of tale-telling that made him the greatest humorist that I met in the A.I.F. He had a thirst that had become chronic and, when in the humour, told stories of the inside of Sydney's lockups which were classics. He furnished me, for one, with unbounded amusement for many months to come.

The command of our battalion passed to Lieutenant-Colonel Alan Humphrey Scott, D.S.O., a tall athletic-looking man, still in his early twenties. He had won the D.S.O. at Lone Pine, where he had taken charge of the 4th Battalion when Colonel MacNaghten was wounded.[5] Snowy told

12

us that he had seen Scott during the fight take his turn at bomb-throwing from a trench-block which was stubbornly contested for hours.

The days had grown very warm; drilling on the desert was hot work. From the parade ground we would often see the most wonderful mirages away in the distance – a sea studded with islands, clumps of palms around a small lake, and so on. At night the jackals howled in the desert much to the alarm of Alfie. He let his fears be known; and some members of the tent promptly devised blood-curdling tales of the ferocity of these more or less harmless animals. Alfie would not venture outside of the tent after lights out for a fortune.

A chap from the next tent, knowing Alfie's fears, came one night, and scratched on the outside of the tent above Alfie's head, making a low growling noise while doing so. Alfie passed that night, sitting with his back against the tent-pole. A few nights later Jacko secured from somewhere unknown a large tom-cat. After lights out we one by one feigned sleep. Alfie, with his blanket over his head, settled down for the night. Suddenly Jacko threw the tom-cat on Alfie's recumbent form, simultaneously yelling 'Jackals!' It was hard to say which was the more alarmed, Alfie or the cat. Alfie rose in a panic, and knocked the rifle-rack from the tent-pole. The tent shook as we all tried to dodge the maddened torn, and the frantic Alfie in their search for the outlet. Alfie reached it and burst through into the night with the tom-cat a good second.

For a month our training was strenuous. The day's work began with physical jerks before breakfast, during this hour we were kept on the move, and came back into camp generally at the double. Then after breakfast and the inspection, we were taken into the desert and graduated through rifle exercises and platoon drill to company and battalion drill. We had been issued with khaki drill uniforms and sun helmets. The cotton drill trousers were as hard as boards and cut our legs badly during the desert route marches. Generally we returned to camp with our clothing saturated with perspiration, and in many cases with thighs bleeding from the chafing of the cotton material.

These desert marches were the hardest training imaginable. Carrying the seventy pounds of the fully equipped infantry soldier, we sank deeply into the soft sand of the desert at every step. The perspiration streamed from our faces and bodies, the sun burned down on us and seemed to strike upwards, too, with a hot breath from the sand. The desire to drink had to be curbed; our officers were most strict in forbidding the guzzling of water; often men fell unconscious under the strain.

This training caused many weaker men to break down. But those with the strength and determination to stick it out were so hardened by it that they afterwards lived under conditions that would have cracked-up men who had not gone through the gruelling that we got while the

13

56th Battalion was being moulded by the leaders who had seen what modern war demanded of men. The climax to it was the brigade's famous dreadful desert march from Tel-el-Kebir to the canal defences at Ferry's Post, via Moascar, on 27, 28, and 29 March.

On the first day reveille sounded at 4.30 a.m. Blissfully ignorant of what was in front of us, we breakfasted in the dim light. Water bottles were filled, and packs adjusted. A heavy fog hung low over the desert; through this a silent line of Indian troops in charge of big camels picked up our blankets, which had been rolled by sections and platoons. The battalion moved off; after marching for about half an hour we reached the assembly point. By this time our clothing, boots, and equipment were wet from the moisture of the blanket of fog through which we had come.

After some little delay we got on the move. Our battalion was in line of companies, in column of route. On our left was another battalion in the same formation, and several hundred yards in our rear were the two other battalions of the 14th Brigade in similar formation and covering those in front. Within the companies the fours were opened out to twice their usual distance and interval to give marching room, minimize the dust, and allow all the air possible.

As the brigade moved off the sun broke through the fog bank; this heat so early in the morning gave us warning that we were in for a scorching day. We marched to a schedule; on the move for fifty minutes; rest eight minutes; at two minutes to the hour, fall in covered off at the slope; move on the hour. This was observed throughout the day. The brigadier-general commanding the brigade and his staff-officer were mounted. The brigadier was a long-legged professional soldier from South Australia. I feel sure that most of the survivors of the 14th Brigade who took part in this march have an indelible picture in their memories of his rangy form sitting his black horse.

Captain Fanning was up and down the company as soon as we started, keeping us in proper formation. He must have covered a tremendous amount of extra ground, though certainly he did not have the full pack which we carried. The desert for some distance was shingly and undulating. But by 10 a.m. we had got into country where the sand was very soft. At every step we sank to our ankles, the sun burned his scorching rays on our backs, the perspiration from our bodies began to show in white stains upon our tunics and equipment. The dust rose in fine white clouds, covering our faces like flour, choking our breathing, and burning our lips and mouths. The craving for drink was damnable; but we knew that the surest way to blow out like a broken-winded horse was to gulp water. Officers and N.C.O.s had strict instructions to prevent men from using their water-bottles except at halting-places. Even then only a sip was allowed.

All the morning we marched to schedule. A few men began to drop out – the physically weak, those lacking in determination, or those with sore feet. Officers in rear of companies and battalions kept on sending men back into the ranks who were capable of further effort. Any man genuinely distressed was given a chit which entitled him to attention by the field ambulance which marched in the rear of the brigade.

We halted for our midday meal at Quassain, the scene of a night-attack by British troops upon the forces of Arabi Pasha during the war of 1882. It was on a slight rise, and quite close to the railway line which had the sweet-water canal running parallel on the further side. Of course, none of us were allowed to go near this waterway.

The midday meal consisted of bully beef and biscuits, washed down with a drink from our water-bottles. The sun fairly scorched us; to gain some little shelter we spread our waterproof sheets across our rifles and huddled in this meagre shade. We felt that water had not in our past life been appreciated at its full value. We could have drunk the contents of our bottles at a draught, but dared not. After an hour's halt, we got on the move again. 'A' Company had lost a few men, but considering the heat and the ground over which we had marched we had not done badly.

We still marched to the schedule and, during the heat of the afternoon despite the efforts of Captain Fanning and his company officers, more men fell out. None of us were sorry when, about four o'clock, after fourteen miles marching, we reached our camping ground for the night, near a small station named Mahsama. We lay on our equipment and stretched our weary limbs, the best among us feeling that we had undergone a severe strain.

Shortly afterwards our stragglers were detrained. They had been threatened by a staff officer that they would probably be returned to Australia for falling out during the march. It was dark before our meal was ready – bully beef, biscuits, and a very small quantity of strong tea. Pickets had been posted on the railway line to prevent any men from crossing to the fresh-water canal. After tea our water-bottles were filled for the next day's march. We fell asleep on the sand in spite of the cold and lack of covering.

The heavy dew had us wet and shivering long before daylight. We were astir very early, and glad to get warm at the cook's fire. Breakfast consisted of a very small portion of particularly salt bacon, biscuits, and jam, with a little tea. When we paraded Captain Fanning told us that 'A' Company had lost far too many men for his liking on the previous march, and that this offence was not to be repeated.

At 7 a.m. the brigadier-general blew his whistle and said: 'Your route is due east,' indicating that point of the compass with a wave of his hand, and we were on the move again, formation as yesterday, but with the leading battalions of the brigade changed. We were now in the rear of the leading battalion, and on the right. The heat of the early morning warned us of another scorching day. Once we got warmed up, we swung along at a good pace. The ground was fairly good, and during the forenoon not a man of 'A' Company fell out.

At midday we halted within easy distance of a large oasis, whose tall shady palms mocked our wish to escape from the burning rays of the sun. We ate our tasteless meal on the sand. A picket had been posted to prevent any of us from entering the oasis. We heard that there was a well among the palms. Again we tried to shelter from the sun as we ate under our waterproof sheets stretched from rifles. During the hours of the march on both days I had kept a pebble in my mouth; this had eased my thirst somewhat, but now the roof of my mouth was becoming very tender.

The meal over, we resumed the march in the hottest part of the day. Our route till the midday halt had been parallel with the railway line. But now we turned away from the line to the left and headed for some rising ground, leaving the oasis on our right flank. We had gone in this new direction perhaps a mile, when we found ourselves trying to march up hills of drift sand. At every step we sank to our calves and our packs suddenly became crushing burdens. The sun struck up from the white sand with the heat of a furnace. The company lost its excellent march-formation of the morning; despite Captain Fanning's endeavours to keep his fours closed up, men began to straggle and at last to drop out.

It was like walking on a treadmill climbing that first hill of sand. At last we reached the top, and on the descent we saw, set in a basin below, two small lakes of water, the colour of washing blue, surrounded by steep banks of white glistening sand. To this picture was added several palm trees growing alongside of the lakes. The men baa-ed like a flock of sheep, and in spite of our distress we laughed at ourselves for making such a noise. The sand surrounding the lakes was so soft and steep that we slid down to the water's edge on our backsides. We passed between the two pools of water which were very salty, and began the long climb up another hill of sand. Here the men began to drop like flies.

The brigadier and his staff found that their horses could not climb the hill of drift sand and dismounted. We reached the summit of the ridge in a very distressed condition. Here we were given eight minutes' rest. Our platoon sergeant seemed to be in rather a bad way, but in spite of his apparent distress Captain Fanning told him to pull himself together and look after his platoon. I still had some water left in my bottle, and offered the sergeant a drink. Although a white foam was on his lips he refused and marched until he fell unconscious under his pack.

After the next fifty minutes' marching the general from his horse pointed to our camp which he said was only an hour's march away. Incidentally it was almost three hours later that the first of our brigade reached the indicated camp. From where we halted the tents looked like white thimbles on the sand. Thenceforward the march became a debacle. Men fell unconscious in the sand and were left lying where they fell. Some became delirious and raved. The strongest among us felt that his strength had been taxed to the utmost. Companies dwindled to mere handfuls. Officers (although with empty packs, because of their extra movements in the companies) fell out exhausted, along with N.C.O.s and men. At each halt now I stripped my shirt and tunic off, and sat on my pack with my body bare, trying to get cooler.

Then on again when the whistle blew, with sagging knees, breath coming in gasps, face ashen-white, protruding eyes, and a white froth on the lips. I was young, proud of my strength, had led for years an athletic life without smoking or drinking, and was in a state of perfect physical fitness; still I found my strength ebbing fast. Our platoon officer collapsed in the sand. Shortly afterwards a corporal marching in front of me fell unconscious, and some of us stumbled over his prone body. Captain Fanning was now the only officer left in our company, and the company on our left was without an officer. 'A' Company was not more than twenty strong.

At each halt we looked back. Away to the skyline, we could see forms of men lying huddled in the sand, as though machine-gun fire had swept the columns. As we looked some would rise and totter a few paces, to collapse again. The desert was strewn with clothing, equipment, and miscellaneous articles.

The pitiless sun beamed down upon us. Queer thoughts surged through our brains. The perspiration was white on the backs of our tunics; even our web-equipment had the white sweat stains seen on the harness of a toiling horse. When we rested and lay stretched out, the heat of the sand added to our torment. Still we were kept marching to the schedule of fifty minutes with eight of rest. At last Captain Fanning fell out, and our company of probably two hundred and fifty men had dwindled to perhaps twelve.

Now we struck a stretch of very soft sand; we reeled like drunken men. Our packs seemed to have grown to the weight of mountains. We were now only marching on our determination, foaming at the mouth like mad dogs, with tongues swollen, breath gripping our throats with agonizing pain, and legs buckling under us. Perhaps a mile from our camp my marching-mate, Peter Hughes, during a halt said to me: 'Pull out and let's have a spell. We have seen the majority of the battalion out; besides, there are no prizes issued for the winner of this mad marathon.' I was very distressed, and fell in with the suggestion.

When the whistle blew, we lay on the ground for a few extra minutes, and then staggered after what was left of 'A' Company. We caught the

17

head of the column before they moved from the next halt. But we dropped behind, and were a few hundred yards in rear when we saw the Adjutant, Captain Anderson, muster the remnants of the 56th Battalion and form them up. N.C.O.s and men numbered only thirty-eight out of a battalion over 900 strong.

Peter and I sat on our packs for perhaps another ten minutes, and then, putting our equipment on, did the final stage to the camp, about half a mile. We did not jettison any of the contents of our packs, as many did. As we entered the camp we met Grenna and Jimmy with some oranges. These two were the only members of our section among the first batch to reach camp. Grenna had proved his boast that he had as much guts as any man in the section, in spite of his youth and light build.

New Zealand troops were at this time camped at Moascar, and Peter and I hastened to the nearest cook house. Here we found a ship's tank cut in half containing a small quantity of dirty water. We joined about a dozen men in a mad scramble to drink this filth. We were parched with thirst and went on our hands and knees, buried our faces in it, and drank like famished beasts. One of the cooks saw what was doing and, realizing the state we were in, pulled a dixie of tea off the fire for us. We vomited it up before it had time to do us any good.

Then a great bustle ensued in the New Zealand lines. Word flew around the camp that there were hundreds of Australians still out on the desert. The 'Kiwis' rose to the occasion; without waiting for orders these best of good fellows hurried out with water-bottles to help the sufferers. Large stretcher-parties, ambulance wagons, mounted men, camel-parties, and even an aeroplane flying low, went back over the route which we had traversed. All night long these New Zealanders worked, bringing in men in all stages of exhaustion, some unconscious, others naked and in delirium, others sunstroke patients. Many cases were sent direct to hospital.

At dusk Captain Fanning came into our lines and spoke kindly to every man of his company. Before he left he turned to the company sergeant-major and said: 'Let it be known to my company that I am proud of every man who stuck the march out to the fourth last halt.'

Early next morning the Prince of Wales visited the camp, and then we marched out on the remaining stage of the journey to Ferry's Post, about six miles. Already the sun was very hot; we did not look forward to another day under our packs. Before we moved off I overheard the brigadier say to Colonel Scott: 'So you still have forty-five men un-accounted for?' to which Scott replied in the affirmative.

We marched off, and after going some distance we entered the town of Ismailia, on the shores of Lake Timsah. The streets through which we passed were lined with tall trees whose shade seemed heavenly after the scorching heat of the desert. We crossed the Suez Canal on a pontoon bridge, just above Lake Timsah, and reached our final camp about noon. Captain Fanning saw us into our tents without the ceremony of forming up to be dismissed. During the last two days we had come to realize that this martinet who commanded A Company was also human.

Some days later the battalion was paraded and we had read to us a lengthy screed on the march, from the divisional commander, Major-General McCay. In scathing terms he described what had been reported to him as our 'disgraceful conduct.' This made the men in the ranks scapegoats for somebody's blunder. As punishment, for many mornings after the battalion was marched round and round in a great circle under full packs for two hours to teach us march discipline.

Note

1. The 4th Battalion was among the first infantry units raised for the AIF during the First World War. Like the 1st, 2nd and 3rd Battalions it was recruited from New South Wales and, together with these other battalions, formed the 1st Brigade. The battalion was raised within a fortnight of the declaration of war in August 1914 and embarked just two months later.
2. Fought between 6–10 August 1915, during the Gallipoli campaign, the Battle of Lone Pine was originally intended as a diversion from attempts by New Zealand and Australian units to force a breakout from the ANZAC front on the heights of Chunuk Bair and Hill 971. Launched by the 1st Brigade AIF in the late afternoon of 6 August 1915, the battle pitched the Australian forces against formidable and well defended Turkish positions, sections of which were securely roofed over with pine logs. In some instances the Australian troops had to break in through the roof of the trench systems in order to engage the defenders. The main Turkish trench was taken within twenty minutes of the initial charge but this was the prelude to four days of intense hand-to-hand fighting, resulting in over 2,000 Australian casualties.
3. The son of Alexander and Margaret Inine McPherson Dykes of Darvel, Ayrshire, Scotland, 26-year-old Second Lieutenant Samuel McPherson Dykes was killed on 1 November 1916. He is buried in Warlencourt British Cemetery.
4. Aged 42 when he was killed, Lieutenant Albert Edward Campling was killed on 14 June 1916. From Penrith, New South Wales, he lies in Brewery Orchard Cemetery on the east side of the village of Bois-Grenier.
5. Later Lieutenant Colonel Charles Melville MacNaghten, CMG.

Chapter 3

The Move to France

Ferry's Post – Desert training – The Battalion Band –
In the front line of the Suez Canal defences – Flies and sand –
We leave Egypt for France – The French countryside.
(30 March to 3 July 1916)

Our new camp was on the Arabian side of the Suez Canal. A metalled road ran from the pontoon bridge past the camp, and continued out into the desert for some miles to the terminus of a light railway running parallel with the road. Road and railway were the arteries which fed the front line, perhaps ten miles from the Canal, and held on our sector by the 8th Brigade. On the high banks just above the canal was constructed a trench system with wire entanglements. Lake Timsah stretched away in the right rear of the camp. A pipe-system gave the camp a rather limited water-supply available only during certain hours and of such low pressure that it was barely sufficient for drinking and cooking purposes. For washing we relied upon the waters of the canal, which were so salt that they left a white powder over face and hands.

The chief duty here at Ferry's Post was picket-guard on all fresh-water taps at which long queues of mess-orderlies daily lined up, and concerning which there were the most stringent orders against waste. On the right of the road the desert stretched away in a series of unrelieved low sand-hills.

In this scene we settled down to a period of drilling and training in outpost duties in the reserve line of the Canal defences. Captain Fanning had by now got us drilling rather well, and his pride in the company made each of us take more interest in the old movements which for weeks had been so monotonous. But any slackening-off on our part would bring him down upon us, and the fear in which we held him allowed him to dominate us like a potentate.

Between our camp and the parade ground were artillery and A.S.C. lines past which we marched in from parade. Invariably when we passed these lines Captain Fanning would have his company covered off and marching like clockwork. Then he would give us rifle exercises while on the move; the manner in which these movements were executed was really excellent.

One day the men looking on from the artillery lines clapped us. By the pleased expression on Captain Fanning's face we knew that none appreciated the compliment more than he did.

We were frequently exercised in the attack, deploying from column of route into artillery formation, and then to a series of attacking waves moving across the desert in short rushes. Running in the heavy sand was hot work. The waves would move in short rushes, then down, with the section commanders giving the range and fire orders. We would work the bolts of our rifles to give covering fire to another portion of the line that was advancing. Then it would be our turn to rise, push forward, and throw ourselves into the prone position, here to maintain fire to assist further advance. When within charging distance of the objective, the firing-line would be reinforced to the utmost strength, bayonets fixed and, a wave of sweating, cheering, charging men, we would rush forward to the final assault.

This training made those strong enough to stand it as fit as racehorses, and gave N.C.O.s a chance to learn their real work. Probably after the exhausting exercise of these attacks, some 'head' sitting on a horse would fault our movements and we would be marched back to 'Do it again'. Many hours were also spent in bayonet fighting. Bombing was taught only to a small squad of battalion bombers, a mistake for which we paid dearly later on.

But route-marching under full packs was still a big factor in the hardening process used to make real fighting troops of us. Many a morning after breakfast the whole battalion would parade under packs, and we would march miles across the desert always to the plan of fifty minutes' march and eight minutes' rest. March discipline was enforced to the utmost. No matter how our thirst might torment us, only at halts were we allowed a sip of our water bottles.

During these marches Captain Fanning was at his strictest. From the head of his company he would look back over the marching column; if covering deviated by a matter only of inches he would roar: 'Jumping Jerusalem, No. – Platoon, can't you cover off?' Or to the platoon officer: 'Mr Blank, make that bloody platoon of yours realize that they are on a march!'

Or he would leave the head of his company, and come along the flank to some weary soldier, who with the sweat blinding him and his pack riding as if it were a grandstand, had dropped slightly out of alignment with the other three men of his four. To this man Captain Fanning would say, in a very mild voice: 'Sonny, what four do you belong to?' The tired soldier would awake with a start and say: 'That one, sir,' indicating the one from which he had fallen back. 'Well, get up into the bloody alignment, and march as if you were a soldier, and not an old crock.' This used to cause a

21

smothered titter among those within hearing, but heaven help anyone caught by the captain with even the semblance of a smile on his face at any straffing of an offender against march-discipline. Captain Fanning during these marches spared himself not at all. From the head to the rear of the company, he moved, ever on the *qui vive* for the slightest deviation in covering and dressing.

Off parade we availed ourselves of the facilities for swimming in the canal. The lukewarm waters after parade hours swarmed with naked men, who hung on to the rudders of the native sailing craft, or swam alongside the passing liners, and if these were British, collected magazines, fruit or cigarettes thrown overboard to us by passengers crowded at the rails.

One moonlight night 'A' Company was aroused and ordered on parade in fatigue-dress. Captain Fanning led us through the sleeping camp, across the pontoon bridge towards Ismailia, and after perhaps an hour's march we found ourselves at Moascar siding facing a train-load of mules. Fanning called for men used to handling stock. Long Jack was one of the first to answer. The volunteers' work was to enter the trucks, and bring the mules out. Each of us was given two mules to lead to halters. Talk about fun in the stock yard!

The untrucking of those mules would have made a film worth seeing. Some of our fellows had never handled any animal fiercer than a cat. Most of the mules were unbroken and for viciousness were unsurpassed. They could kick a fly off their noses. Some of them bucked, kicked, and dragged us over the sand; others broke loose, and galloped about like mad things with men chasing them.

After a long delay we were ready to move. Day was breaking as we moved through the sleepy streets of Ismailia and natives gazed at us from their resting-places on the kerb. Eventually we reached the pontoon and the fun commenced in earnest. Some of the mules played up on the pontoon, making it rock violently. After much trouble we got them all across and led them past our camp and on to the desert. Here the transport people made some difficulty about taking delivery of the brutes. They had no picquet-lines ready for them; they seemed to expect the fatigue party to act as hitching-posts in the meantime. Captain Fanning solved the problem by ordering us to leave the animals tied to one another in small circles.

Our battalion had by now formed a band, in charge of a Marie Louise type of band-sergeant who gave himself great airs. In the division were some really fine bands, in comparison with which ours was very mediocre. The regimental march wished on to us was a weird tune known as 'Steadfast and True,' commonly known as 'Stuck fast in the Glue.' Reveille would sound, and on the last note our band would make the morning air hideous with this composition, the signal for the whole battalion to burst into loud ironical cheers and roars of laughter. This morning-serenade eventually finished our band. The colonel, not feeling well one morning, told the R.S.M. to: 'Take the bloody band away and drown it.' Shortly afterwards our band sergeant left us, never to return.

One day during Smoke O! on the parade ground, my platoon officer told me to report to Captain Fanning. I went, wondering what I was going to get into trouble for. He gazed at me for some seconds – during which I felt very uncomfortable. He smiled and started to talk about the company. It was the first conversation I had had with this man of thunder.

He spoke of the great difference between the condition of the company now, and that of a few weeks before at Tel-el-Kebir, compared the 56th with the 4th Battalion, and said that before he was finished with us we were going to be the equal of it.

As I stood and listened to him there passed through my mind the oft-told tale of how this man had been sent to take charge of a party of Royal Marine Light Infantry composed for the most part of mere youths, occupying a hot place on Gallipoli. These troops were in a trench that was being subjected to a deadly enfilade fire. Their losses had mounted so rapidly that they had become demoralized. A young officer in charge had lost his nerve and was crouching in the bottom of the trench. Fanning came on the scene.

He dragged the terror-stricken officer to his feet and kicked his backside in full view of his own men; and proceeded so to bully him that he recovered himself. Fanning's roar made these jumpy men buckle down to their job and see it through. Rumour said that a certain officer was awarded a decoration for Fanning's work that day.

He told me as we stood on the desert that he could pick the men in his company who would make fighters and those that would not. 'That march the other day,' he said, 'was some guide. Men that stuck that will make soldiers'. It eventually transpired that I had been called up because I was not wearing the lone chevron that marked the exalted rank of lance-corporal![1]

One of my close friends was Lance-Corporal Grimstone, a short, thick-set man, with powerful arms and chest, a brick-red face, and a laugh that could be heard a mile away. He was the most picturesque swearer in the company. His yarns entertained us by the hour. Grimmy became orderly corporal, easily the worst N.C.O.'s job, in the battalion. He saw to the serving of meals, washing of dixies by the mess orderlies, sick parades, and the cleaning of the lines.

The morning after he took over the duties the bacon issue was very light and had been put into one dixie by the cooks. Grimmy took upon himself the serving out of this ration. The company drew their tea and porridge in the usual way, and then formed in single file upon the bacon dixie. Grimmy handed out to each a portion about the size of a two-shilling piece.

This was accepted by all save one of the latest reinforcements. Into his dixie-lid Grimmy placed the atom of bacon. The new arrival poured out a torrent of abuse upon him. Grimmy tried to reason with the fellow, a chronic growler, at which he became very insolent and threw the fragment of bacon at Grimmy.

That caused the storm to break. Grimmy sprang from a sitting position across the dixie on to the growler and beat him to the sand with two sledge-hammer blows, upsetting the bacon in doing so. Although the rest of the bacon was flavoured with sand, nobody else provoked the pugilistic lance-corporal that morning.

On 8 May we relieved the 60th Battalion (15th Brigade) in the front line defence trenches at Mount Kembla, ten miles out in the desert.[2] The site was in a depression among low ridges of sand. To the front and right the ground rose, so that we could see only a few hundred yards. On the reverse side of the ridge from the camp were the trenches – not continuous, but a series of strong-posts manned by platoons and sections, and dug to a depth of five or six feet. Parapet and parados were composed of sandbags, hurdles, and reed-mats. A short communication trench led into each post, and an emergency ration of water, food and ammunition was buried in each. A belt of wire stretched left and right – French 'concertina' – staked and reinforced with barbed wire. Passages through this belt were so arranged that a post commanded them and during the hours of darkness kept strict watch on them.

Here we learned our first real lesson in trench routine. Listening-posts were pushed out, wiring-parties worked under covering parties, patrols went out, and the men in the trenches were employed while off watch in improving the posts. It was heartbreaking working in the sand, which fell in as fast as it was dug out. Trench discipline was very strict, and smoking after dark was forbidden.

When off watch we slept on the bottom of the trench in our equipment. All night long Captain Fanning and his company officers came round, and heaven help a sentry slow in challenging. 'Stand to' was from 3.30 to 4.30 a.m. We were told that Turks were expected to attack. But they never did.

After stand down in the morning we marched back to camp. Breakfast was a rough meal of porridge and bully beef, and then we paraded for water. An N.C.O. of each platoon stood by the water picket and checked off each man as he drew his bottle full. The allowance of water per day was two bottles per man. Our toilets we performed each in a small tobacco-tin, which had to also serve for cleaning teeth, shaving, and washing with the shaving-brush) in that order.

Flies haunted us by the million. They bit our naked bodies as we slept, the tops of the tents were black with them, and to eat in the middle of the day was practically impossible. In a much cooler type of tent than our bell-pattern the thermometer reached as high as 125 degrees. We scraped holes in the sand and buried our water-bottles in an endeavour to keep their contents drinkable. The slightest scratch became septic in a few days and spread into an ugly fester.

Vegetables were extremely scarce, and three mornings per week we got an issue of porridge. Invariably this was so sand-laden that it was hard to eat, and no doubt laid the foundation of some of the stomach complaints found among soldiers who had served in the desert. But our greatest hardship was the lack of water. We meditated on the sound of running streams and the chance of drinking without restraint. Each day the sun beamed from the cloudless sky upon endless wastes of sand, causing mirages in fantastic shapes to mock us and the heat-rays to dance before our eyes.

The monotony and silence of this God-forsaken stretch of country were stupefying. Lack of sleep was felt very much. We lay in the tents during the heat of the day and cursed the flies and the country in a hymn of hate that came from our hearts. When were we to be taken out of this country? France, Salonika, anywhere, rather than rot in a place inhabited by nothing but flies and asps.

Light horse patrols were out on our sector during the hours of daylight. Sometimes these patrols brought in small parties of fierce, dirty-looking Bedouins who were passed to the rear to be questioned. They were tall, gaunt men with hooked noses and fierce eyes. Their tents would be perhaps miles from water, and their possessions were usually a few goats and perhaps some camels. What they or their animals existed upon puzzled us. They were religious fanatics and had the reputation of being robbers by instinct.

On 29 May we were relieved by the 53rd British Division. While in the Canal defences I was promoted to corporal. We marched to Ferry's Post, spent a fortnight there, and on 16 June left that camp for Moascar to entrain for France. Our delight at leaving Egypt was unbounded.

We learned the details of our entrainment at morning parade at Moascar next day. Captain Fanning marched 'A' Company out on to the desert, sat us down in a circle around him, gazed at us for a few seconds, and then said: 'Men, we are leaving for France and hell. To many of you it will mean the introduction to war. Make no mistake as to what that means – death, privation, wounds, and suffering. Many of us will leave our bones in France. It will take all your enthusiasm and manliness to enable you to play the part of good soldiers. I know some of the names you have called me here. I have been hard on you, harder than any drill-sergeant of the old Regulars; but I have been hard for a purpose. Any man who has stuck out the many hardships and tasks that I have imposed on you I have made a soldier. Those that showed weakness I culled out of my company, which today can bear comparison with any of the original 4th Battalion companies when we landed on Gallipoli. You hate me now. You may think otherwise when we have been in action together.'

Wheeling abruptly he roared, 'Sergeant-major, fall in the company.' It was the first time during all these weeks of his command that the man spoke to us instead of the officer. This captain whom we dreaded and disliked because we thought him the most exacting of tyrants, but whose personality held us more firmly than that of a man who was only just a bully could have done, was to become in the bitter days of real war the idol of all of us. His name today is cherished in the memories of the survivors of the original 'A' Company 56th Battalion, with respect and esteem for a brilliant soldier. He could have no finer monument.

On 19 June 1916, we paraded late in the afternoon and marched to the railway siding. Here we entrained in the long, open, shallow trucks used on the Egyptian railways. About sunset the train started.

Peter Duncan stood up on the end of the truck, and bade a soldier's farewell to Egypt. It was in rhyme, voluble and expressive, and caused much amusement to a small group of Tommy officers standing on the platform. As the train ran out across the barren desert in the twilight we sang ourselves hoarse and cheered like lunatics.

It was a glorious moonlight night with the sky studded with stars; the light of the heavens was reflected back from the sands of the desert stretching away on either side of the line. The singing ceased as a heavy dew began to wet our cotton uniforms. From a doze on the floor of the trucks we were awakened about 2 a.m., bustled out, and marched on to a wharf alongside of which was a vessel of about 8,000 tons.

In formation we lay on the wharf on our packs till day was breaking, when we went on board, stacked equipment and rifles, and found we were in the harbour of Alexandria. It was full of shipping and transports embarking troops. Ours was the *Huntsend*, formerly the N.D.L. *Lützow*, now a prize of war. Light Horse occupied the fore-part of the ship, our battalion was quartered amidships, and the sergeants and pay-office details aft. The officers had cabins on the main and boat-decks.

The transports, five of them in convoy, sailed from Alexandria at 7 a.m. on 22 June. Throughout the passage we saw no submarines but we were always under escort either by British or French destroyers. It was ever a source of interest to us to watch the manoeuvres of these wasps of the sea. Now they would be ahead steering a zig-zag course across our bows; suddenly they turned and scoured the sea away to a flank, dropped astern, raced to the van with their bows buried in the seas, their low decks awash, their wakes foaming. There was a trim smartness, a hallmark of efficiency about every British warship that I saw.

Peter Duncan and I commandeered a sleeping position, or 'posy', underneath a port life-boat on the boat-deck. This deck was reserved for officers, so we used to wait until most of the troops were asleep, steal up the ladder, and dodge around to the boat.

As we lay here Peter told me much of his home people, and why he came to Australia. Born of Glasgow parents in rather comfortable circumstances, he was the youngest of a large family but had been a rover. Much to his father's disgust, he had become deeply interested in boxing, had fought in the Scottish Amateur Championships, and had been runner-up in his division. Peter had been well-educated, and only during this voyage could I understand the difference between the well-dressed, gentlemanly fellow whom I had known slightly as a civilian, and the cock-sure 'hard-doer' of the army. He possessed enough knowledge of the world and men to be able to adapt himself admirably to any company in which he found himself.

One night I arrived on the boat-deck alone, and found three Light Horsemen with their sleeping kit round our possy. I went to place my blankets in our usual sleeping-place when they informed me that the possy was theirs and that I had to go elsewhere. This caused an argument, in the midst of which Peter came on the scene. He dropped his blankets, took off his tunic, and said: 'We are going to sleep under this boat, and anybody who tries to prevent us will have to fight.' Peter and I slept under the boat, and we did not have to scrap for our resting place.

Early in the afternoon of Sunday, 25 June, we entered and dropped anchor in St Paul's Bay, Malta. The ship's gangways were lowered, also some of the lifeboats, arid the warm waters around the transports were soon crowded with naked soldiers enjoying one of the best swims imaginable.

At daylight next morning Peter and I saw from our sleeping place a fleet of fishing boats come out from the entrance of the bay. As the sun rose these came in past our transport; to our astonishment we saw that all had women aboard who hauled on the nets and pulled at the oars like men. These women wore a sort of black cowl, which was known as the 'Hood of Shame,' and said to date from the time of the capture of the island by Napoleon. After breakfast the gangways and a couple of boats were again lowered, and we amused ourselves in the water all the morning. Some of our fellows, naked as the truth, pulled over to a Yankee ship lying in the bay and bandied words with the crew about some of President Wilson's notes.

The convoy put to sea again on the evening of 26 June 1916, and at dawn on the 29th we were in Marseilles harbour. Late in the afternoon we went alongside a wharf. Some of the ship's crew were allowed off but we had to content ourselves with looking over the rails and trying to carry on a conversation in Pidgin English with the gendarmes.

Next morning after breakfast we paraded in full marching order, with blanket and waterproof sheet. We formed up by companies in the street and were issued with three days' rations of bully-beef, biscuits, cheese, and jam. Then we marched to the station. The route became crowded with old men, women, and children. Already we were struck with the absence of any able-bodied men in the crowd. The women called out to us things we could not understand; many of them were crying as we marched past.

In the railway-yards we entrained in first and second class carriages. These were placed at our disposal by the kindness of the French Government, and only later did we fully appreciate this kindness. Eight men were allotted to each compartment; we stacked our rifles and equipment on the racks, and crowded to the windows. We had been warned before disembarking that we were to refuse all alcoholic drinks that might be offered to us. Perhaps this was the reason for our not being paid for many weeks. Many of us did not have the price of a packet of cigarettes; 'bumpers' were at a premium. Over thirty trains, each of great length, were used in the transportation of the division.[3]

About 11 a.m. our train started, pulled by two powerful engines. We slowly steamed through the city; at one of the many stops a French woman opened her window overlooking the line and offered us two bottles of wine. We wanted them badly; but none were game enough to get out and fetch them. The good lady then leaned out and placed them on the brick wall below her window. A man from No. 3 platoon in the next compartment jumped out and got them. This was seen by Captain Fanning, and he took them away, handing the wine back to the good-hearted Madame.

We ran out into the suburbs and then into the country. The beautiful South of France passed before our eyes in a series of panoramas which astounded us. As the train slowly climbed the hills we looked back on red-tiled roofs rising above a white-fringed coast line lapped by a blue sea, whose waters flashed and sparkled in the sunlight.

As this scene was lost in the distance we saw below the river Rhône and its tree-covered banks, and on the hillsides the crops in various hues like checkers on a draught board. Everywhere seemed to be running streams, avenues of trees and fields ablaze with scarlet poppies, blue cornflowers and white marguerites. Perhaps there are more beautiful countryside's than the South of France in the month of June, but to us it seemed not possible.

As our crowded train went past many of the women left their work in the fields and came to the railway line to throw kisses, clap their hands, and call out: 'Vive l'Australie!' After the squalor of Egypt these deep-bosomed, sun-kissed daughters of France seemed to us to vie in beauty with their flower-decked fields.

Next morning we pulled into a station-yard where facilities for washing, etc., were ready for us. Here we had breakfast and seemed to be a great attraction to the inhabitants, who gathered around the station fence and called out many things to us.

The small boys of the village demanded 'biskeets' in a ceaseless chorus, and we obliged as far as our ration would allow. At this station Captain Fanning handed out two packets of cigarettes to every man in 'A' Company, purchased from his own pocket. It was a thoughtful act which we appreciated very much, but sad to relate few of us could smoke the French cigarettes, and we made ourselves popular by giving them to some of the middle-aged men in red trousers, long blue coats, and peaked caps, who guarded the length of the railway-line along which we travelled.

On this day we passed through country even more beautiful than the first. An old seaman, well past the romantic age, said to me: 'A man would gladly die for a land like this', and the statement did not seem extravagant. And so we came to Dijon. We did not touch Paris, but branched off at a junction, and eventually on the morning of the fourth day we reached our journey's end at Thiennes. We stood up as a battalion in the zone of the British Army on the Western Front.

Notes

1. Williams' service papers show that he was promoted Lance Corporal on 8 April 1916, Temporary Corporal on 25 May 1916, and Corporal on 13 July 1916.
2. These positions probably drew their name from Mount Kembla in New South Wales, or the nearby village of the same name which is near Wollongong.
3. The 56th Battalion AIF was part of the 14th Brigade of the 5th Australian Division. The division was the last of the four Australian divisions to arrive from Egypt.

Chapter 4

Allied March Through Paris

Arrival on Western Front – The line in the Fleurbaix sector –
Am detailed to military celebrations in Paris – Great military display.
(3 July to 18 July 1916)

From Thiennes station we marched off at dawn to billets. 'A' Company
had the farthest to march, and the platoons were billeted on farms at some
little distance from each other. While in Egypt we had heard of the troops
being billeted on civilians in France, and in our ignorance pictured ourselves being taken into the bosom of the family, as it were, and having a
real bed to sleep in.

The sun was well clear of the horizon when our Platoon officer led No. 3
Platoon through a wide, white-washed gate and round to the back of a
farmhouse. The good Madame hastened to the door at the sound of our
nailed boots on the brick path, and after saying '*Bon jour!*' called to papa,
'*Soldats!*' Papa, a lanky, raw-boned peasant, came out, and he and Madame
hastened to the stable and led forth a couple of cows, sundry calves, and a
horse.

The building being clear of stock, papa with a wave of the hand gave us
right of entry. The place was ankle-deep in clean straw and smelt strongly
of cows. Gone was the dream of a bed with sheets – and we wished that we
could erect a few tents in the open. However, we stripped off our gear and
went outside to have a look around.

The stable was built at right angles to the dwelling-house. Both had had
a liberal coating of white-wash. From the stable to the back door of the
house was a brick path, skirting a large manure-pit, an evil-smelling black
morass which made us wonder whether typhoid fever was common in
the country. The water-supply for household use was drawn from a well
whose pump was on the brick path. Here we washed ourselves, contem-
plating the extent of soakage from the dung-pit into the well. However,
Madame and papa appeared to be robust enough.

We learned that our billet was situated near the village of Steenbecque.
The city of Lille lay to the east and Ypres to the north. Refreshed from the
wash, we completed our breakfast toilets by stripping our shirts off and

killing some of the lice we had gathered in the train. Many of us had kept practically free of them in Egypt, but from the day of landing in France we became more or less 'chatty', as the army called it. Our rations arrived, carried in a waterproof sheet. Heavens!, we thought, we were in for a banquet after our stinted fare of the Canal Zone: there was bacon, jam, bread, and two tins of butter! Butter had been a stranger to us for many months.

After breakfast the company paraded, and we were exercised in adjusting gas helmets. Gas at this period was the military obsession. Coming over on the transport we had been lectured so much on the subject and its horrors had been painted so vividly, that all of us were a little scared of it. Our protection against gas consisted of tear goggles (like those worn by motor-cyclists) and the P.H. helmet.

This was a dank, dark, grey-coloured thing shaped like the hood of the 'terror' in a Yankee movie thriller. It reeked of phenol, which was proof against the gas then in use. Two glass eyelets, a rubber mouth-piece, and a waterproof satchel pinned on the inside of the breast of the soldier's tunic, made up the outfit. After I had had the helmet on for a few minutes the eye-pieces became clouded and I felt like a cat with its head stuck in a salmon-tin.

Thereafter we did our first route-march in France. The cobble-stoned roads after the months of the sands of Egypt jarred our feet and legs, causing many to become lame, and all of us to feel like broken-down cab-horses. We also saw our first rain for months.

Pay day brought money for the first time for weeks, and a thirst accumulated over a like period. The village was studded with estaminets, and drink was cheap in those days. No. 3 Platoon passed from parade *en masse* to an estaminet close to our billet, and here we celebrated in great style, served by Madame and two buxom wenches, Jeanne and Marie. Each one of us must have asked the two mademoiselles about the prospects of spending the night with them. They did not destroy all hope for us, but fixed the appointment for *après la guerre.*

I suppose it would have been bad for business if they had got annoyed with this persistent request. On the other hand, these people had been used to soldiers for many months, and they knew that it was as natural for a soldier to ask an attractive mademoiselle for permission to sleep with her as it is in civilian life to talk about the weather. I really believe that if an attractive French girl working to quench the thirst of soldiers in war-time did not have the proposition put to her with every fresh drink that she served, she would hurry upstairs and critically examine herself in the looking-glass to learn what was wrong with her appearance. We sampled everything drinkable in the estaminet, and were loath to leave when

31

turned out by the picquet. We reached our billet in all stages of alcoholic exhilaration.

We spent a week in various exercises to restore our condition and familiarize us with anti-gas drill, including practise with the goggles and full helmet in tear-gas and cloud-gas respectively. At the end of it, on 8 July, we were warned that on the morrow we should take over a section of the front line. Late that afternoon a sick-parade was held. I have mentioned the effects of the hard roads on many of the men's feet and legs. Some were so lame that marching was impossible. These, along with the few who always developed a temperature or a touch of 'baseitis' whenever a move of any importance was at hand, paraded before the medical officer.

Captain Fanning took up a position near the doctor's billet and with frowning face scanned the sick-parade. In our company Peter Duncan was one of the worst cases with bed feet. So swollen were they that he could not get his boots on. He paraded sick, and as the line passed Captain Fanning remarked to the bare-footed Peter: 'What, Duncan! I did not expect to see you here.'

At this taunt Peter forgot his sore feet, hobbled across, drew himself erect, saluted Captain Fanning like a guardsman, and said: 'Captain Fanning, did you ever know a Scotsman that squibbed it.'

'No, Duncan, I did not, and there were many Scotsmen in the old 4th Battalion.'

'Well, sir, I am not going to start the rot in the breed, and I will follow your bloody company tomorrow, bare-footed.'

Thus delivering himself, Peter turned about, quitted the sick-parade without seeing the doctor, and hobbled back to our billet. After dark the captain sent Peter several pairs of his own socks to wear on the march.

On the march up through Merville next morning Peter followed the column carrying full equipment, with his feet encased only in socks. To realize his ordeal one must have had practical knowledge of what carrying the pack and equipment of an infantry soldier means. His feet were swollen, and he wore out many pairs of socks on the cobbled road. For proof of a man's spirit this performance would be hard to beat.

The day was hot and oppressive, and the distance to be covered about fifteen miles. Hours after we reached our billets in Estaires, Peter came in, very sour over the fact that a mounted officer of Brigade Headquarters had ridden back over the last mile of the journey and accused him of being a malingerer for lagging behind! Peter was so disgusted that he did not try to explain his case.

We rested next day in Estaires, a fair-sized village in the forward zone and crowded with estaminets, drinking *vin blanc* and eating huge plates of fried eggs and chips, like children at a Christmas party. Late in the afternoon on return to our billet I was met by my pal Fred with instructions to report to Captain Fanning. He had a frown black as thunder on his face.

Suddenly he barked at me: 'How would you like to go to Paris, sonny?'

'Me, to Paris!'

'Yes,' said Fanning. 'Would like to be going myself.'

Then he rattled off his instructions, handed me one hundred and fifty francs, turned abruptly, and left me standing staring after him with open mouth. I hastened to my platoon officer to find the reason for this good fortune. It appeared that the French national day, 14 July, was close at hand, and the British, along with the other Allies, were sending a detachment for a grand review in Paris. Our division had to send two officers and about one hundred other ranks, eight from the 56th Battalion, and I was the corporal in charge of the party.

My pals of No. 3 helped polish up my rifle and gear. Even my clothes were made up from among them, so that I should have the best of everything in the platoon when I moved out in the morning. For me the night was sleepless from excitement. With other parties from the 8th and 15th Brigades ours entrained at Sailly next morning in the trucks customarily used for carrying troops. At many stations along the route we were joined by different detachments – Jocks, Tommies, New Zealanders, Canadians. That night we spent in camp at Abbeville and arrived in Paris next afternoon.

We marched through streets draped with flags and lined with people, who cheered us in great style, to a large barracks, and after forming up on the barrack square we were taken up to our quarters. Ours were on the second floor, and when we had taken our equipment off and claimed a bed each we crowded the windows and gazed down at the crowd in the street. Such a crowd! They clapped us, sang, and continually requested us to respond with 'Tipperary'. They seemed to regard us as martyrs because we were not allowed out.

Presently on the edge of the crowd appeared people with bottles of wine, cigars, and cigarettes. We made ropes and hauled up the good cheer; but before we could accumulate much of the stock several Tommy Redcaps came into our room and made us bring in the ropes. But we had few complaints. For tea we were served with food to which we had been total strangers since leaving Australia – delicious roast beef, three vegetables, pudding, and a can of beer and wine for each man. Our breakfast was another meal for soldiers to remember, with wine and beer again as beverages.

The great march was worth living for. Out in the sunlit streets lined by trees brilliant with summer foliage, our hearts were intoxicated with the most wonderful city of Europe – the music, the roll of our drums, and the feeling that we were representing the greatest empire in the world's history before the eyes of a city whose every structure and monument seemed to speak of glory and bravery. Is it any wonder that we kept step to those drums with feet that barely seemed to touch the ground? I felt as though we were racehorses moving behind the barrier before the start of a big race. My ignorance of Paris denies me knowledge of the route we took, but the most vivid impression remains of those living streets, magnificent buildings, a river, and several stone bridges. After a long march we entered the Tuileries.[1] Here we formed up in close column, piled arms, took off our gear, and were allowed to leave the ranks.

On our left was a full battalion of Russian infantry from a force then in the Champagne sector. Clad in field-grey uniforms with round caps, armed with the French rifle and the long, thin bayonet which the French call 'Rosalie,' these men with their powerful bodies, short legs, and thighs the thickness of young trees, had big dull faces wearing the expression of working bullocks.

On the right of their leading company stood a standard-bearer holding aloft a flag with some religious symbol emblazoned thereon. Starting from the right of each company each file in turn brought his rifle to the present. A group of mounted officers rode up, the standard-bearer dipped the flag, and there went up something between a shout and a cheer from the whole battalion, repeated three times to the dipping of the flag. A grey-headed officer, his breast ablaze with decorations, saluted and gave some orders; whereupon the whole battalion piled arms, with their bayonets still fixed, and broke off.

We went among the Russians and were surprised to see that their equipment did not contain a bayonet scabbard. We learned that they never unfixed bayonets because of some incident of a past war. We appeared to be as much a curiosity to them as they to us. Every now and then a fresh detachment of troops marched on to the ground. A very smart turn-out was a battalion of Belgians wearing a khaki uniform with yellow facings and light-coloured trench helmets. They wore the long tunic similar in cut to the French infantry, and carried a light spade as an entrenching tool.

Across the roadway were formed up French Colonial troops, squat broad-faced men from Cochin China with horizon blue uniforms and large, queer looking caps; fierce-faced, brown men from Algiers; tall, thin-legged, ill-shapen, black Senegalese. Away on the right was a mass of poilus in blue, with their officers in red breeches, blue tunics, and caps gay with golden braid. The Chasseurs Alpins looked what they were, the elite of the French infantry. They were clad in navy blue puttees, breeches, and tunic, and black velvet Alpine caps were set at a rakish angle on their heads, and adorned with a silver bugle for a badge. Their officers were a pattern of soldierly bearing – upstanding, straight as a rush, broad-shouldered, and all about six feet in height.

34

After some time, the fall in sounded. We formed up, and stood at the present, while a cavalcade of officers attendant on the French President, M. Poincare, rode along our ranks. Then the combined march began, out through the great gates of the Tuileries in column of route with bayonets fixed.

Upon a platform on the right stood the French President. Before reaching the saluting base we formed line, and as we marched past he took the salute to the strains of a French military band. Passing into column of route again we marched along streets packed with a cheering, clapping crowd such as we had never seen before.

The excitement of the crowd was wonderful. They pelted us with flowers, and occasionally above the cries of *'Bravo, Australie!'* rang out a coo-ee which was music to our ears. Along the route at intervals were posted French cavalry on coal-black horses – big men with steel helmets, long black plumes dropping to their waists, steel corselets, and great black boots reaching to their knees. With the sun gleaming on helmet, corselet, and drawn sword, they were a picture. In all the excitement of the crowd, we could not help noticing the way in which they kept the route clear.

At last we reached a large barracks upon whose square we formed up, entered army lorries, and therein sped back to our barracks. The wonderful march was over, but the memory will be cherished as something to be looked back upon with joy and thankfulness by all Australians who took part in it.

In the afternoon we were allowed out on leave, with orders to report back at 7 p.m. Outside was a crowd of people impatient to invite us to come and see the sights of the gay city. A big New Zealander was my companion. We declined all invitations and decided to see the city on our own.

It was a glorious afternoon. The boulevards were thronged with a crowd in holiday spirit yet under restraint. Whenever we stood to gaze at the scene we became the centre of a curious group. The kilted Jocks came in for most attention; people seemed to want to know whether they wore trousers underneath – much to the Jocks' embarrassment. The manifest kindness and the interest of the crowds made everybody see the thing in the right spirit. One middle-aged citizen pulled us up, and asked what country we hailed from, and when I told him that I was an Australian, he seized my hand and said, 'An Australian! Welcome to our city. The deeds of your countrymen on Gallipoli have made such a name for Australians that we French people hold you in the highest esteem, and wish to make you the guests of our city.' It was a very pretty little speech and made me wish that I had really been an Anzac.

Back at the barracks in the evening the Australian contingent received a call from an Australian girl who wanted to meet her compatriots. She said she hailed from Melbourne. She had with her two friends, a Dublin girl and a Parisienne. They were loaded with cigarettes, which they pressed upon me and two other Australians. The Melbourne girl told us how well we had looked in the march past; she and the colleen brought a touch of home into the atmosphere. We stripped off our badges and gave them to the three girls. As they left the soft-voiced Irish girl promised to try to find me as we marched out to the train on Sunday.

That departure was another exciting event. It was twilight when we fell in, and we marched out for the railway station with bands playing and the sorrow of leaving Paris disguised in song. The crowd adjoining the barracks was so dense that we only just had room to march in fours. But we had not gone far when we were so crowded that we dropped into file.

Each Allied detachment had its own song. Our 'Australia will be there!' we yelled at the top of our voices. Evidently the song made a hit with the Parisians, for one of their papers published it in French some days later. A mile from the barracks all semblance of march-formation was lost. The Melbourne girl and the colleen found us and struggled with us through a throng of people, mostly women, who caught our hands and tunics as we passed and asked to be kissed. The Irish girl told me that we were going through one of the poorer quarters of the city; nevertheless, its inhabitants turned out to give us a send-off the like of which none of us had ever imagined or will see again. The enthusiasm of the crowd was a frenzy; we were carried away by the spirit of it.

Once the column was blocked for some minutes, and an old grey-bearded man stood on the corner of the street and sang 'La Marseillaise' with a voice as clear as a bell and an expression which touched one's soul. This singer produced a wonderful effect on the crowd. They chanted the song in full deep chorus, and the intensity of their feeling intoxicated us. As the human jam finally gave way and we moved on, a bent and aged woman seized my tunic, saying something I could not understand. The colleen told me that she wished me to kiss a curly-headed child held in her arms. I did so, and also kissed the old lady's wrinkled and not over-clean face. I lost the column, so tightly did she hang to my tunic. At last the colleen made her understand that I had to go on or I would be shot. Only my friend knew the route to the station; but for her I should have been hopelessly lost. At the entrance to the station barriers had been erected and as French police prevented any civilians from entering with the troops, I took farewell of my Irish friend there.

The train deposited us at Hazebrouck on 18 July and thence we travelled to our units by lorry. We of the 56th reached our own at Bac St Maur, to hear that we had arrived back just in time for the 'stunt' at Fromelles.

Note
1. The Tuileries Garden is a public garden in Paris located between the Louvre Museum and the Place de la Concorde.

Chapter 5

The Battle of Fromelles

The Battalion's first action – The German counter bombardment –
Slaughter of brave men – The wounded in No Man's Land –
Division's heavy losses.
(19 July to 22 July 1916)

July 1916 was a momentous month on the Western Front. Attacks by mass formations of German infantry were still being launched on the far right of the long front against the fortress of Verdun. Here the French had withstood a battering whose like had not hitherto been seen in warfare. The whole countryside in the disputed area was torn and shattered with shell-fire, obliterating forts that had been looked upon as impregnable to the heaviest bombardments. Still from the shell-craters the French infantry fought so desperately, and were aided so magnificently by their batteries of 75s, that the Germans made little headway. Their attacks, being launched on too narrow a front, suffered tremendous losses. Apparently both sides had to learn this lesson at heavy cost.

But France was feeling the strain very much. The Verdun battle had been raging for several months, and the French were in danger of becoming exhausted. The Allies had prepared a counter offensive on the Somme, and in the event – because of the heavy toll at Verdun upon the French striking power – the Battle of the Somme became almost entirely a British enterprise. It opened on 1 July. The British Army had now over sixty divisions on the Western Front and immense accumulations of guns, munitions, and material for the offensive.

To cause further division and further, to harass the Germans, the attack at Fromelles, into which we were about to enter, had been planned. This undertaking was to be carried out by General Haking's XI Corps consisting of the 61st British and the 5th Australian divisions. The battle formation of the 5th Australian division was, from right to left, 15th Brigade, 14th Brigade, 8th Brigade. Each brigade was to attack on a two-battalion front using its 3rd Battalion to carry stores, and its 4th as reserves. Both the 3rd and part of the 4th Battalion of each brigade were ultimately drawn into the fight. The opening attack was made by the 59th, 60th, 53rd, 54th,

31st, and 32nd battalions against a 4,000-yards front. The leading wave was to deploy in No Man's Land fifteen minutes before the final lift of the artillery barrage.

The assault was planned for six o'clock in the evening of 19 July. In the 56th Battalion, after our midday meal, and having deposited our packs in the Q.M. Store, we stood about and watched the bombardment on our front. The forward area was shrouded in a pall of dust and smoke and shell-bursts, and we believed that no man could live in such an inferno.

We entered an estaminet, and found the place crowded to overflowing. Madame and her assistants were hard pressed to cope with the rush. The men were in the best of spirits and looked forward to the attack as if it were a football match. All talk was of 'stunt', and the women of the *estaminet* knew the details as well as we did. We were only about three miles from the front line.

We stayed in the estaminet for some time and then strolled back to our billet. As parade time approached all was bustle. We had issued to us an extra bandolier each of cartridges, done up into khaki-cloth formed into pouches, with a loop to slip over the shoulder, iron rations, and some extras that the thoughtful Captain Fanning had secured for us. N.C.O.s had wire-cutters fitted to their rifles. Each man carried a pick or a shovel and several sandbags. Water-bottles were filled, ammunition cleaned, gas helmets inspected. We fell in in the school-yard, children gazing at us with a look of awe on their small old-fashioned faces.

About 5 p.m. we moved forward in artillery formation. From eleven in the forenoon the artillery had been pounding away, and now late in the afternoon it increased in intensity until the whole earth trembled. The Germans were replying to our barrage and concentrated their fire on our front, support, and communication trenches. They seemed to know the hour when these would be packed with the assaulting infantry on their way to the jumping-off line. Very few shells appeared to be coming further back, and our batteries were subjected to no great amount of counter-fire.

We moved down the road with our eyes fixed upon the hell-broth in front of us. Along this same road I had gone, rather 'windy', with the fatigue party on the previous night, but that nervousness had now given place to excitement and expectation. Halts were frequent and of short duration. At 5.45 p.m. we were sitting on the roadway in front of the 60-pounder battery. One of the guns had suffered a premature explosion in its breach, which had made a mess of its crew. We saw the stretcher-party hurry over and collect the wounded. The fire of the other guns was maintained; we could see their shells skimming the tree-tops on their journey. Many eyes among us had been watching the time; at zero hour our platoon sergeant remarked – 'They are over!' Floating back from the front line came the sound of heavy machine-gun fire to tell that the attack had been launched.

Soon we entered a shallow trench which led into the support line. Here we saw the first dead of the attacking infantry. We halted in the support trench and took shelter against the parapet. The line had been considerably damaged by the German shell fire; a lot of dead were in the trench. Fritz was still playing a barrage on the line. Here we sustained our first casualties.

That first experience of shell-fire, the shattering of the trench breastworks, the concussion of the exploding shells, and the smell of the high explosive are still vivid in my memory. I could not but admire our Company Sergeant-Major Dykes. He walked along the duckboards cool as an icicle, ordering us to keep well into the parapet, directing the stretcher-bearers to the casualties, and by his sangfroid inspiring confidence. Just as it was growing dusk the order came for us to move up to the front line. The German shelling and machine-gun fire had now reached a terrific volume.

The communication trench called Brompton Avenue had in places ceased to exist as a defined work; the bodies of dead men lay thickly along its length. Here the supporting battalion, moving up, had suffered severely in the passage. The German shells still searched this sap and blew great craters along its length as we struggled through, trampling underfoot the dead that cluttered it.

All the while we were losing men. Some of the wounded lay in pools staining the water with their blood. Dead men, broken trench material, shattered duckboards that tripped us as we passed, the smell of the fumes of high explosives, and the unforgettable odour of death made this trench a place of horror.

A gas alarm passed down added to it, and we were ordered to put on our helmets. So into the hideous, vile-smelling P.H. helmets we got. The heat of our heads soon clouded the glasses; we floundered through the mire and debris of the shattered trench partly blinded. Alex O'Rourke was immediately in front of me and at one place where the trench had been blown in he, in his semi-blindness, got out into the open, and I as blindly followed him. When we realized that were wandering away from the line of our advance we pulled the helmets off and risked the gas danger for the boon of being able to see where we were going.

As the company emerged into the front line, Captain Smythe of 'B' Company, standing by, roared out to the men, 'Take those damn helmets off!' – so the gas alarm was evidently given by somebody who mistook smoke for gas!

In a wrecked trench to the right, where the German shelling had found our close-packed battalions awaiting zero hour, we found a bay and sat in close to the parapet enveloped in a din from bursts of the deadly German 5.9s. One enemy battery firing from our left enfiladed the trench, destroying whole bays and all who occupied them.

We had not been in the bay for long when a shell appeared to land among us. The roar and flash stunned and partly blinded us. Long Jack was the first to speak, and asked in a strange voice if anybody was hurt. Alfie had caught it in the hand and leg. Long Jack and I tied his wounds up, and I was surprised to see the stolid way in which he took his hurts. We put him in a small dugout close at hand. Presently word came along for our bombers; they went across to assist the infantry who were being ceaselessly counter-attacked in the positions which they had captured.

All night long the remnants of the attacking battalion worked like galley-slaves to establish a defensive line on a site which they had been told was the German support trench. This did not exist, and the leading waves of our attack were now engaged in consolidating what was really a ditch. This work was constantly interrupted by the counter-attacks of the Germans, who with their intimate knowledge of the ground appeared and disappeared with bewildering suddenness. 'B' Company of our battalion was taken over the top and commenced the work of digging a communication sap from our front line to the German trenches.

We took it in turns to observe from the fire-step, but with the dust and smoke we could see very little. Walking wounded drifted back, and huddled themselves in the bottom of our trench to wait for the shelling to ease before passing on to the rear. Through the unceasing enemy barrage on Pinney's and Brompton Avenues, the battalion stretcher-bearers with the aid of volunteers made brave but hopeless efforts to get the stretcher-cases out.

Twice during the night we heard on our right the continuous rhythm of heavy machine-gun fire. Here the 15th Brigade, without much co-operation from the 61st Division, was trying to make headway in the face of the machine-gun nests sheltering in the concrete emplacements of a small rise called the Sugar Loaf.[1]

This fire enfiladed the whole front over which the gallant 15th Brigade battalions were going through an ordeal which was a sheer useless squandering of life. Not only did the initial effort of the leading waves of the 15th Brigade fail to reach the German front line, but, acting under instructions from Corps, these battalions were again committed to an assault that was supposed to be in conjunction with another effort by the left brigade of the 61st Division. Too late were the 15th Brigade advised that the attacking waves of the British division could not be got into position by zero hour, with the consequence that the battalions of the Australian brigade were swept out of existence by the deadly machine-gun fire from the Sugar Loaf, the position which was to have been attacked by the 61st Division.

The survivors of this attack made a desperate effort to consolidate along a ditch near the German wire. But they were for the most part killed. The 59th and 60th Battalions of the 15th Australian Brigade lost 718 and 757 men respectively in this fighting. Throughout the night our battalion with others provided parties to carry sand-bags, ammunition, and wire to the captured positions through heavily-shelled saps.

Very little of this material reached its destination and the communication trench became more and more choked on account of the breaking down of these carrying parties. We learned that our 14th Brigade had carried its objective, but whether it could hold on was doubtful, seeing that both the 61st Division and the 15th Australian Brigade on their right had failed to gain a footing in the German lines. The 8th Brigade on our left had also to give way under concentrated German attacks during the night. Some defended posts of this brigade fought till they were annihilated in the positions they had won.

Our 'B' Company completed the sap across to the German front line. They had suffered heavy casualties in this work, but did not have to meet the enfilading fire which the 8th Brigade men experienced on a similar task. Never for an instant did the German barrage slacken on the line we were occupying. Our casualties were mounting fast; in the din, concussion, and horror of it all we went about our jobs as though stunned. I suppose the numbing concussion was really a good thing in that it dulled our senses to the horrors about us. Captain Fanning was constantly along our line and walked about talking to us as though not a shell were falling. His conduct was a wonderfully steadying influence.

Towards midnight an increasing number of wounded began to stream back to us. Many were in a state of exhaustion and bleeding from wounds that had not been bandaged. They told of the almost hopeless task of trying to form a trench line while the German bombing parties appeared from everywhere. We were not surprised when about 2 a.m. our platoon officer and a sergeant came and told us that our troops were about to retire.

My section was moved farther along to the right. We entered a bay that had been badly damaged, and I was instructed to have the parapet manned and to make an attempt to build up the trench. Just as we entered the bay a 5.9 skimmed the parapet and burst on the duckboards behind. The explosion knocked a man clown and he raved like a lunatic, calling out to his mother to shut the gate and other nonsense until, exhausted, he moaned in a way horrible to hear.

The shelling upon our line increased in volume. The Germans were raining shells upon it to hamper any attempt to reinforce the captured territory. On our right front a savage bombing fight was in progress; along

41

our parapet surged a storm of machine-gun fire. All the while we worked feverishly at the task of repairing the damage to our bay. In this Alex O'Rourke with his superhuman strength was magnificent. I really believe he did not know what fear or exhaustion was.

At last daybreak came, and in its light we saw the battlefield in all its ghastliness. In the long rank grass that covered No Man's Land of yesterday were lying the dead and wounded. Many of the latter were trying to crawl back to us, and in doing so made of themselves a target for the German machine-gunners. Among us were many of the wounded of the attacking battalions, their uniforms caked with mud and blood from their wounds.

Lieutenant O'Halloran of 'B' Company came and told me to take a party and get boxes of bombs from a dump farther along the trench and to distribute them. When I returned he was standing in my bay telling the men how to use the Mills grenade. It seemed wrong after all the months of training in Egypt that we should be put into an attack in which bombing played a big part without even an elementary knowledge of this weapon. Certainly there was in each battalion a section of bombers. But the remainder of us had been given no instruction in using hand-grenades and many boxes of bombs had been given out without being detonated.

The German barrage now dropped to behind our front line and along the two saps that led to the rear. In the captured portion of the German trench a heavy bombing fight was in progress. In this were engaged the bombers from our battalion and the rearguard of our retiring force, fighting hard to gain time for a withdrawal. But the Germans sensed victory and pressed their bombing attacks from left and right flanks.

We plainly saw an Australian jump out of the trench and from the parados bomb the leaders of one of the German attacks. Through the sap that 'B' Company had dug during the night our infantry were coming back. Upon this trench the German fire then concentrated.

The enemy's bombing attacks could not be held long enough to allow all to retire through the sap. Therefore the remnants of the rearguard, at a given signal, leaped out of the German front line trench to run back over the open. We were powerless to assist them, and had to watch them being shot down at point-blank range. Regardless of anything else we stood up on the fire-step to assist this race with death. It seemed an eternity of time until the lucky ones reached our parapets, to be pulled in by willing hands.

No sooner was our field of fire clear than we blazed into the Germans who had lined their parapets to punish the retiring troops. Few of the rearguard escaped. Many of them disobeyed the order to save themselves and continued to fight in the German line to give their comrades a chance to retire.

The remnants of the 53rd, 54th, and 55th Battalions were led through saps to the rear, leaving the 56th Battalion to hold the line. The shelling gradually died away, until about 11 a.m. not a gun was being fired, and even the crack of sharpshooters' rifles from both sides had ceased.

Our senses gradually returned to normal and we looked around us like men awakened from a nightmare. The ordeal of the night was plainly visible on all faces, ghastly white showing through masks of grime and dried sweat, eyes glassy, protruding, and full of that horror seen only upon men who have lived through a heavy bombardment.

We realized in a dull way that we were hungry, so we sat on the remnant of the fire-step and munched bully beef and biscuits. Then Peter Hughes and I went along to a dump to get a tin of water. Our path was strewn with dead men, lying mangled and huddled in the ruins of the bays or along the duckboards. We reached the dump and helped ourselves to a gallon-tin of water. These tins had lately contained petrol, of which the water tasted strongly.

On my way back I stood on a corpse and, to my horror, I recognized the body of a man who on the first night in Liverpool camp had spread his blankets beside me. The day before I had left the battalion at Estaires for Paris I had met him, then a lieutenant in a battalion of our brigade. He had stayed behind in Liverpool, and passed through the officers' school. Now he was lying alongside the duck-boards practically cut in two by a shell.

The dead were saddening to look upon, but a worse sight was the wounded lying out in No Man's Land beyond our aid. On the left an Australian officer and an N.C.O. had gone across under the white flag during the morning and asked a German officer for permission to collect the wounded still lying there. The German sent to the rear for instructions, which were in the negative. So we had to see our wounded lying there to suffer the torments of the damn.

They called out unceasingly for help and water. The sun and flies persecuted them. Those of them who were able to crawl were sniped at by the Germans. One man almost in front of our bay crawled inch by inch towards us, drawing a badly wounded pal with him. He got within a few yards of our parapet when he was fired upon by a German sniper.

The two then took shelter in a shell-hole, and called to us for water. A bottle was filled and heaved over the parapet to them. One of them called out again that they would wait until dark before moving. Another lying in a slight depression in the ground worked with his entrenching tool to build head-cover for himself. Most of these we got in when darkness came down. Then there were others who had lost all sense of direction and seemed not to know which was the German line and which ours. One such was seen to crawl towards the German line; within a few feet of it he was bombed by them.

Within our trenches the wounded were now being removed much more freely. Some of them had been hit early the day previously and because of the heavy shelling had been left in the front line. My pal Fred was a walking wounded case, hit in the back by shrapnel. He paused to say a few words to me, and asked if I had heard anything of Jimmy. He went out, never to return to France.

Shortly afterwards Alfie came, with his hand and knee bandaged. He crouched as he walked, and did not stop to speak as he went past. I watched him being picked up by a stretcher-party, and he waved his hand to me as he went around the traverse. He also went back to Australia.

About noon General McCay[2] and a staff-officer came down the now quiet line. The general stopped before a party of us who were working on the trench and remarked: 'The Boche beat us today, but very shortly we will attack again when there will be a different tale to tell.'

As soon as darkness fell stretcher-parties from among us went over the top and worked all night collecting the wounded.

The following morning broke with the usual hymn of hate. Everybody seemed to wake up at stand to, with a brisk exchange of artillery, machine-gun, and rifle-fire. Then in a heavy ground mist after stand down, as though both sides were weary from the watchful night, all firing ceased. From the fire-step we peered out into the fog.

Suddenly a cry, so clear and unexpected that it made me start, rang out: 'Stretcher-bearers! Stretcher-bearers!' and 'Come on, New South Wales'. Despair punctuated the words. It was a wounded man overlooked at night in No Man's Land, too stricken to help himself but still conscious enough to know that there were men ready to chance their lives in an endeavour to rescue him if only he could guide them to him. Company Sergeant-Major Dykes, my pal Jimmy Sowter, and two others went out with a stretcher.

After a time we saw them picking their way back up our parapet. Willing hands eased the stretcher down into the trench. On it was a sergeant of one of the 14th Brigade battalions. A machine-gun had made a wound in his hip so large that a fist could be inserted; while he had lain unconscious flies had blown his wound. With ashen face, clothes soaked with blood and mud, he lay face downwards on the stretcher, shivering in the raw morning air. He said that he had been hit on the Wednesday afternoon during the initial stages of the advance, had lost consciousness, and could hardly believe that this was now Friday morning. Willing hands gave him a warm drink and hurried him away to the aid post.

Two bays away on my left the corporal in charge of No. 9 Section, 'Skinny' Elliott, went out over the parapet on his own. Well out in No Man's Land he came across a man who had been disabled with a bad leg wound. Although he was only a featherweight and the wounded man was heavy, Elliott managed to get him to hang on to his back and started for our line. In the sodden, shell-torn ground, and heavily laden, he struggled a few yards at a time, the wounded man suffering damnably.

The fog had now begun to lift, and a sniper started to fire at them. The wounded man begged Elliott to leave him in a shell hole, but Skinny refused. Up they struggled a few paces, and then exhaustion and the sniper's bullets forced them into a shell hole. At last they were within a few yards of the parapet. A spell – and then a final dash for the borrow-ditch, which they gained. Here Elliott was easing the wounded man down when a bullet from the sniper pierced his felt hat fore and aft without injuring the wearer.

As the fog had now practically disappeared, the wounded man insisted that it was madness for his rescuer to try to scramble up the parapet. He told Elliott to leave him in the ditch until darkness came, and to throw him over a bottle of water. Skinny fell in with this plan, made a rush, and beat the sniper's bullet to the shelter of our trench. A water-bottle and some food were thrown out to the wounded man, and Skinny and two others brought him in when darkness came. Only those who witnessed this performance and Skinny Elliott's particular pals knew of this exploit. The corporal of No. 9 Section was very proud of his punctured hat, and guarded it like a family heirloom.

When darkness came we learned that we were to be relieved during the night. After stand down Alex and Peter returned to our bay. They had worked like horses carrying out the dead, and Alex, mellow with rum, bustled about in the darkness getting his kit ready; he became highly indignant because he could not find the pick that he had brought into the fight. Peter advised him to carry out part of the parapet and a dozen or so duckboards to console himself.

Our relief, we found, was from a 15th Brigade battalion. Just as they had taken over a German bombing party from the darkness of No Man's Land bombed our part of the trench; but they did not persist. The relief completed we began to file away through Brompton Avenue towards the rear, It was a beautiful moonlit night and, forgetting our tiredness, we made as much haste as the shattered sap would allow.

In front of Peter and me was a tall, shy bushman, who had within the last twelve hours been near to collapse. Like a sick dog he had spent the day in a little dugout, refusing to eat and speaking to nobody. Half-way down Brompton Avenue his slung rifle was caught by the wire-cutter attached to the muzzle in a telephone wire.

The sudden check almost dragged him off his feet and appeared to make him panic-stricken. He plunged and pulled like a steer in a wire fence; his mad antics threatened to brain the man behind him. After he had calmed

45

down Peter and I released him and he scampered along the duckboards to catch up, with hunched back and flogging equipment. We laughed, but the poor chap was dead in a couple of days from pneumonia.

As daylight was breaking we halted at the level crossing of Bac St Maur to allow stragglers to catch up. Then in column of route we moved into the village, which was just astir.

This was Saturday morning. Surely it was much longer ago than last Wednesday evening when we left here to take part in the battle! How different the scenes! We entered the fight with the spirits of a well-trained team taking the field for a hard game. Now we felt old and broken, hoping only to drop to the ground and sleep. Such are my memories of the costly blunder called later the Battle of Fromelles.

Gradually, during the next few weeks we learned the tale in all its details of bungling and waste of brave men's lives. Some of the battalions of the division were nearly obliterated: 60th Battalion lost 757 men, the 59th 718, and the 32nd 695. The 53rd, 31st, and 54th Battalions lost more than half their strength. From noon on 19 July to noon on 20 July the division lost 178 officers and 5,335 other ranks. I have heard it stated that this is the heaviest casualty list of any British division during the war in the same space of time.

The 61st Division which co-operated in the attack lost 1,313 in the action. There can be no excuse for the manner in which our assaulting troops were misled on the very vital point of the situation of the German second line of defence. These troops, after taking the German first line on the 14th and 8th Brigade fronts, wandered far afield in vain endeavour to locate the position of this second trench system upon whose existence the battle orders were most definite. Can the XI Corps staff absolve themselves, when the 61st Division had failed to take the Sugar Loaf, and when the initial attack of the 15th Brigade's right battalion had been almost swept out of existence by the fire from this strong point on their flank, of committing the 15th Brigade to the attack again on the assurance that the 61st Division was to make another attempt on the strong point – whereas the 61st Division failed to make the attempt?

The 5th Australian Division was sacrificed on the altar of incompetence. But at least by their gallantry and tenacity they proved in those bloody hours that they were fit to rate with the best fighting divisions on the Western Front. Men who had fought on Gallipoli from the landing to the evacuation, admitted freely that Fromelles was the severest test they had seen.

Notes

1. The Battle of Fromelles was fought midway between the British-occupied village of Fleurbaix and that of Fromelles which lay behind the German lines. Part of the Allied

intention was to capture a salient just to the north of Fromelles. The salient, which was contained within all the area's available high ground, pointed north-west and was nicknamed the 'Sugar Loaf' by Allied troops due to its distinctive shape. It was held by the 6th Bavarian Reserve Division. The salient's small size and height allowed the Germans to easily survey and cover No Man's Land on either flank.

2. Commander of the 5th Division, and later Lieutenant General Sir James Whiteside McCay KCMG, KBE, CB, VD.

Chapter 6

Into The Somme Battle

Two months in the 'Nursery Sector' – Gas alarms – Army school –
We move South – The march up into the Somme battlefield.
(24 July to 20 October 1916)

There followed a period of two months of trench garrison duty for the division in the Fleurbaix sector. Reinforcements were drafted into all units to replace the battle losses. Some N.C.O.s received commissions as officers and were sent to other companies – among them our Company Sergeant-Major Dykes and our Platoon Sergeant Creber.

Battalions in each brigade took their turns at front line duty, and when relieved went out to support or reserve billets for fatigue duties and training in turn. In the morning mists of this low and swampy country gas alarms were frequent, and though often false alarms they served to provide training to all hands, especially the reinforcements, in the systematized trench drill for the occasion.

Most of these alarms were caused by windy sentries. Still, we were all so keyed-up with the lectures that had been pumped into us about gas that we took no chances. During one of these alarms our platoon-cooks provided us with some comic relief. It was our custom to subscribe a small sum each towards a messing fund. This bought us such things as pickles, sauce and jam from the canteen in Fleurbaix a mile or so in the rear. The cooks were our messing foragers; after tea they went out of the line to do the purchasing. They returned laden with sundry sand-bags and with a good cargo of *vin blanc* under hatches, as the sailors say. They retired to bed without doing any beauty exercises, and slept like men without a trouble under the mellowing influences of Madame's wine.

It so happened that around midnight a gas alarm on a big scale was sounded. Gongs were banged and we were all bustled out of dugouts to stand to. Gas was on us this time! When the excitement had simmered down a little someone noticed that the two cooks were missing from their posts in the trench. Heavens! They were still in their dugout and sure to be gassed!

Two N.C.O.s hurried along, and after much shouting and pulling by the legs aroused the two cooks. Fuddled with sleep and wine they struggled into their equipment and gas helmets and pawed their way out of the dugout. One of them, filled with blood-lust, scrambled to the top of the parapet and opened rapid fire towards the front line. He had been told that a gas cloud had to be fired into, and did not wait to distinguish anything before opening up. He was dragged down and placed under arrest. His pal fared worse.

Across the duckboards which ran along the rear of our position was a field in which fillers of sandbags had left a shallow hole of large dimensions. This, waterlogged, was now a miniature lake. Cook No. 2, in his hurry to get into his helmet, had put it on back to front. Right way on it was never very clear to see through, and the effects of the wine prevented the cook from discovering his mistake. Out of the dugout he floundered across the duckboards and into the pond where he sprawled full-length. He arose dripping like a sea-god, blinded with his wrongly-adjusted helmet, the most laughable and easily the most terror-stricken man in the British army. From his predicament he had to be rescued by two men. The cooks lost their positions as caterers to the platoon.

Next day a large fatigue party of New Zealanders went through our trench, heavily laden with Stokes mortar ammunition and the awkward 'plum puddings'. These were the heavy trench mortar shell fixed to an iron rod, named from their shape.[1] Upon exploding they made a deafening noise, but aim with them was mostly guess-work.

The New Zealanders told us that they were going to 'stir Fritz up a bit' that night. Their division linked ours on the left, and they were the most aggressive troops we ever saw.

About 11 p.m. the commotion duly commenced. Trench mortar, artillery, and heavy machine-gun fire was opened upon the German line in a savage burst. Then under a display of coloured S.O.S. lights sharp explosions of hand-grenades told us that the Kiwis' raiding-party had got to work. Our troops in the front line caught some of the strafe, but no shells came our way. This performance became very frequent with the New Zealanders. If they did not put over a raiding party, they harassed the Germans with heavy bombardments.

One day after dinner a runner came and told me to report at once to Captain Fanning at company headquarters. Turning over in my mind possible offences I reached company headquarters and asked Company Sergeant-Major Dykes what the captain wanted me for. He said I was in for a hell of a row. At Captain Fanning's dugout I clicked my heels and handed the smartest salute I was capable of. The captain returned the salute, and gazed at me for several seconds. Then he growled, 'What have you been up to, sonny?' I replied that I had no recollection of committing any offence. At this he laughed and said, 'Come inside; sit down over there', waving to his bunk.

He filled his pipe with an absent air, and as he puffed gazed at me with piercing eyes and uttered not a word. I felt like the Christmas rooster that hears the axe being sharpened. Then he began talking about the fight and after half an hour, during which I cudgelled my brain wondering why he should send for a corporal of his company to discuss these matters, he said abruptly: 'The battalions are very short of junior officers, and I have recommended you for a commission.' If he had told me that the war was over I could not have been more astonished. 'You will leave the battalion, and probably the brigade.'

I replied that I did not want a commission. He angrily demanded why not. 'Don't you think that you could make an officer? You thought once that you would never make a corporal.'

I hastened to reply that I did not want to leave the battalion or 'A' Company. There I touched his vanity. To him his company was his handiwork, his hobby, his own charge to swear at, to bully, but to pride himself about as only a soldier can.

'All right, sonny,' he said, 'you say you do not wish to leave my company. Go on as you have done these last few months, and if you do not get killed I will make an officer of you in the company before the end of the year. You can go now.'

In a trance I saluted and tried to walk away from the dugout with an air of unconcern. Turning into the sap which led to Hudson's Bay I broke into a trot, elated as if I had won a great prize. I hurried to tell the news to my pals. I found them gathered around wondering what had happened to me. They listened to the end of my story and then Barney broke in with: 'Well, you are a bloody fool. You would have got a good trip out of it, and don't forget you can just as easily be killed with two stripes on your arm as two stars on your shoulder straps.'

Until this time the fashion had been to sit under the German shelling and try to look pleasant. Our people were hampered by the paucity of shells. But now the British Government was shipping munitions in plenty. We were told that our guns would give shell for shell, keep going until the Germans stopped, and then add a few more for good measure. Troops in the front line were instructed to give rifle-grenades in the same proportions, and trench-mortars, two to one. Gradually it began to dawn on the Germans that it was not healthy to promote a strafe, and thenceforward in this sector our guns dominated theirs. They lashed away at the German trenches until in fairness to his own infantry Fritz retaliated, when our guns promptly shelled him into silence.

There were some amusing incidents out of the line, as there always were when the Australian soldier in rest billets set out to savour such entertainment as the rear areas offered him. About midnight one night I was rudely awakened by being pulled out of the dugout by the feet. The moon was shining brightly, and I found Peter Hughes and Tibby laden with several sand-bags and bottles. My fellow occupant of the dugout, Long Jack, was also hauled forth, and the sand-bags were emptied for us to admire their contents.

The two braves had four bottles of champagne, a bag full of MacConnachie rations,[2] another of bacon, cheese and jam, and of all things in the world, a large-sized box respirator against gas. This was brought as a special present for me. At this period box-respirators were issued only to artillery officers. A bottle was opened and we had a drink while the two unfolded their tale.

In an adjacent estaminet they had picked up with the batman of a major of artillery, and under the mellowing influence of sundry bottles of wine they became bosom friends, so much so that when closing-time came the batman invited them along to the battery position. His major happened to be absent. So the batman entertained his new-found friends in the officers' quarters and served out the major's liquor.

When parting time came the batman, generous of heart, loaded his two pals up with eatables, and they helped themselves to what he forgot to give them. In fact, Peter said that he considered bringing home a horse, but refrained when he thought of the lack of room in his dugout. Our section lived like fighting-cocks for some time on the plunder, but I never learned how the liberal-hearted batman fared with his officer.

Just before one of our tours in the line No. 3 Platoon was taken over by Lieutenant Joe Morrison, lately a sergeant in 'C' Company. Tall, thin, fresh-complexioned, and very quiet, Joe was not a man who impressed at first, but when we came to know him we found that he was as cool as an iceberg, game to the core, did his job without any brag, and was never flurried. Long Joe Morrison was as good an all-round platoon officer as a man could wish to serve under.

In 'A' Company was Sergeant McGee, a fire-eating old Scot, old enough in years to be teaching his grandchildren how to play soldiers. In him burned the Scottish warlike spirit. To this old warhorse Captain Fanning was most considerate. They had served together in the 4th Battalion, and our captain knew that although the right spirit was in old McGee he was physically unfit for the strain of the front line.

One night in the line Captain Fanning sent for me, and said, 'I want you to act in the capacity of sergeant. McGee is an old man and I want to spare him as much as I possibly can.' Although I was doing McGee's tour of duty it only wanted the Germans to shell the line, and the old sergeant would be out along the duckboards, with his bare bayonet down the swivels of his

51

rifle, pushing into every bay with the order: 'Get y'r bayonets ready, boys; he'll be coming over.'

With all the deadly weapons to hand to repel the Germans if they did come across, McGee always pinned his faith to the bayonet. This old Scot knew the traditions of the Scottish regiments as a child knows its ABC. Well over military age, he had enlisted at the outbreak of war in the 4th Battalion, which had a decidedly Scotch flavour about its personnel and was commanded by that old fire-eater Colonel MacNaghten.

This battalion was one of the best in the peerless 1st Australian Division. I have already mentioned the calibre of the officers and N.C.O.s that came across from this battalion to take command of the 56th. Somehow in these men (of whom McGee was a sample) there seemed to burn a military fervour akin to a religious fanaticism.

At every opportunity McGee would talk to us of the greatness of the old 4th Battalion. We gathered from his remarks that this was the only unit under the British flag that could be mentioned in the same breath as the Highland Light Infantry or the Royal Scots. McGee was evacuated just before we went into the Somme battle and never returned. He died shortly after he reached Australia.

Our stay in the so-called 'nursery sector' at Fleurbaix was broken for me by a month's absence at Second Army School, near St Omer. When the British Expeditionary Force in France had grown to over sixty Divisions, there sprang up behind the lines many schools – Army, Corps, Division, and even Brigade Schools. These instructed in infantry training, bombing, machine-guns, signalling, gas, trench-mortars, and even cooking. In specialty subjects these schools were an excellent means of training selected men from various units. They were staffed by experts. Besides, they offered an excellent rest from the front line, and individual soldiers in this enormous army, gathered from all over the Empire, found an opportunity at such schools to learn something about each other.

By 7 October 1916, I was back at the battalion, which I found in reserve billets and waiting to be relieved by the New Zealanders in order that we might be moved down to the Somme battle. The New Zealand Division had already been engaged in that 'blood bath', and was now coming back to Fleurbaix to recuperate.

We marched away through Fleurbaix as dusk fell on 13 October and turned our backs upon the little village, never to return to it. Arriving at Bac St Maur we entered lorries, and in a long stream of these jolting vehicles, a crowded singing battalion of men, we entered the first stage of our journey to the storm centre of the Western Front.

When we had sung 'Never take a walk with Daisy,' 'Down home in Tennessee,' and all the other old favourites until the star songbird of No. 3 Platoon was hoarse, we found our lorry entering a town of considerable size. We 'debussed,' formed up in the street and, with Captain Fanning in the van, led out into the countryside. After a march of several kilometres we entered a farm. The dogs barked furiously and after some delay we were shown into the billet; No. 3 Platoon occupied a large barn. Long Jack and I climbed upon a winnower and, making our beds there, were soon asleep.

In this place for a long weekend we spent our time training at attack formation in the wake of an imaginary moving curtain barrage. This was the new scheme of attack on the enemy's fortified field positions. Our waves of assault were checked as to pace in advance to a time schedule laid down beforehand, Captain Fanning supervising our company's movements with his customary thoroughness.

On the Sunday I was told by Captain Fanning to take a man and make a number of bayonet blobs. I took Peter Duncan. The trees in the area were few and the hedges grew no sticks suitable for the purpose. Peter and I decided that the battens of an unused farm gate lying behind our billets would answer our purpose well. We dared not take it unless unobserved by the family, for fear of having the A.I.F. billed with a sum that would construct a whole barn. About 11 a.m. Madame and her family arrayed in their Sunday best departed along the road apparently on the way to church.

Much to our disgust a boy about ten years old hung around our cook-house and appeared as if he did not intend to leave. Peter told him a couple of times that he would be late for Mass and finally, this admonition having no effect, Peter said: 'Let's break the damned gate up. This garcon intends to stay here all day.'

So we started on the gate. Before we had the second batten off the boy was in top-gear travelling in the wake of monsieur and Madame along the road. This decided us. We nailed the battens on again and were sitting smoking by the cook's fire when papa and boy returned hot-foot. They could not disguise their surprise to find the gate intact and of apparently no interest to us. I trust that papa found consolation for having missed his devotions. That night we knocked some palings off his fence and completed our supply of bayonet sticks.

The chief incident here was the ballot taken in pursuance of the Australian referendum on conscription.[3] It was amazing to me that most of our men seemed resolved to vote 'No'. The main reason was the reluctance of the men (all volunteers, and still willing to fight for the cause that brought them overseas) to vote in favour of forcing their countrymen to join up and help in the fight. It was typical of the Australian soldier that he would face all the dangers that came his way, but would not vote to compel others of his countrymen, who had just as much to fight for as he had, to risk their lives in the common cause.

53

We marched out in the afternoon of 17 October to entrain for another stage of the journey to the Somme. Packed like sardines in covered railway trucks, forty men to the truck (as the legend on its side allowed), we made a most uncomfortable night journey from Bailleul West station through Hazebrouck, Calais, Boulogne and Abbeville.

With darkness, rain came down, causing us to pull-to the sliding doors and sit, with small pieces of candles burning on the floor, talking or singing to while away the tediousness of the journey. Sleep in our cramped position was practically impossible. Long Jack, Sergeant Skinny Elliott, and myself were close together and after telling many tales played cut-throat euchre, interrupting the game occasionally to stand up and stretch our cramped limbs. As day broke our train pulled into the yard of a large station, where we were ordered to detrain, formed up in a raw wind, and marched into the main street of the large village of Pont Remy.

'A' Company halted a little distance up the street from the station, and Captain Fanning, following his usual custom, bustled the men into their billets out of the cold rain. Some confusion occurred over No. 3 Platoon's billet. Captain Fanning promptly settled this by ordering Lieutenant Morrison to take us into an adjacent barn.

Hardly had we stripped off our equipment when the officer in charge of the battalion Lewis guns came along and ordered us out of the building. Captain Fanning reappeared and told the officer that he was not going to keep his men standing in the rain while the Lewis gunners messed about getting clear of the train. His (Fanning's) men were in the billet, and the Lewis gunners could look elsewhere for accommodation.

That was one thing we admired about Captain Fanning. He never kept us standing about under our full packs while the question of billets was being debated. And if he put us into a building no one could bluff him into ordering us out. He himself would flay us unmercifully with his tongue in criticism, overlooking nothing that bore the slightest semblance to slackness. But he was our champion against all the rest of the world, and heaven help the person who tried to take from his company what Fanning considered was its right.

And now our orders came. In the small hours of 20 October we were aroused, and had breakfasted and paraded before daylight. Soon the battalion was moving down the silent cobbled street, our ears and hands tingling with the bite of the frosty air. The rhythm of our marching feet drew some of the inhabitants from their beds to peer through their windows at the brown column swinging through the faint first light of day.

Out into the country we moved. It was an ideal morning for marching. We were fit in body and care-free of mind, and the very beat of our feet seemed like music that kept us in perfect step and march formation. Up came the sun. It turned the frost on the grass and shrubs to diamonds and made the least poetic of us feel that life was grand and nature magnificent.

Whether it was the surroundings or the keen blood of our youth a tingle with the anticipation of something big and dangerous ahead I cannot say, but never had 'A' Company marched better – and it could march under Captain Fanning better than any troops it has been my lot to see. Step was perfect, distance and covering superb. We knew we were doing well, for Captain Fanning kept looking back, would stand by the road-side to watch us pass, then hurry to the van again uttering no word but with an expression of satisfaction upon his face easy to read. And we responded to it.

After marching eight or nine kilometres we halted for a rest. Another battalion of the brigade went past, their equipment often hanging anyhow and their step, their dressing and covering according, and their column concertinaed badly. It was no surprise to us when Captain Fanning called the officers of his company to him and, nodding towards the passing troops, said: 'Gentlemen, you have seen my company march this morning; look at this one.'

Little did we dream that we were showing ourselves off to the satis-faction of our great captain for the last time. He was leading us into the hell-broth of the Somme, a clean, soldierly-looking company disciplined by a master hand. Many of its members were to enter on their long sleep in the mud of Flers, Gueudecourt, Le Transloy, and Bullecourt, and the gallant Fanning was to be among the first to die.

A few kilometres further on we entered a long line of French motor wagons, drawn up on a poplar lined Amiens-Abbeville road. In these we travelled most of the day, through a seemingly endless series of villages mostly crowded with troops; late in the afternoon we 'debussed' on a hill overlooking the village of Buire. We had not eaten since a hasty breakfast before daybreak. Certainly we carried the usual reserve of iron rations, but these we could never use until bidden to do so.

We were cold and stiff after our long bus-ride, and the wind cut through us as we stood in platoons on the hill waiting for the command to move off. But, to our disgust, not into billets in the village below. We marched through it and then on until the next came in sight, and then on through still more villages, each more battered than the last. The sun went down. Still we marched on. Villages now ceased to exist except as rubble heaps.

Along this roadside the whole British army appeared to be camped in shell-torn ground churned into a sea of mud. Everywhere in sight camp-fires twinkled and horses and men fed. Here and there groups of soldiers sang and smoked around their fires. Still we marched on. Darkness came. The road was inches deep in mud which soaked through our heavy boots and clotted our puttees as high as our knees. We were weary and hungry and becoming exasperated at the apparent forgetfulness that we had been on the move since before daylight, and had had nothing to eat since.

Some of the weaker ones dropped out. When were we ever going to stop? The packs that were featherweights when we marched out of Pont Remy were now weighing us down like crushing burdens. Long Jack was my marching mate, and we found ourselves marching at the head of the column with Captain Fanning a silent figure in front.

At last we turned to the left from the road, and sank to our knees in the mud. Not a shelter of any kind was to be seen. 'Here's your bivouac,' said Captain Fanning.

'Where are we going to sleep?' piped a voice from the darkness.

'Right here in the mud,' said Captain Fanning in an angry voice.

We stripped off our equipment. Men were posted on the roadside to guide the stragglers in, and presently our blankets were dumped off some wagons. We made a fire by splitting up a ration case with our bayonets and so at last came to bully beef, biscuits, and tea.

Notes

1. The British 2-inch Medium Trench Mortar, also known as the 2-inch Howitzer, was nicknamed the 'Toffee Apple' or 'Plum Pudding' mortar.
2. Maconochie is a stew of sliced turnips and carrots in a thin soup, named for the Aberdeen Maconochie Company that produced it. It was a widely used as rations for British soldiers in the field during the Boer War and First World War. Though the stew was described as 'tolerable when famished', many soldiers detested it. As one soldier put it: 'Warmed in the tin, Maconochie was edible; cold it was a mankiller.'
3. The referendum of 28 October 1916, instigated by the pro-conscription Australian Prime Minister Billy Hughes, asked the Australian people the following questions: 'Are you in favour of the Government having, in this grave emergency, the same compulsory powers over citizens in regard to requiring their military service, for the term of this War, outside the Commonwealth, as it now has in regard to military service within the Commonwealth?' The referendum was defeated with 1,087,557 in favour and 1,160,033 against.

Chapter 7

Death of Captain Fanning

Delville Wood – Flers – Horrors of the Battlefield – The mud –
A disastrous bombardment – Loss of a great leader.
(21 October to 1 November 1916)

We were aroused early and gazed upon surroundings which would have dampened the spirits of the founder of the House of Optimism. Perhaps it was fortunate that we had arrived in the darkness, for to have grasped fully this scene of desolation in the mood in which we had finished yesterday's march would have blistered our souls.

A biting wind blew, clouds hung low, the earth was a waste of yellowish mud. In the near distance were the blasted remains of what had once been trees. Shell holes, broken wire, smashed trenches, surrounded us. Below was a ravine, and running past our bivouac was the road upon which we had marched last night.

Even at this early hour it was crowded with two lines of transport, one proceeding towards the line, empties returning. The amount of traffic on this narrow roadway had to be seen to be realized. Even from beneath the horses' feet and the wheels men of the labour battalions scraped the slush, using long rods with cups at the end, and filled in ruts and holes with loose metal or bricks from shattered buildings. The streams of traffic never paused for these repairs. Save for the crude shelters made of boxes, tins, or hessian, and some low-roofed stalls for horses, buildings did not exist. In this welter of mud and destruction caused by the drum-fire of the opening phases of the battle of the Somme human beings lived and floundered in the slime, which varied in depth according to the amount of traffic through it.

This was, or had been, Montauban, once a fair village settled on a slight hill. It had been pounded into rubble-heaps by the British barrage, and had fallen to the first British advance on 1 July. From the ruins of the village and the adjacent brick-fields the 6th Bavarian Regiment, mustering 6,000 men, fought desperately to repel the British attacks. They failed, and lost 3,000 men in the attempt.

Hereabouts had been used for the barrage that queen of field guns, the 75 of the French Army. The front line by now was some miles farther forward; this was a sort of staging camp for troops going to and from the line. Engineering material had not yet arrived to make the comfortable closely-hutted areas, the corduroy roads and the duck-board tracks we were to know later on. Breakfast over, word was passed round that we were to take over the front line that night. To confirm this rumour the acting company sergeant-major warned me and a small party of N.C.O.s and men to be ready to move out with Captain Fanning in an hour's time.

Some of the boys had consumed much liquid refreshment during our short stay in Pont Remy. Peter Hughes was one of these, and upon this raw cheerless morning he badly felt the need of a reviver. The only oasis in this desert of thirst and mud was the company quarter-master's store, housed beneath a tarpaulin thrown over two forks and a ridge pole. Temporarily in charge was the quarter-master sergeant's clerk, known as Old Harry. He was sandy-headed, watery-eyed, flabby of skin, and verging on middle-age, and as cranky as a houseful of old maids. Had Old Harry paid for everything in the store from his own purse he could not have been meaner with it. But the troops suspected that when opportunity arose he treated himself handsomely to rum and other things. Peter Hughes hated him but, driven by the crying need of a nip, he approached Old Harry, and in the nicest tones at his command, said: 'Harry, give me a nip of rum?'

'Indeed I will not,' snarled Harry. 'You won't, you rum-thieving old bastard!' said Peter. 'I'll have rum to drink when they are trying to grow lilies on your grave!'

This little passage raised a laugh among a small group that overheard it.

With my party I reported to Captain Fanning, and he led the way to the roadside, where we were joined by a party from 'D' Company in charge of Captain Sheen. Along the sloppy road we proceeded in single file, wending our way in and out of the two lines of transport which took up most of the road space – G.S. wagons, limbers, and mule-teams laden with shells carried on pack-saddles.

A mile or so past the remains of Bernafay Wood the wheeled transport halted where the road was obliterated in a waste of shell-torn ground, and we came upon a sight that must have made the angels weep – Delville Wood, or Devil's Wood, as the soldiers called it.

Shell fire had torn its great trees into blackened jagged stumps and littered the ground with the trunks and branches. Trench systems had criss-crossed through the wood, separated in places by only a few feet: huge shell craters pock-marked the ground, many of them partly filled with greenish water, and the desolation was completed by a carpet of the rotting corpses of the men who had lost and won the wood.

British and German lay here unburied. The ground was strewn with equipment, rifles, cartridges, and all the other debris of an untidy battle-field. Here had been staged one of the fiercest fights of the Somme offensive. From 15 July to 18 July every inch of the wood had been con-tested in hand-to-hand fighting, and the survivors of each attack and counter-attack consolidated behind hastily thrown-up, cover, consisting often of the bodies of the dead.

In this hideous place the gallant South African Brigade and Scottish troops of the 9th Division had met in a death-grapple the 3rd Guards Division and the 5th Brandenburg Division of the German Army. Throughout the three days and nights the battle had raged. The South Africans paid a terrible price for their gains of a few yards at a time, and finally the enemy, driven out, concentrated upon Delville Wood all the heavy artillery that he could bring to bear. The South Africans suffered such a tornado of a bombardment that it was incredible mortals could live under it. But they stuck it out, beating back repeated counter-attacks. When relieved, their few survivors were in the last stages of exhaustion. It was not, however, until several weeks later that the whole of Delville Wood was captured by British troops.

The tide of battle had now rolled on, leaving Delville Wood to its unburied dead and to form a doubtful screen for a battery of heavy artillery firing from its western edge. Our little party was very silent as we picked our way through it. Forward our way led into a hollow devoid of cover where our field batteries were firing at full pressure. Away to the left were the battered remains of High Wood, another scene of heavy fighting.

Coming towards us over a low rise were many walking wounded on their way back to the aid posts. We came to a trench known as Turk Lane, narrow, deep, and heavy with mud. We struggled along it, sometimes knee-deep in the stinking slime. Turk Lane had been until recently German, and bodies of dead men were lying on parapet and parados throughout its length.

Presently we halted. A boyish-looking Tommy with white face, staring eyes, and blood-stained tunic came along. He asked me to light his cigarette, and if we were going to relieve the front line. I replied in the affirmative, and he added, 'My God, you are going into hell up there.' I quite believed him.

A Tommy sergeant-major got up out of the trench, and walked along the top to a battered German dugout which apparently was being used as a headquarters. Captain Fanning emerged from this dugout, passed the word back for me to report, and ordered me to accompany him with my party.

We entered a shallow communication trench at right angles from Turk Lane. The bottom was so slippery that we had to catch hold of both sides to lever ourselves along. We came into a badly knocked-about trench in which were a small party of men and two officers from the Manchester Regiment of the 30th British Division, caked with mud, unshaven, and exhausted. Two of the officers' batmen were endeavouring to boil a dixie of water over a small fire.

Captain Fanning called out to me to follow him. The Manchesters' captain, clad in an officer's trench coat and carrying a walking stick, led the way. Out of the trench we climbed, and in the bright sunlight of early afternoon the three of us walked slowly along the company front which we were to take over that night.

The only semblance of trench that existed was perhaps a stretch of about thirty yards, and in depth about three feet. The front line troops were lying in posts which were nothing but shell-craters. The Germans were only some three hundred yards away; we walked along in full view of them. The Manchester captain and Fanning talked casually as they strolled along, Captain Fanning turning to point out to me where the platoon sectors commenced and finished. I marked these by sticking rifles (which lay around in profusion) into the mud, so that I would be able to lead the platoons to their positions in the darkness.

We went to where the company front linked with the 9th Scottish Division, which had brigaded with it the South Africans. We returned to the support trench by a sunken road that ran from the front line to the supports. I was not sorry to get back into the trench, for throughout the walk I had expected every moment that a sniper would open up on us. Coming from a sector in which it was almost certain death to show even the top of a head over the parapet during hours of daylight, it certainly appeared to me as if we were asking for our tickets to walk along this sector in full view of the Germans.

The sergeant-major of the Manchesters gave me a full jar of rum. I entrusted this, along with my overcoat, to a lance corporal of my platoon known as Peter Doody (on account of his dismal outlook on life), with strictest instructions that he was to sit on the jar of rum and if he valued his skin not to lose sight of it.

During the whole afternoon the shelling from both sides was very heavy. But as darkness fell the Germans put over a barrage which lashed the sector into an inferno of bursting and whistling shells. The din was so great that we had to roar at the top of our voices to carry on a conversation. Lieutenant Dykes came into the support trench just as the strafe commenced, and told Captain Fanning that the company was in Turk Lane waiting to move in. While the shelling was at its height a Tommy officer came hurrying along the trench. Upon seeing our little group he called out to Fanning – 'Colonel's compliments, sir, and will you relieve the front line at once?'

'My compliments to your colonel,' replied Fanning, 'I will relieve the front line when it is dark.'

In a few minutes the Tommy officer was back again. 'Colonel So and So's orders are that you are to relieve at once.'

'You tell your colonel from me to go to Hell! I will not take my men over the top to relieve in this barrage while it is still light,' said Fanning, and he did not move his men until it was dark.

When darkness came, I led Lieutenant Dykes with Nos. 2 and 4 Platoons into the right sector, and then Lieutenants Creber and Morrison with Nos. 1 and 3 into the left. The platoons were immediately spaced out, and before the Manchesters were clear of the line we had commenced to dig. Captain Fanning walked along the company front and to each group said, 'Dig like hell tonight, Boys. The deeper you are tomorrow the safer you will be.'

When I returned to my section, I found it had already suffered two casualties. Stretcher-bearers were not available. I got my wounded back into the support-trench, and set about looking for the lance-corporal whom I had left in charge of the jar of rum and my greatcoat. I found him minus both. He had become flustered when the barrage came down and forgotten everything else. I heard later that the support company did themselves rather well on the rum. No regular issue reached us during the time we held this line.

Later in the night Captain Fanning sent me with a fatigue party to bring up boxes of bombs from battalion headquarters. When I went to the right sector with their share of bombs Captain Fanning was sitting on the fire-step talking to Lieutenant Dykes, and puffing at his pipe. I was about to move away after my work was finished, when Captain Fanning said: 'I was glad when we had finished that walk this afternoon, sonny. A German with half an eye could have seen that we were officers by our sticks and trench coats. As an English Johnny set the fashion, I had to follow in all details.' I was glad to know that I was not the only member of the party who did not wish to tarry on that stroll.

All night long we dug, and the shelling never abated. In this sector the guns fired without ceasing day and night. We dug furiously and when daylight came we had a good trench built. At 'stand to' the Germans basted us with a terrific barrage. The earth trembled under the concussion, and our line became an inferno of bursting shells hidden by clouds of smoke. Earth shot into the air in geysers, and great clods rained down upon us as we crouched low on the fire-steps. The sun came up in a cloudless sky. No rations or water had come up to us during the night, so we ate bully-beef and biscuits from our reserve rations. In the bright sunshine of the early morning the shelling eased somewhat, and we had time to look around.

In the rear were the still-smoking ruins of the village of Flers. To the left front was a queer sort of a large mound which we afterwards learned was the Butte de Warlencourt.[1] Directly in front could be seen the tops of trees and the roofs of the villages of Le Barque and Ligny Thilloy. Past these was the town of Bapaume.

In front and between the line and the support trench the ground was strewn with the bodies of men of the Royal West Kent Regiment and the Seaforth Highlanders. Across the shell-torn ground, a few hundred yards away, a line of thrown-up earth marked the German front line trench. Now and then we noticed a German walking along the top of the trench, a practice we soon adopted. This explained why we were not sniped at yesterday. Both sides apparently left the killing to be done by the artillery unless an attack was launched.

As the morning went on, the shelling increased in volume. Many 'planes crossed and re-crossed our lines. Directly in front one of ours was caught with a direct hit from a shell and fell, a crumpled and burning mass, behind the German line. In the early afternoon another British 'plane came down out of control and landed about 100 yards in the rear of our trench. Willing hands, in spite of the barrage, rushed across and assisted the observer into the support trench. The Germans deluged the vicinity with shells until they destroyed the 'plane with a direct hit.

While this strafe was at its height, along the trench at a trot came a swarthy-skinned lad from the Australian outback, bleeding from two shrapnel wounds in his head and one in his arm. He was quite delighted, and stopped to have a word with Long Jack and me, lighting a cigarette while he told us, 'This will do me for my cut'. Receiving directions to the aid post, he left us at a trot, with the blood running down over his shoulders.

The left platoon rescued a Tommy who had been buried alive by a shell the previous night. But the worst sight of all was an English chap from No. 3 Platoon with shell shock. He had been wounded at the battle of Fromelles, and had rejoined us only a few days before we took over this sector. Bent double, sometimes on all fours, the poor chap came along the trench foaming at the mouth and babbling insanely. It was hard to recognize in this awful wreck the tall straight young Englishman who had been with us since the early days in Egypt. He was the most pitiful sight imaginable. He never came back to the battalion.

When night fell the Germans got the wind up rather badly. They threw up S.O.S. rockets and their artillery barraged our line with a terrific hail of shells. A machine-gunner standing a few yards along the trench from my post was caught by low-bursting shrapnel. He was killed instantly and his uniform was almost stripped off him. I helped to throw his body over the parapet.

62

In the midst of this barrage Captain Fanning came along the company front and spoke to each post, telling them to keep well into the parapet. He was of the opinion that the Germans had noticed the work that had been done on our line over night, and were evidently expecting an attack to develop from it at dawn or during the hours of darkness.

After the bombardment had died down we set ourselves to repairing the trench works. No food or water had been got up to us and the demand for the latter was so great that some men drank the stinking water from the shell holes. We found iron rations in the haversacks of the dead men who lay about.

Towards midnight Lieutenant Morrison came to tell us that we were to be relieved, and an hour or so later the relief came along, a company from one of the 15th Brigade Battalions. Our stay in the front line had been for only two days, but we were exhausted by the heavy digging, incessant shelling, and the lack of all food except our iron rations – or water save what our water bottles contained when we went in.

Sleep, day or night, had been out of the question. After a weary march through mud we found ourselves back at Montauban. During our absence much engineering material had been dumped on the ground, uprights over which tarpaulins had been thrown were erected, and a few bell-tents had risen for officers. Into each of the tarpaulin-covered shelters a platoon was packed. Long Jack and I made ourselves a small kennel out of material from the dump, ate a meal, crawled into our rude shelter, and fell into the deep sleep of utter exhaustion.

I awoke next morning with a feverish cold. A dull raw day turned to rain; I lay in the little kennel sick and miserable. Late in the afternoon, Jimmy (looking spotless in a new uniform and fresh from Blighty leave) brought my friend of pre-war days, Big Bert, to see me. We had not met since Tel-el-Kebir. Since then Bert had been wounded and had had a turn in hospital in England. He was now the roughest-looking diamond in the A.I.F., with several days' beard on his face, the seat out of his breeches, a hat which had apparently been used to beat out fire, and a laugh that was good to hear. He jeered at me about being lousy. Was not the army a great thing to be in? Were we not winning the war quickly? Germany was only so many hundred miles away. He blathered away in this strain until I began to feel a new interest in life and was sorry when he had to leave.

After another night's rest I awoke feeling a new man. Apparently the quickest way to cure influenza in the army was to lie on the sodden ground with little covering and the temperature near freezing point in a biting north wind.

Word had got round that on the morrow we would return to the line and carry out the attack. We cleaned our rifles, oiled our cartridge-clips, checked our iron rations, and filled our water bottles. This finished, Long

Jack and I strolled down into the ravine where the 1st Australian Brigade were encamped in the mud.

Here I saw Big Bert, his brother, and their pal S————. These three were battalion bombers. We spent an hour discussing the war, and enjoyed Big Bert's flowery description of his treatment in a Canadian hospital, and the girl in the green bathing costume whom he had taught to swim at some bathing-resort in the Isle of Wight. Upon leaving Bert wished me a wound and a clean shirt.

They moved into the line that night and took part in a raid, in which S———— was killed and Big Bert and his brother wounded. Bert was awarded the D.C.M. for his work during this operation, and his wound got him his ticket to Blighty. I met him next in much cleaner surroundings.

Our own attack was again postponed. The rain was ceaseless, and the north wind biting in the extreme. As for the mud – a Dickens, a Zola, or a Victor Hugo might be able to describe it. Around our bivouac it was knee-deep. The whole terrain was a sea of mud. The only place in the vicinity where anything like a sound footing was to be found was along the road that ran past our camp. Even this, with the ceaseless rain and the ever-moving lines of transport, was several inches deep in. mud, though constantly scraped by the labour battalions. The mud caked our boots and puttees into one yellow cloying mess, inches thick. Our feet were saturated and so cold that they felt as if they were encased in ice-blocks.

To wear an ordinary military greatcoat one had either to cut it short like a reefer-jacket, or tie up the tail round the waist. The mud round Montauban was not only dirty; it was foul, slimy, and reeked of corpses. The sand of the desert had been maddening to look upon for any length of time, but the mud of the Somme during 1916 drowned men's spirits with horror. For the next six months winter, rain, and mud were to be worse enemies than the Germans.

Yet at night when we had piled into our braziers wood chopped from German dugouts, we sat round the fires singing and telling stories as light-heartedly as if we were on a picnic. It was the companionship of men with hearts of gold, learning to live only for the hour, which enabled us to conquer the utter misery of these surroundings.

Another day of rain in this so-called rest-place, and on 30 October we were ordered up to relieve the line. On the way up we were drenched in a heavy thunderstorm and Turk Lane when we entered it was hip-deep in water. At one place I put my foot on a broken duckboard and fell headlong into the slush. Those behind gave me a cheer.

Entering the front line we took up our posts as near as possible to those we had occupied during our previous tour in this sector. The trench was now a quagmire along which it was almost impossible to move. The sides had caved in, leaving holes as large as rooms across the trench.

The sides were so soft and slippery that where the trench was deep it was impossible for a man to climb out of it without assistance. Long Jack, Grenna, and I formed a post.

First we dug a shell-slit in the parapet, wide and high enough for a man to stand in while he kept watch. In the parados we cut another where the two off post could sit with their feet across the trench to avoid the slush of the bottom. In short reliefs we watched all night in the lashing rain driven by a bitter wind which through our sodden clothes chilled us to the marrow. The rain and wind did not cause the shelling to slacken on either side. It was the worst night I ever had in the front line. Cigarettes and the optimism of Long Jack kept us alive.

One man expressed the general feeling with the opinion: 'If I do not have pneumonia tomorrow, there is something wrong with my lungs.' Undoubtedly it was the army's hardening process that saved us. We had become so hardened that we complained of nothing so long as we still lived.

Late next afternoon word was passed along for Lieutenant Morrison to report to Captain Fanning. We were sure this meant that we were 'for it'. Sure enough he brought back details. We were to attack at daylight next morning – not the general advance on a wide front that we had been led to expect, but a minor operation carried out by our 14th Brigade in conjunction with the 50th British Division on the left. This operation had as its objective 'the improving of the line' (as the communiqués called it), an operation generally notable chiefly for the number of new white crosses it set up which altogether outweighed any advantage gained.

We were to be relieved by another company of the battalion, and were to spend the night in the support trench about fifty yards to the rear. At dusk the relief came. We moved back to supports and took up a position to try to get a sleep. Long Jack and I found ourselves in a part of the trench that had been blown in by a large shell, making a nice sloping bank of mud with a water frontage. However, it would have to be worse than bad if we could not sleep in it.

Just as we settled down, Jimmy came along the trench looking for me. He had some rum, procured heaven knows where; we had not seen any since coming to the Somme. He gave Long Jack and me a good nip, and under the blessed influence of that Great Spirit we fell asleep, not caring that our bed was wet mud and our feet were in the water. Before daylight we were aroused to find that the attack had again been postponed.

But this day (1 November) was a day of tragedy.

We had come back to our possy in the trench from a prowl in the vicinity, and were about to eat when a company runner came hurrying around the traverse. He was white and breathless as he asked for Lieutenant Morrison. The latter was lying down trying to sleep. The runner told him that Captain Fanning had been badly wounded and that Lieutenant Dykes had been killed. All thought of eating was banished from our minds by this tragic news.

Presently word came along that a chance shell had done the damage. Lieutenant Dykes had been decapitated as he sat in the side of the trench, a signaller had been killed, and Captain Fanning had an arm and a leg badly shattered. My pal Jimmy, the company sergeant-major, was wounded in the knee, Barney hit in the shoulder, and Peter Hughes suffering from concussion. It was a disaster for 'A' Company.

Sammy Dykes, the fighting Scot with his long Gallipoli service, had risen from the ranks step by step to wear his stars only a few months – and then go west. He was Fanning's right-hand man, coolness itself under fire, respected and admired by every man in the company. His body was put over the parados and buried in a shell hole, to remain there till many months later when his pals Bobbie Myles and Bill Brunt walked several kilometres to give him a decent burial and put a white cross over his grave.

How long afterwards I cannot recollect, but early in the afternoon we heard we were to be relieved and had to get ready to move out at once. I found myself leading No. 3 Platoon at the head of the march out. Turk Lane we found impassable. We legged each other out of the trench and started to plod our weary way along the top. Each platoon as it came to the junction clambered out of the trench until the whole company was in file, struggling along in full view of the Germans.

The enemy soon opened up on us with 5.9s. Fortunately many were 'overs' which burst with a roar and flung the mud high in the air around us; but some he put right on to his target. To walk through the mud would have taxed the strength of an ox; to men in our condition it was exhausting in the extreme. Every few yards men would sink down panting like broken-winded horses, and lie full length in the mud, so done up that close-bursting shells mattered little. Then up and on for a short distance until their strength petered out again.

Hampered with a wrenched ankle I gradually dropped back to the end of the line, Long Jack keeping me company. As we came to the end of Turk Lane, we met our relief coming down the opposite slope. The Germans quickly availed themselves of this choice of targets and shelled very heavily.

By the time we had topped the rise Long Jack and I were losing ground steadily and the short evening was drawing to a close. Stretcher-bearers from the 14th Field Ambulance were coming up the reverse of the hill to pick up the wounded that had been conveyed to this point by the battalion bearers.

Two stretchers were on the ground, upon one of which Long Jack recognized Captain Fanning. I went across and spoke to him. In his deep voice he growled: 'I am not too bad, sonny. My left arm is badly shattered, and my right leg is nearly to pulp.'

He continued: 'You know, these battalion bearers are wonderful. But through the mud the journey has been hell for me. Can you see anything of the sledge?' This referred to a horse-drawn sledge upon which stretcher cases were pulled over the mud to the field aid post. I looked around and told him that it was coming at that moment. I saw him on to the sledge, but his face had already the greyness of death which even the mud upon it failed to hide.

I turned away as the sledge started, and walked across to Long Jack with my heart in my boots.

'How is he?' asked Jack.

'Well, by his talk he will live, but there is death in his face,' I replied.

Captain Fanning was taken to the casualty clearing station at Becordel and hurried on to the operating table, where he died. His death was an irreparable loss to the company, and a grievous loss to the battalion; in fact, the A.I.F. was the poorer by the passing of a man, whose name, if he had been spared, would have become famous in the division. Soldiers on active service have short memories for those who have crossed the Great Divide, but Captain Fanning was never forgotten.[2]

Months later, when we were near Becordel, on the only afternoon that we had off from parade a voluntary fatigue party went across and attended to his grave. Right up to the beginning of 1918 when we got our last reinforcements from Australia the boys would gather round the braziers at night in the billets, and would entertain the newcomers with stories of Captain Fanning and what 'A' Company was like when he commanded it.

I would preserve this last story of him. As he lay on the stretcher at the regimental aid post, some men of the 54th Battalion nearby recognized the captain. One turned to his companions and said: 'That's Captain Fanning, badly knocked. 'A' Company of the 56th is buggered now.'

Fanning overheard the remark, and he asked for the man to be sent to him. The soldier came, no doubt expecting to be reprimanded. Instead Fanning said, 'I don't know who you are, sonny. But you have paid me the greatest compliment of my life.' Perhaps in this unexpected tribute couched in the rough words of a soldier Captain Fanning found some consolation in the agony of his last hours.

Notes

1. The Butte de Warlencourt is an ancient burial mound that lies alongside the Albert-Bapaume road, north-east of the village of Le Sars. Though the first attack on the Butte was made on 1 October 1916, it was finally captured by British troops after the German retreat to the Hindenburg Line in February 1917.

2. The son of Lieutenant Colonel F.G. and Mary Fanning, of Coomeragee, Casino, New South Wales, 25-year-old Captain Frederick Fanning is buried in Dartmoor Cemetery which is located just to the north of the village of Becordel-Becourt. The cemetery was begun (as Becordel-Becourt Military Cemetery) in August 1915 and was used by the battalions holding that part of the line; its name was changed in May 1916 at the request of the 8th and 9th Battalions of the Devonshire Regiment. In September 1916, the XV Corps Main Dressing Station was established in the neighbourhood.

Chapter 8

The Gueudecourt Sector

The Gueudecourt Sector – The icy mud of the trenches –
Horrors of trench feet and of rescuing the wounded – Christmas in Buire.
(November and December 1916)

Mid-November saw us again exchanging billets for the line, in another of those relays which enabled the British army to survive the duties of garrisoning the Somme trenches in the appalling winter of 1916–17. We spent several days in the fatigue camp at Fricourt where in gangs we scraped mud from the road all day long. Then we moved on a stage to Montauban.

Here a wonderful change had taken place. Rows of Nissen huts had sprung into being with raised duck-board tracks well above ground level, and a wide corduroy track ran from the main Albert Road to the huts containing the quarter-master's stores.

The weather was very bad. Sleety rain fell without ceasing; at night icy winds blew. Below the camp in the ravine a large dump had been made of coal, wood, and engineering material. This was in charge of Tommy engineers, who mounted a guard over it. The day after our arrival Peter Duncan came to the stores hut, occupied also by 'A' Company's sergeants, to inquire if a bag of coal were worth a nip of rum. The quarter-master sergeant, Bobbie Brew, said that it was, but asked where the coal was coming from.

'Don't ask questions' said Peter, 'but have the rum ready.'

He returned to his platoon's hut, had a secret confab with four pals, and afterwards a quiet talk with Sergeant Elliott. Presently a party of four privates armed with bags fell in to the commands of Peter, who for the occasion wore the chevrons of a sergeant. The party marched off into the ravine, and after some little time struggled through the mud into camp laden with four bags of coal. Two were deposited in the platoon hut, the sergeant's tunic removed, and Peter with his braves appeared at the quarter-master's hut carrying two bags of coal. One was bartered for rum, and the other he presented to Lieutenant Morrison in exchange for more rum.

This episode caused great amusement among the boys when they learned how the coal had been procured. Knowing the awe with which Tommy privates regarded any rank from lance corporal upwards Peter had, in his borrowed sergeant's tunic, marched his party to the engineers' dump under the very nose of the sentry, halted them smartly, and then rapped out the order: 'Fill your bags.' The sentry had looked on without misgiving.

From Montauban we moved to Bernafay Wood, where accommodation consisted chiefly of holes in the ground. Long Jack, Grenna, Collins, and myself took possession of one such hole. Its walls fell down in large cakes when touched. Its roof was of timber with earth heaped upon it. As the roof was only a matter of a few inches above ground level, it often happened that in the darkness stragglers walked upon it, to be shooed off with lusty curses.

Here the fatigue duties were unloading trains, carrying material, and building huts. The weather continued to be shockingly bad, the rain seemed never-ending, and the cold was intense. Living in the poor shelters caused much sickness. The first Nissen huts that were completed were used as resting-places for those who fell ill but were not considered bad enough to be evacuated.

At this time a soldier had to be almost at death's door before he was sent back. It was the only way to keep the battalions anywhere near strength. Men evacuated sick might recover in a few days, but be held at the base for weeks. Rum was our best doctor. To work and live in wet clothes, sleep in a hole in the ground under those conditions, and keep healthy would have been impossible without the rum issue. Taken neat on an empty stomach first thing in the morning, it went down like molten fire and, however wet or depressed we might be, it sent our spirits soaring and created such an appetite that we could have eaten a dead man's boot.

Still, there were old women of both sexes at home and in the army who moved heaven and earth to have this ration stopped. They ought to have been made to see the Somme forward area in winter time. It has often amused me since to hear the stay-at-homes talk about the rum issued to soldiers in France. The general opinion seems to be that before we went over the top we were well dosed with rum. Every experienced soldier knew that in an attack he wanted all his faculties and a clear brain, and that to fuddle oneself with rum would be almost to commit suicide.

On 30 November 1916, we moved up to relieve the line at Gueudecourt. Our new company commander, Captain Smythe, told us that we were to move into supports that night to do four days in the front line at a stretch. If we made up our minds to fight sickness and trench feet and stuck out the four days, we should not be sent in again while the Division was holding this sector. But if under losses through sickness we had to be withdrawn

70

after two days, then we should have to come in for another stretch. At this time of the year under the prevailing conditions four days in the line was almost an eternity. Trench feet and sickness had taken a heavy toll of the battalions which had lately been holding the line, and every endeavour was being made to lessen this wastage. It was given out that any man contracting trench-feet would be crimed with loss of pay.

The trenches of the Gueudecourt sector were situated on the far side of a ridge, which during even the darkest of nights was under observation under the enemy's flare lights. The company sector was not held in a continuous line but consisted of a series of communication posts. The trench was in a bad state, and passage along it was impossible on account of the mud. All carrying parties and reliefs had to go overland during the night.

When darkness came we started for the front line. Once we left the duckboard tracks our progress was painfully slow. The mud was atrocious. We sank to our knees at times and had to help each other along. It must have taken us two hours to cover a mile at the rate we progressed. Eventually we crossed the crest of the ridge against which we had been warned as the danger-spot. Evidently we were not seen; only the normal amount of shelling took place. A broken aeroplane was lying just in rear of Company headquarters. Here No. 3 Platoon turned to the left and followed the trench for some distance almost direct toward the German line. Then it bent away sharply at right angles to the left.

We reached No. 3 Platoon's headquarters, the most strongly held post on the left sector. The trench here was wide and junctioned with a sap which ran out directly towards the German line for about twenty-five yards and ended in a formation resembling the half of the letter T.

In this communication trench were two partly-made dugouts, one at the junction of the communication trench with our main line and the other a few yards farther along. The sap had wide open sides, was narrow at the bottom, knee-deep in water; and the Germans could look along it for some distance. Where the upper part of the T joined the lower was placed the headquarters Lewis gun and crew. At the end of the T was situated a bombing block in charge of Long Jack.

The latter post appeared to be well sighted, but this could not be said of the position of the Lewis gun. Here the trench was shallow, and as wide as a room. I told Lieutenant Morrison that I though this post too exposed, and under too constant observation without sufficient cover. He agreed with me, but said we had relieved a Lewis gun post in this position and therefore must occupy it until otherwise ordered.

Our rations were poor in the extreme. Even the water had to be measured. Bread worked out at a loaf to six or eight men, not the two-pound loaf of civilian dimensions but the very much smaller army loaf. Meat was generally corned pork. There was a small issue of rum, served out at stand down in the morning, and whale-oil for our feet. The rations had to be brought up by fatigue parties through the sea of mud, generally in the rain. When it reached the troops in the front line the food was anything but appetizing. The bread would be sopping wet and mud-stained, whilst the meat had adhering to it the fluff from the wet bags in which it had been carried. Still, we ate it gladly. Although the cold was intense, and it rained practically the whole of the time, we had nothing hot either to eat or drink.

The conditions of the front line were dreadful. The whole terrain was glistening yellowish brown slime which clung to everything that touched it. Over our rifles we kept breech-covers of waterproof material, but even with this protection we could not have used our bolts for rapid fire if the winning of the war had depended upon it. The wet coldness numbed our bodies and our senses. The only shelters were our waterproof sheets covering shell-slits in the side of the trench, into which we crouched when off duty.

Our hands swelled with the cold so that the men almost cried with the pain. Our faces puffed up into a bloated appearance. Often did I open my tunic and shirt and thrust my wet muddy hands against my skin in an effort to get them warm. Our feet were blocks of ice. Twice a day we rubbed them frantically with whale-oil and changed our socks, partly drying the wet ones by putting them around our waists.

The days were an eternity in length during which movement (except within the narrow confines of the posts) was impossible. Sleep was prac-tically out of the question. Exhaustion certainly caused sleep of a kind, but the cold soon interrupted even that. The nights were occupied with watches and work, and did give us an opportunity to get out of the trench and move about. All the while shelling was constant and accurate.

Why our people held these waterlogged, badly-battered trenches through the winter, when only a few hundred yards in the rear was a position that gave better observation and would certainly have been less hard on the infantry, can only be explained by the army's policy of holding every inch so dearly gained in this ghastly country. As we used to say, we were so many yards, feet, inches, nearer to Germany.

By the time we had been two days in the line many of the men were plainly showing signs of the strain. Nearly all had their feet swollen, the white spongy-looking flesh which was one of the first signs of trench-feet. Our platoon officer and the N.C.O.s went to great pains to see that the men rubbed their feet twice a day with the whale-oil on issue. After this was done they had their feet inspected by the officer, or an N.C.O. in charge of the post, before again putting on their boots.

Trench foot was a loathsome thing. Beside the swelling, the nails became discoloured, and when the disease was in an advanced state the feet gave off the odour of putrefying flesh. Many an amputation was necessary from this disease. Some authorities declared that it was caused by a germ bred in the filth of the ground. This germ was supposed to enter the feet under the toe-nails.

Trench feet made the wastage high in battalions holding the line during the winter months. It was pitiful to see the men who suffered from it plodding their way along the duck-board tracks. No boots would fit them and they had to swathe their feet about with many sand-bags. All men who saw much service in the front line of the Somme had the malady in a more or less serious form. Not only did our feet swell and become spongy, but our faces took on the same swollen bloated look. Our hands became puffed, and the backs bore a horrible purplish tint. Some were evacuated with what was diagnosed as 'trench-eyes'.

There was only one worse state than having to stand garrison day and night in this mud. That was being bombarded in it. The German barrages used to do a lot of damage. They regularly used high explosive shells, many of them the dreaded 5.9s. Our line would occasionally at evening be marked by a cloud of heavy smoke, pierced with the wicked orange flashes of the bursting shells. They whistled through the air to burst with a nerve-shattering roar, flinging the mud high and making the trench almost rock under the concussion. Only when our artillery became active and basted the German front line did the fire slacken and eventually cease. The labour of the stretcher-bearers in getting out the wounded beggars description. Even to bury a dead body took an incredibly long time.

In one bombardment a 5.9 shell obliterated that exposed Lewis gun position against which my instinct had rebelled. It was just after stand down one morning when all but the post garrisons had crawled from the more open mud to seek sleep. We heard the burst very close, and immediately afterwards were called by a runner.

Lieutenant Morrison led as we ploughed our way to the post and were met with the worst sight I saw during the war. Not a man of the gun team had escaped. Five were dead, and several others were shockingly wounded. The body of J———, still sat in the shell slit where I had spoken to him only five minutes before. His face was entirely blown away, leaving just the back of his head; one hand and forearm were also missing, likewise a knee; but his corpse had not moved.

We turned from this ghastly sight to bind up the wounds of those still living. Our field bandages were inadequate and somebody had to get shell dressings from battalion headquarters. Little bandy-legged Grenna jumped at the job. The trench was impassable. The journey of about 300 yards had to be done practically the whole way overland. Grenna pulled his equipment off, Alex O'Rourke and I legged him up out of the trench, and he started to run as fast as the mud would allow.

He had only gone a matter of yards when zip came the bullets from a German sniper. Then a machine-gun spoke. At this Grenna dived into the trench where he was hidden for a few minutes, to reappear some yards farther along the top crouching as he ran. Again the rifle and machine-gun spoke and again he dived into the trench. Then he was lost to our view, but when the firing continued at intervals we guessed that he was still being missed by the German marksmen.

At length he hove in sight on the return journey, travelling on top until the German sniping got too hot, when he would dive for the trench, soon to reappear as before. Just as he came upon the rear of our parados the crack of a final rifle-shot sounded. Grenna jumped into the trench holding the bandages in his hand, and shouted triumphantly: 'Missed me, you cows!' It was a brave act – for which he was not even recommended for the poorest decoration given by the army.

The Germans had no mercy on stretcher parties, and after experience of their shelling of rescuers struggling in the mud orders were strictly against removing stretcher cases from the line in daylight. The day seemed a year in length. Before it was quite dark Alex O'Rourke heaved the first stretcher out of the sap. The Germans soon commenced to snipe, first with a single rifle shot and then with a machine-gun. Alex never even bothered to look round, but heaved and tugged at the stretcher until he had it on the top. Then he and his mate George Lupton plodded off through the mud. Only the quickly descending darkness quietened the enemy's fire upon them.

The burying of the dead was a terrible task. It took an hour to get the first body carried out through the sap and buried in a shell hole behind the fire trench. The others, therefore, we buried in some of the big shell holes in front of the fire trench, and it occupied us for most of the night.

Upon returning to my post, I heard a man being violently sick in the bottom of the trench. He told me that he was one of the reinforcements that joined the company only the night before, and these were the first dead he had been called upon to handle. I saw that he was only a lad, so I said, 'I am really sorry, sonny, that I took you on that job. But I did not notice that you were a newcomer when I detailed you in the darkness.'

Then in the pale dawn came the rations and an Australian mail. To sit in my little burrow with a waterproof curtain dropped to hide a lighted candle, and read lines of pity from a girl at home, who corresponded with me because I was a pal of her friend, nearly broke down my last human reserves.

We were relieved that night by the 55th Battalion. The German gunners left us alone until we reached the crest of the hill in rear of our line, when he sang his hymn of hate round us with a barrage of whizz-bangs.[1]

Through that and the bog which stretched to the duckboard track in Switch Trench, we plodded like weary beasts of burden and came to rest at last in a long low structure of galvanized iron at Bernafay Wood. Rest, did I say? We had just rolled into our blankets when an adjacent six-inch naval gun fired, and the explosion brought our tin roof upon our heads. With much cursing we turned out to readjust it, and then fell asleep under even the regular discharge of that gun.

After eight days in reserve and support trenches we were obliged, after all, to do another two days in the front line. That two days' front line duty was as much as the battalion could endure without collapse speaks for itself of the conditions of weather and trenches and the reduced physical strength of the men under the assaults of bombardment, sickness, and dysentery.

Some of us began to appreciate now the hard training we had undergone in the desert. We often remarked that the men who had been trained in Egypt withstood the hardships of the front line much better than the men who came to us on draft from the training camps in England. The rigorous training which the battalion underwent hardened those who survived it to the toughness of working bullocks. It was the mainstay of many of us now in the mud of the Somme winter.

When we left the line upon relief each platoon had to send off its 'lame-ducks' several hours ahead of the effective remnant; this was the only means of retaining organization in the battalion during the march out, for the sick and crippled could not move for more than a few yards without resting.

Four days before Christmas we journeyed by field train from the forward area to the unfestive looking village of Buire, our rest camp. The village was typical of those on the fringe of the Somme battlefields. Some of its houses showed signs of shelling. Its one main street was churned into mud with the ceaseless stream of transports and marching infantry passing to and from the line. Its inhabitants consisted of aged men, frightened-looking children, and women with care-lined faces – also fowls which 'got into top gear and beat it for a hiding-place' as soon as the head of an Australian column hove into sight. Every second house was an estaminet which dispensed *vin blanc* and *vin rouge* of dubious vintage. These places were open for troops only during certain hours. To the villagers soldiers had long since ceased to be anything but customers with a thirst.

'A' Company was billeted in barns round a large yard. Amusement did not exist, notwithstanding the fact that an impoverished-looking Y.M.C.A., with papers and magazines, months and years old, squatted at the end of the village. Buire was anything but exciting; but its immediate merit was that the army here provided steaming hot baths. Our Christmas Eve bath here was our first for many weeks, and no words can describe the desire for it of men whose bodies and clothes were overrun with vermin and foul with trench mud. Inside the building we stripped, handed our underclothing into a store, and entered the bathing-room. Here each man, equipped with a piece of soap, stood under steaming hot showers. These ran for long enough to wet us, and were then turned off while we lathered.

When we were well soaped, the water came on again, and we would hop about to the smarting of the lice marks on our bodies. Dried, we went to the store and were issued with garments in lieu of those we had handed in. Sometimes this underclothing was new, but mostly it was the laundered and disinfected wear of others who had been through the baths. Invariably these contained the eggs of lice which survived treatment and eventually hatched out. In any case our blankets, dugouts, and billets quickly re-infected us. But to object to that was to be hyper-critical.

Christmas was black cold day, but an Australian mail brought many parcels from the home folks, also an issue from the Comforts Fund of tinned plum puddings, sweets and cigarettes. The company's dinner was bully beef stew, but living with us of the company sergeant's mess was the regimental sergeant-major, who held that there were traditions to uphold. He was an ex-Imperial soldier with a string of ribbons on his chest for South African and Indian wars, and moreover an Irishman who had been a soldier from his teens. What Dooling did not know about the army had probably gone out of date with King Richard the Lion-hearted.

On parade straight as a gun barrel, wax-moustached, and gruff-voiced, he inspired awe in the hearts of the men and made inexperienced N.C.O.s dodder at the knees. Living among us he was a jovial soul who could conjure strong I liquor out of the empty air. An inalienable right of the sergeants' mess was the most adequate procurable dinner on Christmas night. With money subscribed, the R.S.M. disappeared for some hours. He returned with a crate of bottled beer, and disguised in a sandbag a jar three-quarters full of rum – from heaven knows where obtained.

A room was rented from Madame farther down the street. Some poultry appeared from a dubious source and were hidden in a blanket, and the cooks were bribed to supply the hot-water for plucking purposes and also to do the cooking. Grimmy and I undertook the dressing of the fowls. As officers and men were constantly coming to the billet we had to do this under a bunk behind a blanket over the edge.

While we were so engaged Captain Smythe came to the billet with some instructions for the company sergeant-major. It was a distinct relief when he took his departure. One of the purloined roosters was the largest we had ever seen; we judged by the work necessary upon him that he dated back to the Napoleonic period.

The dinner was a magnificent carousal. The only jarring note of the evening was that Grimmy broke his gold tooth on the leg of the ancient rooster. He was the toughest meat I have ever tried to eat, but we devoured him to the bones. We ate, sang, recited, and drank until we grew sentimental, and then concluded the evening in an adjacent blacksmith's forge. Here we were joined by the old smith and a fine, smart-looking French infantryman. Primed with our liquor the young poilu at our request sang us *La Marseillaise*. He sang it standing rigidly at attention, his face alight with enthusiasm, and his voice throwing every fibre of his being into the song. With our blood stirred by the magnificent air, and our senses gratefully buoyant in beer and rum, we drifted away to bed.

Note
1. Although the term was used widely by Allied (most often British and Commonwealth) servicemen to describe any form of German field artillery shells, the 'Whizz Bang' was originally attributed to the noise made by shells from German 77mm field guns.

Chapter 9

German Retreat From The Somme

Fourth Army School – Le Transloy sector – Patrols –
The enemy's retirement – War in the open – Our fight at Louverval.
(1 January to 3 April 1917)

My stay with the battalion in rest billets was broken early in the new year by orders to proceed on a training course at the Fourth Army School at Flexicourt. Captain Smythe, our company commander, was also for the course, as were other officers and N.C.O.s from the 5th Division. Here we spent a hard-working and invigorating four weeks among a collection of good fellows and experienced soldiers from all divisions of the Fourth Army – Tommies, Jocks, and Australians.

Apart from the excellent field-training and the enduring friendships formed at these schools they were of great moral value in bringing together men of all countries and characters; the mixing of English and colonial soldiers in this way broke down many ignorant prejudices. Thus we learned the traditions and the real quality of many of the British regiments – often ignorantly slandered in the A.I.F. on the score of short-comings in some newly-raised war battalion; and on their part they learned that Australians were not all the boasters they had heard of who delighted in insulting English officers and flaunting the fact that we were the best-paid troops in the field. The clean life again after months of living like caged beasts in the trenches was itself a wonderful tonic.

On 13 February I rejoined the battalion in reserve at Bernafay Wood, and three nights later we moved up into the line at Le Transloy, with that village (or its remains) on our right front. Our company trench for the most part followed the crest of a rise which sloped away in front into a flat piece of country for several hundred yards and rose again to a low ridge occupied by the enemy. Our position was well elevated – a change from Gueudecourt – but part of the flat country in front could not be seen from our line. This dead ground was evidently a matter of some concern to our

78

people, and to the British division on our right, and it was well patrolled during the hours of darkness.

The ground had been heavily fought for; in front of our line the dead lay about in great numbers. German corpses were strewn in waves; it was here that they had counter-attacked the British Guards after the fall of the village of Les Boeufs on a low hill in rear of our present position.

The German dead attracted the souvenir-hunters in the company, such as were found in every battalion – men who always seemed willing to risk their lives to gather a few postcards, a watch, a ribbon, a cap, or the like from dead Germans or from the living. One man, an officer's batman, came to our shelter really upset because he had found the body of a German officer lying in a frozen shell hole in which the ice, he complained, was so hard that he could not turn the body over to obtain a pistol believed to be attached to it.

Another improvement upon the earlier winter was the hot meal of stew or soup now brought up to the line at the end of each day. It made a vast improvement to the health and spirits of men in the mud. The meal was cooked behind the line, put into containers, and brought by the 'Imshi Anzac' light railway to the support line dump. Here it was picked up by the front line ration party and carried into the line.

The battalion in supports generally furnished this carrying party. Rain, mud, snow or shells did not prevent these fatigues from getting the food up. From the officer in charge to the last reinforcement the will that hot rations must be got up at all costs was paramount. I heard of one new arrival who tapped the rum-jar one night, and he was spoken of with as much disgust as though he had committed the most heinous crime in the calendar.

At the end of February upon our next tour of the line after the regulation interval of relief, I had my first experience of patrol work. Battalion patrols were to be the new order; Lieutenant Jock Gordon was to be the officer in charge, and I was made his sergeant. Gordon was a popular officer with much experience and as brave a man as ever pulled on boots. Patrols worked usually in diamond formation with one man as 'tailer' who had to watch the rear of the main group and guide any necessary retirement.

Our early patrols were without special incident, but on 9 March we were almost caught by a large body of Germans. We went out eleven strong with Peter Duncan as tailer. It was he who saved us. We had followed a shallow sunken road that ran towards the German position, Lieutenant Gordon and myself in front. A light fall of snow lay on the ground. Suddenly we were halted by a low whistle from Peter and we all crouched down. He moved up to the head of the patrol and pointed to a couple of objects lying on the ground. We made out several dark forms lying in pairs. Lieutenant

Gordon thought that they were dead, and he and I started to edge towards them. He had his revolver in his hand and I had my rifle at the ready.

We had moved only a few yards when we heard a breach-lock close. Gordon said: 'They are waiting for us, Darkie.'

We lay flat on the snow and could distinguish a large patrol lying out in pairs in crescent formation. They appeared to number at least thirty. We discussed the situation in whispers. Out-numbered as we were, we wanted to avoid fighting; even if some of us got away we were almost certain to lose some killed or wounded. So we wormed our way backwards, still keeping our formation and our faces towards the Germans, with one man turned about to guide us, and so out of the centre of their formation.

Inch by inch we edged backwards on our stomachs through the snow, expecting every minute that they would rush us; but they did not come on. In view of the events of the next few days, I am sure that they were pushed out into No Man's Land to prevent our patrols from reaching their wire in case we learned anything of what was now taking place in their lines.

Before being relieved by the 53rd Battalion we put in much work wiring our forward posts and deepening the trenches. The enemy heavily bombarded us as soon as he noticed the operations. In digging out the frozen mud at the bottom of the trench we came upon another set of duckboards and full boxes of ammunition and of bombs, all trodden out of sight in the mud before the later duckboards were laid.

We might have spared ourselves much of this labour, for hardly were we back in the support line at Needle Dump when we got news that the Germans were suspected of being about to retire on a wide front. The units of our division on the left had nightly been pushing forward to find here a length of trench, there a village, evacuated. On the sector which we had been holding around Le Transloy the Germans were showing no signs of leaving. It was afterwards learned that Le Transloy was the pivot from which during his retreat the enemy swung back his line at right angles to the main Bapaume-Cambrai road.

That night (16 March 1917) the 53rd Battalion were to push forward; if the 53rd made headway, we were also to move forward with a right and left patrol of considerable strength preceding the company. Lieutenant Morrison was to be in charge of the left, and I was to have the right patrol.

I was awakened next morning as day was breaking. All fire had ceased. An unnatural stillness hung over the countryside that for months had heard no cessation of gun fire. The horizon was ringed with burning villages. Word had come through that the 53rd Battalion had already moved out across what was yesterday No Man's Land. On the duckboard tracks infantry, engineers and pioneers were moving forward in Indian file. Some Light Horse detachments also appeared. The 18-pounders had their teams up and were floundering in the mud dragging guns from the gun pits.

Our own orders to move did not arrive till dark. Just before we moved off somebody started – from God knows where – a hare. A crowd of men went in pursuit, and as the valley was full of troops the poor hare was soon bamboozled and caught. Where that poor beast had lived in that shell-swept region was a puzzle to us all. It was killed and strapped to a haversack to supply a meal for its captors.

We crossed our now deserted front line of yesterday. The late front line of the Germans was garrisoned by some of the 53rd Battalion, and we halted along the main Le Transloy-Bapaume road. Our 'A' Company was still the right of the Australian line, and our flank was some little distance from Le Transloy, some of the outlying ruins of which were now in the line. Posts were mounted, one of which was pushed out to the edge of a wood that skirted a burning village on our direct front.

A strong patrol was sent out under Lieutenant Morrison, my patrol followed on Morrison's return at midnight. Lieutenant Reid joined us as we started. We advanced across the deserted countryside, and visited the advance-post under Corporal Court pushed forward earlier that night. They were occupying what had been a German 5.9 battery position with a very comfortable dugout. We noticed that adjacent to each gun-pit was the mounting for a machine-gun, evidently as anti-aircraft defence. This system had yet to be adopted by our artillery; we were still learning from the enemy the uses of machine-guns. All around were burning villages and clouds of smoke billowed about over the scene.

We divided our patrol, sending one part off under Peter Duncan, while with the other Lieutenant Reid and I pushed on through the wood into the outskirts of the burning village of Villers-au-Flos. Neither of us found any signs of the enemy on a wide beat. We returned to the battalion at day-break, hungry and sleepy. But the company moved at once, and we break-fasted eventually in the wood beyond Villers-au-Flos.

On our right front, about a mile away, was Haplincourt village and wood, and here Grenna picked up movement of the enemy.

During the morning (18 March) the 15th Brigade had moved through us to take up the duties of advance-guard. Their advance opened the skirmishes with the retiring Germans soon to develop into pitched battles around vantage-points along the line of the retreat into which almost every battalion in the division was ultimately drawn. During these fights the Australian infantry outfought the picked troops which formed the German rear-guard and drove them from every position until they entered the famous Hindenburg line. The fights of the 15th and 8th Australian Brigades for Morchies and Beaumetz, and the determined counter-attacks which they repulsed, followed in the next few days.

The 14th Brigade's turn to take up the advance came on 29 March. Peter Duncan was in ominously pensive mood during the evening before. Generally the wit of our sing-song gatherings around the camp-fire he alone would not sing this night, but gazed moodily into the fire. When we rallied him about it he broke into that mournful Scotch dirge, 'The Land of the Leal.' This closed down our concert as abruptly as if a 5.9 had landed into our fire. I went to bed feeling sure that my bosom pal, Peter Duncan, was not coming out of the fight that we were about to enter, and for weeks afterwards his voice singing that dirge rang in my ears like a funeral bell.

The battalion moved forward to Fremicourt on the Bapaume-Cambrai road and there halted for two days awaiting orders for the attack. Colonel Scott gave these out to us in the afternoon of 31 March.

The German position now ran across the main road through the villages of Doignies to the right of the road and Louverval to the left of it. The 56th Battalion's mission was to capture the village and wood of Louverval while the 55th attacked Doignies. To the left of Louverval was a small wood which was 'A' Company's particular objective. A trench system connected the two villages, and a factory on rising ground was on the main road. The position was one of considerable strength.

We were to attack without an artillery barrage. The Germans had dug trenches in front of Louverval, had erected wire entanglements, and were known to hold the wood with machine-gun posts. Just in advance of our outpost line the ground sloped from the crest of a hill down to the wood. This gave the defenders a clear field of fire over some three hundred, and in places five hundred, yards. On the right flank of the wood, and in front of Louverval, ran a deep trench protected with wire of the heavy apron pattern; behind the village and wood the ground rose steeply and offered many good machine-gun positions. We were to move from our billets at midnight and get into position under cover of the high ground just in advance of the outpost line ready to attack at dawn. 'A', 'B' and 'D' Companies were to carry out the battalion's attack, with 'C' in reserve.

Each company was to attack in four waves of platoons, about fifty paces distant, excepting 'A', on the left, which had three lines of platoons, with my platoon (No. 3) in a single wave on the extreme left of the attack. 'A' Company's objective was the sunken road on the far side of the wood; 'B' Company's the village and trench system covering it; 'D' Company's the sugar factory, trench system, and sunken road connecting the villages of Louveral and Doignies.

The 55th Battalion was to form up behind us, move off, and, when 'D' Company of the 56th had reached its objective, to incline to the right in three columns and attack Doignies.

Several officers and N.C.O.s, myself among them, spent the next day in a personal reconnaissance of the German position from near Beaumetz.

1. Australian soldiers on camels in front of the Sphinx, Egypt, 1915.
(*Courtesy of the State Library of Queensland*)

. The exposed expanse of what was
Jo Man's Land, between the Allied
nd German front lines, on the
romelles Battlefield. This photograph
'as taken on 11 November 1918, over
wo years after the action in which the
roops of the 5th Australian Division
nd the 61st British Division suffered
eavily. The remains of the River des
aies line of trenches and old German
·illboxes, which formed part of the
efences in the Sugar Loaf Salient, can
e seen, marked by the wooden stakes,
n the right of the picture, though
nickly overgrown with grass.
Courtesy of the Australian War Memorial)

3. Waiting for whatever lay ahead. Taken on 19 July 1916, this photograph shows a group of soldiers from the 53rd Battalion waiting to don their equipment prior to 'going over the top' at Fromelles. Only three of the men seen here came out of the action alive – and those three were wounded. The 53rd Battalion arrived in France on 27 June 1916, and entered the front line for the first time on 10 July. (*Courtesy of the Australian War Memorial*)

. Another photograph showing men of the 53rd Battalion in a trench in their front line a few minutes before the attack at Fromelles. For the Australian Imperial Force this was to be their baptism of fire on the Western Front, for although other divisions from 1 ANZAC had been sent down to the Somme they had not yet been committed. (*Courtesy of the Australian War Memorial*)

5. An oblique aerial photograph of the area in front of the village of Fromelles – ground over which part of the battle was fought in July 1916. This is almost certainly a target identification image taken from a fixed German Drachen observation balloon. Fromelles itself is just out of the shot to the bottom right. The German trenches are nearest the bottom of the view (one is marked 'Layerbach') whilst the Allied lines are furthest from the camera. (*With the kind permission of Dr Franz Kessler*)

6. A well-defended German bunker in the Fromelles salient, July 1916. (*Deutsches Bundesarchiv, Bild 146-1994-105-20*)

7. A soldier from the German garrison at Fromelles pictured with the village's badly damaged church as a backdrop. This area was held at the time by the 6th Bavarian Reserve Division. The German archive images are reproduced here with the kind permission of Dr Franz Kessler, whose grandfather was a *Oberleutnant* serving in the artillery in the 6th Bavarian Reserve Division. (*With the kind permission of Dr Franz Kessler*)

8. A view from the German observation post located in the Church at Fromelles, looking over the area where the British and Australian soldiers attacked on 19 July 1916. The Sugar Loaf Salient is beyond the shattered tree line on the left side of the image. The site of the new Commonwealth War Graves Commission Cemetery at Fromelles can be seen in this photograph – it is on the left hand side of the road, immediately before the damaged house on the bottom left-hand corner. (*Courtesy of the Australian War Memorial*)

9. A German soldier pictured in the battered village of Fromelles. It is believed that one of the German soldiers involved in the fighting was Adolf Hitler, then a 27-year-old Corporal and a message runner in the 16th Bavarian Reserve Infantry Regiment. This unit was one of those which were defending the Sugar Loaf Salient. Hitler served in the Aubers-Fromelles sector from March 1915 until September 1916. (*With the kind permission of Dr Franz Kessler*)

10. A German photograph depicting a large group of German, Australian and/or British bodies in a wooded area behind the German lines near the village of Fromelles. Taken in the aftermath of the fighting of 19/20 July 1916, this photograph was one of series that was printed and circulated as postcards aimed at boosting morale in Germany. One postcard in the archives of the Australian War Memorial, with the same image as that shown here, bears a caption at the bottom which reads 'Gef. Englander n.d Angriff b. Fromelles 19.7.1916' – which, when translated, reads as 'Fallen British from the attack at Fromelles on 19.7.1916'. Note that many of the bodies have been covered with ground sheets or gas capes – the remains of such items being found during the recent excavations at Fromelles. (*With the kind permission of Dr Franz Kessler*)

11. Remnants of shell and bullet-torn items of uniform and equipment from men who were killed in the attack at Fromelles, 19 July 1916, litter the battlefield. Note the two water bottles in the foreground. (*Courtesy of the Australian War Memorial*)

12. A First World War postcard that is purported to show German soldiers burying Allied casualties in the mass burial pits at Pheasant Wood, Fromelles.

13. Temporary graves pictured in July 1916. It is believed that these graves, beside what appears to be a battered German trench, are of men killed in the Battle of Fromelles in the salient that was known by the Allies as the 'Sugar Loaf'. (*With the kind permission of Dr Franz Kessler*)

14. An aerial view of part of the countryside around the village of Fromelles, looking towards the Allied lines at the time of the attack. In this shot you can see both the original Pheasant Wood site of the mass graves (top right-hand corner, the green strip in front of the belt of trees) and the location where the new cemetery will be built (centre left, the half-ploughed field).
(*Courtesy of the Commonwealth War Graves Commission*)

5. Members of the Oxford Archaeology team begin to excavate by hand the site of the German burial pits at Pheasant Wood, Fromelles. By the time that the four-month-long archaeological operation was completed, exactly 250 sets of remains, along with some 6,200 individual artefacts, had been recovered from the site. (*Courtesy of Oxford Archaeology/Tim Loveless*)

6. Martial Delebarre, a member of the Commonwealth War Graves Commission's staff and keeper of the Fromelles Museum in the Town Hall, with battlefield debris removed from the site of the Fromelles (Pheasant Wood) Military Cemetery. (*Courtesy of the Commonwealth War Graves Commission*)

17. A military issue pocket watch, dated 1916 and stamped with the number 61900, pictured soon after being uncovered from the site of the mass burial pits at Fromelles. (*Courtesy of the Commonwealth War Graves Commission*)

18. The same watch having been opened during the subsequent conservation process. (*Courtesy of the Commonwealth War Graves Commission*)

9. A 'Rising Sun' collar badge uncovered during the excavations at Fromelles. Worn by soldiers of the 1st and 2nd Australian Imperial Forces in both world wars, the 'Rising Sun' badge has become an integral part of the 'Digger' tradition in that the badge with its distinctive shape, worn on the upturned brim of a slouch hat, is readily identified with the spirit of ANZAC.
© *Commonwealth of Australia 2008*)

10. An aerial view showing the construction of Fromelles (Pheasant Wood) Military Cemetery underway in late 2009, early 2010. (*Courtesy of the Commonwealth War Graves Commission*)

21. A view of Fromelles (Pheasant Wood) Military Cemetery.
(*Courtesy of the Commonwealth War Graves Commission*)

22. The completed Fromelles (Pheasant Wood) Military Cemetery pictured in July 2010 being prepared for the burial service of the final soldier recovered from the site of the original German mass burial pits at Pheasant Wood, Fromelles. (*Courtesy of the Commonwealth War Graves Commission*)

3. The consequences of the Battle of Fromelles can be seen at V.C. Corner Australian Cemetery and Memorial. It contains the graves of over 400 Australian soldiers who died in the attack at Fromelles and whose bodies were found on the battlefield. But, incredibly, not a single body could be identified. There are no individual graves, but a memorial listing the names of all the Australian soldiers killed. (*Courtesy of the Commonwealth War Graves Commission*)

4. The Australian Memorial Park. The central feature is the sculpture 'Cobbers' by Peter Corlett of Melbourne. The sculpture is modelled on Sergeant Simon Fraser of the 57th Battalion, a 40-year-old Victorian farmer turned soldier who rescued many men from the battlefield. He is carrying a man of the 60th Battalion.

25. Australian soldiers with a German A7V tank, nicknamed *Elfriede*, that was captured in the fighting near Villers-Bretonneux in April 1918. The names chalked on the hull can clearly be seen. (*HMP*)

26. The Battle of Amiens. This painting by Australian official war artist Will Longstaff depicts the view towards the west, looking back towards Amiens. A column of German prisoners of war is being led into captivity. Meanwhile horse-drawn artillery is advancing to the east.
(*Courtesy of the Australian War Memorial, ART03022*)

7. German prisoners captured during the Battle of Amiens, 8 August 1918. The smoke is from howitzer ammunition set on fire by German gunners before retiring. In the fighting, the Germans lost 27,000 men, including 15,000 prisoners and 400 guns.

8. All that remains of the Amiens Gun – the barrel – on display at the Australian War Memorial in January 2009.

29. The ruins of the church in Villers-Bretonneux after the town was recaptured by Allied troops in April 1918. (*HMP*)

30. Australian soldiers on the quayside at Cape Town during a break in their return journey to Australia in the winter of 1918/1919. Harold Williams embarked for the home on 2 January 1919. He died on 13 May 1955. (*Courtesy of the State Library of Queensland*)

On our return I found Peter Duncan by his fire rolling cigarettes.

'Well, Dick,' he said, 'if we both come through this stunt, we will get our leave and I will take you to my home in Scotland, where my people will give us such a good time that we will forget the war.'

'Yes, Peter,' I replied, 'we will come through the stunt all right, and I'll be delighted to come with you.' 'I wonder?' he said, as he gazed with a fixed stare into the dancing flames as if they held the answer to the riddle. Again the feeling that Peter was going to be killed, and that he knew it – wanted to tell me, but held it back – came into my mind. Premonition of coming death was frequent during the war. Many thousands of those who died knew when their end was at hand. In some cases their best pals knew as well as they did.

After tea we sat in our billets and talked and laughed in a manner that would have led a stranger to believe anything but that before the sun came up tomorrow we had to walk down an open field upon a position held in force by a fully-equipped enemy. About 10 p.m. a rum issue was served out. None of us wanted to sleep.

Alex O'Rourke and Peter Hughes came to see me and Quarter-Master Sergeant Brew gave them each a nip of the rum. Alex wanted to borrow a Colt revolver that had come into my possession. He and Peter were going over with the last wave of 'A' Company as stretcher-bearers. Of course they were supposed to carry rifles, but a rifle (Alex thought) would be an encumbrance. I gave him the belt and revolver after loading the weapon for him. That was the last I ever saw of big, good-hearted Alex O'Rourke.

At 11 p.m. the cooks had two dixies full of steaming tea. We drank this around the fires, and then the whistle blew and platoons fell in among the slush of the littered village street.

The tramp of many feet on the cobbled streets of the battered village awoke strange echoes. Here and there little groups of transport men, engineers, and others watched the column pass and called out 'Good luck' to their pals. Then out into the main road with its leafless avenue of trees. At last we inclined to the left and followed a fold in the ground to the point from which we were to attack. A screen of scouts was pushed out, and then the companies deployed into battle formation. As each platoon got into position the men lay down on the frozen ground to await the zero hour.

Over the ridge the enemy occasionally threw up his flares. Farther back his guns barked and the shells droned over our heads to explode with a crash and a shower of sparks along the main road. A pale moon gave a faint light, and wisps of mist lingered in the gullies. Peter Duncan came in with his scouts and lay down beside me. It was bitterly cold and our teeth chattered.

After what seemed years of waiting, and just as a faint light began to show in the east, a company-runner came with orders to the platoon commanders to have the men up on one knee. No sooner was this completed than the word to advance was given. Peter Duncan moved out with his screen of scouts, to meet death just over the rise.

A few hundred yards, and we were on the crest of the ridge. A startled German threw up three flares in rapid succession and had a bayonet driven through his body before he could rise from the ground. Then the racket broke loose. The German machine-gunners poured belt after belt of bullets into the waves of men coming down the slope towards them. The enemy's S.O.S. went up in a snaky chain of sparks, to burst into the familiar golden shower. The noise of the machine-guns was deafening. Their bullets cracked among us like stock whips, and seemed to strike fire from the frozen ground. But those waves of Australian infantry would have done credit to many a battalion on the parade ground.

At a walk they went forward firing no shot, keeping their alignment, and closing up gaps as casualties fell. In the excitement of it all their steadiness was exhilarating to at least one among them. We had no artillery barrage to punish or shake the morale of the well-entrenched Germans. We had to walk right down on to that wood and trench spitting death from machine-guns and rifles and covered by shell-fire, until we were close enough to rush the defenders.

From the crest of the ridge our losses began. Lieutenant Reid, leading No. 1 Platoon of 'A' Company, was one of the first to fall, and all the length of the incline was dotted with men struck down as the fire became a hail of bullets. But the lines never faltered – in fact an officer of 'A' Company was in front calling out to the platoons to keep their dressing as they advanced. Captain Smythe was at the head of his company, armed with nothing more deadly that his walking-stick, and his coolness and disregard of the bullets that cracked around him was a wonderful example for every man he led.

At last we reached the German wire. For an instant the leading wave seemed to pause, and then with a rush and a yell went through it. It was then our turn. Some of the Germans died at their posts. Others tried to escape, and were chased and shot down as they ran. The sugar factory on the right was rushed by a platoon of 'D' Company, led by Lieutenant Watt, whose reckless bravery was recognized throughout the battalion. 'B' Company mopped up the trench system in front of the village of Louverval, and then treated the village in like manner.

The machine-gun nests at the edge of the wood took a heavy toll of 'A' Company, but their crews were either killed at their guns or driven helter-skelter through the wood. The Germans tried to hold the far edge, but were forced into the sunken road and our Lewis gunners did great execution among them as they fled along it. As the wave in which I was entered the wood, 'B' Company had just gained a footing in the trench.

Some of the Germans tried to escape down a communication sap, and a party of us set off after them. One German stood and shot one of our little band at point-blank range through the head. He himself was shot down instantly. We killed several more and the chase after the others through the village led us out of 'A' Company's sector. When I realized this I said to the only other 'A' Company man whom I could recognize that we had better turn into the wood. As I entered I saw Lieutenant O'Halloran moving to the edge of the wood with a small party. He was shot dead a few minutes later.

On the northern edge of the wood I found 'A' Company driving out the Germans past a large tin hut and across the sunken road. Lance-Corporal Monkhouse with No. 3 Platoon gun-team opened fire on them as they came into the open and swept many of them away. My attention was attracted by Joe Wallace calling out from some distance beyond the wood. He dropped to his knees and fired several shots. I ran out with some of my platoon and we came upon a party of Germans who decided not to make a stand when they saw that Joe was not alone. We shot down several as they made off, and Monkhouse coming up with his Lewis-gun got in some deadly work.

From here we saw a large post in our rear which had been missed in the advance. A shot from this place bowled over one of our men walking up towards it. We saw that it was full of Germans. An officer and a number of our men appeared on the edge of the wood and the officer called out to me. I walked across and he wanted to know what my party were doing out on the flank of the wood. I told him of the enemy post in our rear, and urged that we should attack it.

He was a new officer just across from England, and he refused; more than that, I was immediately to withdraw my gun team and stay in the wood. I went to tell my team to come in, when a machine-gun opened on them from this post, killed Monkhouse and wounded another man. The three survivors came running in with their Lewis gun and the news that a large body of Germans could be seen coming from the direction of Pronville.

Captain Smythe had been wounded, and Lieutenant Reid, and the officer that I had just been speaking to on the edge of the wood. So I went to Captain Roberts of 'B' Company and reported these German reserves moving up. He told me to collect any men who were about the edge of the wood, and to report to Lieutenant Gordon who was entrenching near the châteaux.

As I went off on this mission I saw what had been evidently a machine-gun post which part of 'A' Company had met. Ten men were lying out in a semi-circle, the closest not more than fifteen yards from where the gun had been firing. Eight of them were dead. This will show how the Germans fought their guns that morning. One of the wounded was a fine fellow from my platoon; he had a cruel wound from a machine-gun bullet which had gone through his upper thigh. He had bled very much before he was bandaged; I got a stretcher for him and McCrory, 'B' Company's bearer, got him out. Two years later, back in Sydney, this man met me in Pitt Street and was most profuse in his thanks, but I referred him to McCrory.

The 55th Battalion had by now taken Doignies. We heard several loud explosions as if mines had been sprung, and the enemy began shelling the village very heavily. Inside an hour the whole of the position was ours, and the work of consolidating it was being pushed ahead with all speed against an expected counter-attack.

Hardly were the German infantry driven from the position when their artillery opened fire upon the wood, trenches and village. The high explosives blew the buildings into brick-dust, and the whizz-bangs never ceased. Our casualties mounted up rapidly. Many walking wounded were killed on their way out by shells or by machine-gun fire from the heights beyond the village. To add to our misery, especially that of the badly wounded, it snowed all the afternoon.

The battalion stretcher-bearers deserved all the decorations in the army. Three-fourths of them were killed that day. Their numbers were reinforced by volunteers from the fighting ranks who knew something of wounds from personal experience. They were few, and our wounded many. Many a fine young life would perhaps have been saved if it had been possible to get the wounded out quickly.

I reported with the men that I collected to Lieutenant Gordon and we set to work. During the afternoon Grenna came along and told me that Alex O'Rourke and Peter Duncan had been killed. Alex had been carrying out wounded since the first few minutes of the attack, and about noon was returning for more wounded when the Germans caught the party with a shower of whizz-bangs as they came down the slope. A large piece of shell went clean through Alex's body, killing him instantly. So died this brave man who devoted his tremendous bush-bred strength to succouring many a stricken man. I never saw him angry; he was always ready to laugh; and he had the disposition of a child. He did not know what fear was. I have seen him many a time under heavy shell-fire going about his job as though the shells were only crackers. He was never given a decoration, but he deserved one if any man in our company did. His only apparent reward is a white cross in some cemetery in the Somme battlefields, but that cannot be the finish of such as he. I searched for his body that afternoon but could not find it, and later, as I was telling Grenna of this, someone said that Peter Duncan's body was lying on a road near the châteaux nearby. I went to look for this, too, but it was not there.

It snowed very heavily all the afternoon. During a heavy burst of shelling a corporal from a post on the far side of the wood with his face smothered in blood, came along to Lieutenant Gordon with the news that Lieutenants Watt and Bowman had been badly wounded in the tin shed, and that the Germans could be seen advancing across the open ground on our left flank in several waves. Lieutenant Gordon told me to cease work on the trench, and take a party to reinforce a post on our right which covered a crossroads.

The threatened attack was broken up by our artillery. We learned later that the Germans had concentrated seven times during the day to launch counter-attacks, but each time our artillery had shelled them so accurately that their attacks were withered before they could develop.

Night came on and we toiled at the digging. What a night! The wind blew half a gale, and the snow turned to rain and hail against which our waterproof sheets were poor protection. We shivered in sodden clothes, and peered into the darkness for a counterattack that never came. Instead, the Germans shelled the wood heavily all night.

Towards morning I was digging to keep warm when one of the others came along to take post beside me. He was rather a boaster and was known as 'Brasso.' During the attack that morning a German had been busily firing into us when Brasso broke through the thicket right on top of him. The German immediately tried to put up his hands but Brasso shot him dead. Now as he stood beside me in the darkness and rain, he said: 'I feel bad about shooting that German this morning.' He talked in this strain for some time, and, his pal coming to keep him company, I said that I would have a smoke. Brasso took my pick, and as I crouched down under a waterproof to light my pipe, he said: 'Take Lai's possy farther up the trench, so that I will have more room to dig.'

This I did, and just lit my pipe when a shell landed in the trench. I rushed over and picked up Lai Hanna, who was badly wounded just above the knee, but poor Brasso lay on his back with the pick still in his hand, quite dead from the concussion.

In a wintry sunlight next morning the carriers brought up our rations. These consisted of sodden bread, wet through the bags from the night's rain, cheese, jam and, best of all, a small ration of rum. We drank the rum neat and at once it went through our numbed bodies like fire. Warmed and cheered, we ate the wet bread with an appetite, and then buried Brasso in a shallow trench.

A runner came with word that my post could withdraw deeper into the wood during the hours of daylight, but with my party I stayed on in the position that we had dug overnight. At about 10 a.m. a German 'plane flew low over the wood, and within half an hour we were shelled very heavily. I sat down in the trench with Joe Wallace (who was asleep) next to me.

Presently a shell landed close to us and almost immediately one directly in front and one to the rear. One of our fellows remarked how close the three were, and I answered that the gunners had to put one right into the trench to get us. The words were scarcely out of my mouth when there came the whistle and roar of an exploding shell. I was hurled to my face in the bottom of the trench, and felt as if a draught horse had kicked me in the solar plexus.

My mouth was open and rigid, my hands clutched my stomach, and my limbs felt as if they had been petrified. My face was turned to the spot where only a few minutes before I had been relieved on post. Instead of a man there was a heap of tumbled earth that still smoked from the explosion of the shell, and intermingled with the smoking mass was blood, flesh and fragments of clothing. My face, arms and head were smothered with the poor wretch's minced flesh and warm blood. Jack Brewster and another man lifted me up, and when I could catch my breath I moaned with the hurt of my stomach and ribs.

Joe Wallace had been lying within three feet of the sentry and was not affected in any way apart from being spattered as I was. The shell must have struck the sentry a direct hit on the chest and exploded. It was many minutes before I could stand, and then only in a bent position, and for days afterwards my senses were as if I had been stunned. When I could walk I decided to take my post farther into the wood as Lieutenant Gordon had given me the option of doing earlier in the morning. I have not a very clear recollection of further events this day. When men spoke to me their voices came from miles away, and it took me an appreciable time to realize what they were saying. Even the noise of the shells appeared not to matter. My stomach, back and ribs ached damnably.

During the afternoon we learned that we were to be relieved that night. Towards dusk I again took my post forward. I left behind one man, a noted 'dismal Jimmy', to act as guide for the relief to my post. The night wind was again bitterly cold and the rain unceasing. We were in a state of utter exhaustion, without sleep since Saturday night and this was Tuesday. Sodden clothes and the lack of a hot meal in that time had greatly reduced us.

About 10 p.m. we could hear the relief of the posts on our left being carried out, and expected every moment the tramp of feet which was to mean that our relief had arrived, but each time we were disappointed. About midnight I sent to the post on my immediate left, and word came back that the whole of 'A' Company had moved out two hours previously.

About 3 a.m. we heard a party coming through the wood from the left. We challenged, and a well-known voice answered and asked, 'Is that you, Dick?' It was Sergeant McHugh of my company with the relief. Then we learned how we had been left in the lurch. The guide that I had sent out had on reaching battalion headquarters reported sick, without saying that his job was to guide a relief in. The company had been relieved and marched back to the vicinity of Morchies before the fact that my post was missing had been noticed. Then Sergeant McHugh, dead beat himself, had volunteered to return and bring the relief in. It was an unselfish action, and typical of the soldier that Sergeant Jim McHugh always was.

I handed over and reported to the company commander as we passed out. Just as we got clear of the wood Jack Brewster collapsed in the mud. I told McHugh to take my post back and said that I would come along with Brewster. They moved off and I was alone in the darkness with a game man whose shame at his exhaustion made me pity him. I took his rifle, and with him hanging on to my equipment we plodded up the rise down which we had advanced seemingly years ago.

It was daylight when we reached the sunken road with Jack Brewster's weight hanging with both hands to the braces of my equipment. Ready hands helped him down the bank, and showed me to a place that had been kept for me in the shelter of some waterproof sheets. Somebody gave me a nip of rum, I dropped to the wet ground, and fell asleep till midday.

Chapter 10

Blighty Leave

London – Horseferry Road soldiers – Bert among the Londoners –
The girl in grey – Peter Duncan's people – Scotty in our West End platoon.
(23 April to 6 May 1917)

On its day I wrote down 23 April 1917, in my diary in letters of gold. It is St George's Day and Shakespeare's day; but chiefly it was the day I got Blighty leave. While Lieutenant Morrison was inspecting No. 3 Platoon, a runner came to him with a message form. He read it, and calling out to me said: 'Your leave-pass is at the battalion orderly room; if you hurry you have a chance of catching a train from Albert this morning.' He shook hands and wished me luck; telling me to hurry off at once. It was many years until I saw again that good fellow and excellent soldier, Joe Morrison. He was shot through the head at Bullecourt during my absence, lived by some miracle, and returned to Australia to fight his way back to a semblance of his former health by the sheer dogged pluck and perseverance which always characterized him in the battalion.

I ran to our hut and bounded up the steps, both hands undoing the catches of my cartridge-pouches, and threw the clips into a heap on the floor. The C.S.M. helped me to fix my pack, and within a few minutes I was at the orderly room. There were five passes allotted to the battalion; when the party was complete the orderly officer would inspect us; I was to be in charge. It seemed as though the fifth man would never put in an appearance; but at last he came and we were sent off. We made all haste to decamp.

Just as we were leaving the camp a man came running after us calling me by name. I recognized Bill Brunt, the battalion 'two-up king.' He thrust a roll of French money into my hand, saying: 'Take it, take it, and have a good time.' I started to explain that I had good credit in my pay-book, but Bill turned abruptly on his heel and walked away. I counted the money as we moved along; it represented in English currency £10. There was no certainty that Bill would ever see me again, but this was the spirit among the men of the Australian battalions – what's mine is yours, what's yours is mine, and it applied to everything from ready money to boot-polish. It was one of the things that the Tommies could not understand about us, but it helped to found the fighting qualities of the Australian infantry. I repaid Bill his unsought loan when I returned from leave.

The journey to Boulogne passed somehow. We over-nighted at Coppin's Billet, with the great sentry-guarded gate, well known to most troops going on leave, and marched down to the leave-boat next morning.

It was a beautiful sunny day at sea, and our spirits needed no fillip. My pal and I got into conversation with a group of Tommy A.S.C., whose station was Boulogne. We learned that they received Blighty leave every three months, and knew to the day when they returned from one leave when they would be setting out on the next – that is, unless they should develop mumps or fatty degeneration of the heart. We wondered why it took us nearly two years to obtain such a boon, but we supposed it was a penalty for stupidity in joining the infantry.

We focused our gaze upon the white cliffs of England, and even while our eyes dwelt upon them, it seemed we were drawing into the quay at Folkestone. The first train was packed before we reached the platform, and was signalled out. We scrambled into a carriage of a second train and were quickly off. No snail's pace here. We were swept into the charm of the English countryside, and learned that the narrow strip of the English Channel separated not merely two countries but two entirely different worlds.

Early in the afternoon the train pulled into Victoria Station and we were in London, the city of the soldiers' dreams. Our own most roseate dreams fell far short of what it really was to us Australians so far from our own land, who craved for a city peopled with our own kin. At Victoria we Australians were paraded under warrant officers from A.I.F. Head-quarters, and were marched to Horseferry Road. Here our passes were inspected, our rifles and equipment put into store, and ration tickets issued. Then to the pay office, where I drew £35 to add to nearly £20 worth of French currency for my ten-days' leave.

That over, I searched for my pal Big Bert, who after being discharged from hospital had got a position on the H.Q. staff. The building was like a rabbit-warren with long passages and rooms full of girls, and well-dressed, sleek staff-sergeants, each very full of his own importance and as hard for a line-soldier to approach as a rajah in his palace. My appearance caused much giggling among the girls, engaged with their typewriters and their teas and their flirtations with the fine-looking sergeants. I must have pre-sented a great contrast to the latter – hair as long as a spring poet's, elbows sticking out of my tunic, worn breeches, puttees torn with barbed wire and mud-stained beyond redemption, and steel helmet covered with hessian.

I found Big Bert. He gave me a great 'Ha, ha!' and told me where I could get a bath and some clothes. The A.I.F. Store was short of uniforms, and I

91

had to buy a pair of breeches from an oily looking alien Jew. I could not procure an Australian hat anywhere and told Bert so. 'Wait a moment,' said he, and taking my tin hat, returned presently with an Aussie one stolen from the hat-rack of one of the rooms that housed the well-dressed sergeants.

Standing on the corner of Victoria Street waiting for Bert, bathed, barbered, and with clean clothes on my body – if I live for a century I shall never forget that re-birth into civilization. The street traffic of peace-time again, the streams of pedestrians hurrying along, the young, clean, neatly-dressed women who walked with the step of youth and their heads held high.

It was the womenfolk who fascinated me. Slowly it dawned upon my bewildered senses that these girls, with their fresh faces and happy gait were of my own race, that any one of them could talk in my language, and the realization of this made me long to make any one of them understand that I was a lone Australian who for months past counting had lived the life of an animal corralled in a landscape of mud and beastliness. And then suddenly it came to me that I was on leave, that this city was open to me with money in my pocket, that I was changed from the flabbergasted unwashed creature that had been laughed at by the girls at Horseferry Road into a fellow who had the right and the chance to make this leave a whale of a good time.

Bert came along to help me begin it. But first we went to an establish-ment in Victoria Street conducted (if I remember rightly) by the Australian Red Cross. Here I paid into the keeping of a young lady with a ready smile all my money except £15. Then a bus took us to some restaurant with a palm court, obsequious waiters, champagne, music by an orchestra, and a meal such as I had not seen for years. I mellowed under it all as in a dreamland, heard and forgot in fleeting amusement Bert's concern that I had arranged no lodging for the night, and as lightly accepted at once his offer to take me to his diggings at Chiswick.

Next day, Anzac Day, my battalion mate, Bob, and I explored London and its soldiers' haunts till evening, when Big Bert rejoined us. In festive mood Bert led us to an upstairs bar near the Palace Theatre, his greatcoat flying open as a gate. The swing-doors he opened by pushing one and pulling the other, and he strode into the crowded lounge in the full majesty of his huge frame and 6 feet 2 inches of height. His voice was equally huge and strong, and I twitted him with frightening the little girl behind the bar, saying, 'I suppose that's how you bluffed the Huns when you won your D.C.M.' After a round of drinks I egged him on to talk of this exploit.

He related the story as seriously as a man would talk about a bun fight. At Christmas time in 1916 on the Somme his battalion had decided to put over a raid. Bert, his brother, S——, and a fellow called Joe were the bombing section. They were all over six feet high.

The raiders under cover of darkness crawled as close to their objective as possible, and rushed in after the box barrage had lifted. The German on guard was bayoneted before he had time to give the alarm, and then the raiders' bayonet men and bombers got to work. The bombers would bomb a certain length of trench, and the two bayonet-men, Bert and Joe, would rush around immediately the missiles had exploded and use their bayonets with terrible effect. Some of the Germans were stuck like pigs before they could get out of their shelters. The required number of prisoners bagged, and Fritz bombing from both flanks, the raiders started to retire to their own lines.

The Germans threw up their S.O.S. signals, lit the heavens with their star-shells, and peppered the retreating raiders with machine-gun and rifle fire, and bombs. Bert, Joe and S——, with two prisoners, were forced to take shelter in a shell-hole in No Man's Land Here S—— was shot through the head, and Bert wounded in the leg. They were forced to stay in the shell-hole all one day, with the dead body of S—— and the two prisoners, who were scared stiff at falling into the hands of these gigantic Australians. When darkness came they reached the battalion line. Bert was evacuated with his wound to a hospital in England.

We left the bar at closing-up time, and I was amused to watch Bert shouldering through the crowd to the tube, with his greatcoat still flapping around him. In the carriage he hung from a strap, and respectable sub-urban citizens returning to their homes were evidently amused at this huge Australian, whose great bulk swayed with the movements of the carriage, while he aired his opinions upon Lloyd George, the conduct of the war, and the weakness of the English beer, in a voice that could be heard all over the carriage.

One morning while I was waiting for Bob in the palm court of a large West End hotel, my attention was attracted to a strikingly pretty girl in grey, sitting alone. She gave me a half contemptuous glance and turned her face away from me. At last Bob arrived, looking as if he had rather a lot of sins to atone for, and said that he was so dry that his tongue felt as if it was covered with black ants. I drew his attention to the girl in the grey costume. 'Gee, she's a stunner,' was his comment. I told him that I was going to speak to her even if she called the police and had me thrown into the street. I walked over to the table at which she sat and said. 'Pardon me, but may I sit down?'

She ran her eye over me with utter disdain.

But brazenly I sat at her table.

Suddenly she wheeled round on me and said, 'Look here, Australia, what do you take me for?'

I leaned across the table and replied, 'The prettiest girl that I have seen in London.'

For an instant her face was expressionless, then she threw her head back and laughed. 'There is no doubt about you Australians; your effrontery carries you through.' She went on: 'Well as long as you do not take me for one of these women who frequent these hotels to be picked up by you Colonials, we know where we stand.'

I hastened to add that not for a moment did I class her as such. I told her that I had only arrived from France a few days ago, that I was hungry for the company of a decent girl to take about to the theatres and to dine with, that I had spoken to only one such woman of my own race for a few minutes in almost two years.

She asked me about where we had been, and when I mentioned Egypt she was all interest. From this she drew me on to tell her of the life of the men in the trenches in France. She listened intently, with her chin resting in one of her hands and gazed at me with eyes that never left my face.

I was interrupted by a waitress putting a note into my hand which read: 'What damned tale are you telling Angel-face? What about a drink?' I apologized to the girl and asked her would she join Bob and me in morning-tea or a drink. Both she refused; she was expecting a 'distant relation' to have lunch with her – but she agreed after some hesitation to go with us to a show at the Coliseum in the afternoon.

That night we four dined in the West End – the girl in grey, Bert, Bob and I. At a table with a soft-shaded light we sat listening to the orchestra, enjoying the good food and wine. The girl sat with a smile about her lips, and egged us on to talk about our life in the army. At the sallies of the big and humorous Bert she sometimes threw her dark head back and laughed with all the abandon of her youth. It was an enjoyable evening, and it was late when we saw her to her hotel. We repeated the outing on the following night.

But next afternoon she was leaving for her home in the south of England. She lunched with me in a little restaurant in Soho, and I took her to Paddington Station. I rallied her on her silence in the taxi and then she said in a sort of burst: 'I feel sick at heart when I think that within a few days you will be back in France again. You and your pals laugh at the dinner-table over the life in the army, but I know that there is a hideousness that you do not speak of, for it is in your eyes in your unguarded moments. You and your pals have given me a wonderful time these last few days. I want to keep the memory of this short while which I have enjoyed immensely; I shall always remember it and will many times think of you.'

I secured her a seat in the train, saw her baggage aboard, and she stood talking to me on the platform. When the warning-bell sounded she turned to me with outstretched hand, a quiver on her lips, and said: 'Goodbye, cheeky Dick, I am glad you were so persistent in the hotel lounge the other morning.' I kissed her, she sprang lightly into the carriage, and the door closed behind her. One little wave from the moving train and she had gone, but down all these years I still remember the freshness of her youth with her dark head and eyes of limpid brown.

The days were running out, and to keep my promise to Peter Duncan's sister I had to leave for Glasgow. I had written to her after Peter's death; her reply was one that only a brave woman could write. She sympathized with me in the loss of a close comrade and friend, and said that when my leave came I was to keep Peter's appointment and go to see them as arranged. Her black-lined frayed envelope is still in my possession, stained with the mud and wet which it accumulated in my tunic pocket during the remainder of the war.

After a journey by night train to Glasgow I searched out the Duncan's house in the still early morning, and only as I rang the bell and received no reply did it occur to me that, in casual Australian fashion, I had not written to say that I was coming. I cursed my stupidity.

However, a lady in the next-door house challenged me as 'Peter Duncan's Australian friend,' and told me where to find Peter's brother's place of business. There I found Archie Duncan, who took me to a shell-case factory where his sister Agnes worked in the office. A message was sent up to her, and presently she came running down the stairs, dressed in a blue-and-white uniform. She put her arms around me and kissed me, telling me how glad she was that I had come to Glasgow, so that her family could thank me for what I had done. I felt myself blushing to the roots of my hair. She went away to tell the manager she would not be at work for several days, and reappeared in a black costume and small black hat. She took me to lunch at the best restaurant in the city, and pointed to the table she had engaged for a week for the leave that Peter and I were to spend with her in Glasgow.

All through the meal she chatted brightly, never mentioning the sorrow that had come upon them. Only later, as we sat by the fire at her home, waiting for her brother, did Agnes at last turn the conversation to what she had avoided all day – the life of her brother Peter in the army.

She sat and listened to the tale of our friendship in Egypt onward, and laughed at the many amusing incidents of our life together in France, but I could see that beneath her self-control and outward calm she grieved very much at the loss of her brother. I pitied and admired her as she sat with the firelight playing on her fair hair and mobile features. As she arose to prepare the meal she said, 'Why did God make me a woman? If I were only a man, I could go and be a soldier among men whom through you and Peter's letters I seem to know so well. My thoughts were always across in France with Peter and his friends.'

After a vaudeville show that evening, to which despite my protests they took me, we three sat around a bright fire and talked into the early hours of the morning about France and Egypt. Next morning Agnes took me to Fairlie, on the Clyde, to see her mother, a soft-voiced lady who greeted me as warmly as if I had been her son. The shock of Peter's death had affected her keenly, but she hid her grief away as Agnes had done, and their doing it so as not to cloud my holiday touched me very deeply. Then, back in Rutherglen, two of Agnes' girl friends appeared at the house. One stayed overnight, and after the other members of the household had retired to rest we three again sat around the fire and talked till 3 a.m. This girl friend was engaged to an officer in one of the Highland regiments. Before the little group broke up, she asked me point-blank about the life that soldiers were reputed to lead when behind the line.

I asked what she referred to, and she replied: 'Oh, we hear horrible tales of the houses where you soldiers visit women.'

'Try to imagine,' I answered, 'the weeks and weeks that these soldiers live in the conditions of the forward trenches. They come out of this fatigued, filthy, and nerve-racked. They perhaps are billeted in a village where the war can still be heard in the distance. Only a little while, and they will be in the line again, to gamble their lives again with death in its most horrible forms. Temporarily they must forget this, or go insane. Are they to be blamed because they drink wine with their pals, and perhaps consort with these women, not because altogether they want them so much, but as a distraction to help them forget what they have been through and must face again?'

It was strange to talk like that to those two girls. Next morning, as Agnes and I sat over a late breakfast, she said to me: 'My friend and I talked a long while after you went to bed. To a girl whose fiancé is in France the rumours of the life behind the lines is not pleasant, but the reply you gave last night put the subject in another light, and you can think of us as less critical.'

Agnes, Archie, and a troop of their friends came to see me off. They loaded me with chocolates, a large tin of Scotch shortbread, and a bottle of whisky. I felt weak at bidding farewell to these devoted people, and the fair-haired, soft-voiced Agnes, I thought, was another example of the bravery of these British women. While Scotland breeds women of this stamp, there is no longer need to wonder at the bravery of their men, renowned in battle for centuries.

Then London again, while the morning was still young of my last day of leave. I still had over £10 left, and decided that it should provide a fitting grand finale to my time. Bert and Bob met me; shaved, shampooed and bathed we adjourned to a lounge-bar in Shaftesbury Avenue. As we were entering a girl of perhaps twenty years of age accosted us and said: 'Take me in, Aussie!' A rule of some West End hotels forbade the entrance of women unaccompanied. The girl had a Scotch accent, was well dressed, and wore a saucy little hat. Being still thrilled with the voices of Glasgow, I replied, 'Yes, Scotty, come in and we will buy you a drink.'

We got a table and I turned to study the girl. I had remarked that she was young, but now I realized that she was also good-looking. She had hair of silky fineness and the colour of honey, her eyes were large and dark brown, her teeth were even and white, and she had an air of superiority about her in distinct contrast to most of the women who haunted the lounge-bars and palm-courts of the West End. She seemed satisfied to stay with us; we lunched together at an Italian cafe and finally adjourned to Madame Tussauds waxworks in rather a mellow state.

I caused a loud 'Ha, ha!' by presenting our tickets on the first landing to a waxen figure in a gorgeous uniform, which I mistook for a doorkeeper. We visited all the murderers' effigies, and Bert was making a great speech from the dock of the Old Bailey, when he was interrupted by one of the attendants. I am afraid that in our hilarious mood we were not very impressed with the horrors of the place; and I am of the opinion that one must be either very melancholy or half tipsy to spend an afternoon among such scenes.

Back in the West End we left Scotty, but invited her to join us later at dinner, for which she seemed grateful. We met again in our favourite restaurant off Piccadilly, where by now we were known to some of the waiters. Our table was in a smaller room off the main dining-saloon, and when the second bottle of wine had been emptied we were a lively little party. Bert aired his views of things concerning the war in his usual high humour and in a voice which allowed many other diners to be vastly entertained. He picked on the wine-waiter, an Italian of gigantic proportions, and wanted to know why he was still running drinks to thirsty soldiers when he could be employed in the Trentine rolling pebbles down upon the Austrians. The waiter did not altogether enjoy these remarks, but under our tips he suffered in silence.

After midnight, when we rose to leave, Scotty, who had been showing signs of feeling the weather, collapsed. 'The female portion of the platoon is down,' said Big Bert, and drawing Scotty to her feet, he took her arm and walked out as though he had been drinking ginger-ale all night. Bob and I followed precariously in their wake, while the tables began to converge upon me, first in slow motion and then with a rush. But I reached the palm-court without a collision, and here I found Bert on a settee supporting Scotty, now dissolving into tears. As I stooped to inquire the cause of the weeping, Bert pushed me and I fell backwards over a large palm. The waiters assisted me to my feet and opened the door its widest to let us pass out.

Scotty was now sobbing tragically. We decided to take her home, but could not get any directions from her as to home's whereabouts. Leaving Bob to support her, Bert and I went out for a taxi. These seemed scarce, but after I had fallen over a low railing which was around a garden plot we found one. The taxi collided with another as we turned out of the street, which brought a policeman upon the scene. Bert wanted to get out and engage him in mortal combat; I restrained him and at last we reached the place where we had left our two companions.

Scotty was still tearful, but Bob's resource had discovered in her bag a card bearing her address. This was in a suburb some distance out; it took a lot of persuasion on our part to get the taxi-driver to start for it. We placed Scotty in the cab, and clambered in after her. When we reached the suburb, Bert rode on the running-board of the taxi to keep a look out for the street. Eventually we found it and then the house where Scotty lived.

After a furious ringing of the bell an elderly woman came to the door in a dressing-gown. She said, 'Bring the poor girl in.' In we brought her, and while the good lady busied herself turning down the bed, Bert and I relieved Scotty of her outer dress, put her night-gown on, and lifted her into bed. We had a great task getting her long boots off.

This job done, we prepared to leave, when the good-hearted landlady said, 'Where are you two boys going at this hour?'

'Back to London,' I replied.

She offered us a room for the night, but before accepting we told her that there was another of us outside in the taxi, and that two of us had to catch the leave train next morning. She promised to have us up betimes. It was still dark when a tray with breakfast was brought into us. We arose feeling not nearly so bright as when we went to bed. The good-hearted old lady did not want to accept money for our night's lodging and our meal, but we did not stand for that. We said good-bye to Scotty, who was still in bed and very sorry for herself. She told us she intended never to repeat the performance. We gave her two of our last pound notes as a solatium. Poor little Scotty!

With ten shillings left I boarded the leave-train. When our ship left Folkestone I could not bear to look back upon the receding coast. At Boulogne we were marched in a long straggling column to a large camp on a hill – one of those cheerless detail camps where a man always felt like a stray dog. Here bully-beef and biscuits greeted us and, having washed it down with weak tea, we turned into our blankets, seeking only unconsciousness.

Chapter 11

Officers' Course, Cambridge

Withdrawn from the Somme – Training for a new campaign –
Flanders again – Am selected for a commission – Cambridge –
The New Zealanders – Officers in the making – Back to France.
(May to December 1917)

On arrival at the battalion camp at Bécourt, near Albert, we found that only the nucleus was there, for the battalion had been hurried up to Bullecourt. During the latter end of my leave in London, the newspapers had published news of the fighting for the Hindenburg Line around Bullecourt. Following the abortive attack of the 4th Australian Division at that place on 11 April, later attempts had gained an important footing in the German defences. But the position made a marked salient in our line, and the sector (now held by the 5th Australian Division) was heavily enfiladed by enemy guns on both flanks.

A continuous artillery battle raged along the whole front. But the enemy's artillery was concentrated night and day, particularly on the sector near Bullecourt. The 5th Division had been drawn into the fighting in May, and the 54th Battalion of our brigade had distinguished itself in overwhelming one severe German assault. During this fighting all battalions of the 14th Brigade had been under heavy bombardment, and in the 56th Battalion (in support) Lieutenant Morrison was severely wounded in the head, and my old friend, Peter Hughes, in the back.

Our division was now withdrawn into corps reserve and it was generally known that we were to be moved very shortly from the Somme sector. By 15 June we knew we were destined for Flanders, where the British Army staged the opening attack at Messines for a new campaign. The battalion left Bapaume that day by rail for a training area behind Albert. In this region we spent a hard-working six weeks, and then on 25 July we entrained for the north. We found our destination at Ebblinghem, outside St Omer. In farm billets in that region we promptly resumed intensive training.

For weeks we had heard the 'furfies'[1] that all the Australian divisions were to be made storm troops. Apparently the authorities were determined that for our next attack we were to be trained like athletes. An acid test of fitness was the frequent route-march. This was carried out by companies under full packs. A dismounted captain (carrying no equipment) would lead and he would set a solid pace.

We would march fifty minutes, rest eight, and at two minutes to the hour we would be standing in column of route at the slope to move off on the hour. At each halt the leading platoon retired to the rear of the company so as to give each a turn at the head of the column. Under the pace and the weight of our packs the perspiration streamed from our bodies. Most noticeable was the ability of the older hands to outmarch the new drafts trained in England, who had joined up since we left the line. But, above all, the survivors of those who had undergone the desert training in Egypt were as tough as ironbark.

We arrived back at billets with our shirts wringing wet, and on sunny days it was a common sight to see the yard full of soldiers, naked to the waist, while they wrung their shirts out and hung them in the sun to dry. Then at nights we slept on the damp earthen floor in our sweaty clothes, bedded next door to the farm horses. However, never since we came to France had the health and spirits of our fellows been so high. We laughed and skylarked off parade like overgrown boys, wrestled, punched one another about the body; and I have seen two men, their noses streaming blood from this horse-play, shouting with laughter while they struggled with each other on the ground.

I remarked one day that, if all the division were as fit as our company, it would require super-men to stop them when they were put into an attack. My surmise was correct. In their attack at Polygon Wood on 26 September the 5th Division started its advance with its right flank open, but took all its objectives on time, dug in, and repulsed the German counterattacks with such superb confidence that the men called out to one another to let the attacking waves get closer so that they would have less chance of missing their targets.[2]

But I was not to see this fighting. Six weeks before it happened, on 11 August, I was ordered to parade before the 14th Brigade commander, Brigadier General Hobkirk. He informed me that I had been recommended for a commission, was to go through an officers' school in England, and if I got through the course I would be appointed to my own battalion. I came away from the interview feeling more than proud.

To every Australian soldier, his company, his battalion, was his home. Here lived our truest and most trusted friends and companions, brothers who would share their last franc or crust with each other, bound together till victory or death. Home and civilian associates were only misty memories; it took an effort to conceive what by now they really meant to us. It seemed as if we in the company had always been soldiers and cobbers. Away from the company any one of us felt like a lost dog and on return was greeted with yells and what would be regarded in other walks of life as obscene insults.

I left for England on 22 August. At the station and in the crowded train I made friends with Sergeant Archie Forbes, of the 30th Battalion, also bound for Blighty for a commission, who became one of my closest friends. The journey to London passed rapidly, and after Horseferry Road[3] had given us short leave we were given our rail warrants for the officers' school at Cambridge.

In the train we fell in with a C.S.M. from the 55th Battalion, Bert Matthews, and a sergeant from the 53rd, Stinson. The former was short, thick set, with a large red face, a perpetual grin, and an inexhaustible fund of humour. Stinson was a tall leather-faced bushman. At Cambridge we reported to 'C' Company, 5th Officers' Cadet Battalion, in Trinity College.[4]

After reporting, Archie and I stood beside our packs and stared at the scene before us. Taxis and big private cars were constantly pulling up at the arched gateway to disgorge their occupants. The taxis were full of Australians and New Zealanders, but the private car passengers were young men in fashionable civilian clothes, wearing straw boaters with gay hatbands, while chauffeurs in livery saw to the unloading of piles of cabin-trunks. We were to learn later that these gilded youths had been called up under the Conscription Act, had been sent into training schools, and then drafted into the cadet battalions as the final step towards gaining a commission.

In the weeks that were to come we came to know these young fellows, and realized how unfitted many of them were to become leaders of men in the field. How could they be compared as leaders with those smart soldiers among the senior N.C.O.s of the Imperial Army whom many of us had met at the army schools in France?

We were posted to platoons. The Australians were allotted by brigades to their platoons. Thus Archie, who belonged to the 8th Brigade, was in No. 11, whilst we four of the 14th Brigade were in No. 12 Platoon. The 15th Brigade men were sent to another company, whose parade ground was in the inner courtyard. The posting over, we were marched to our quarters. No. 12 Platoon's was in the inner court. Our rooms consisted of one large room with three army bedsteads, with an ante-room containing a fourth bed. Bert Matthews and I decided we would be room-mates.

On the walls of all rooms were posted a copy of the school regulations, in which was laid down that not more than two Colonials or two Scotsmen were to room together. To our room were then detailed a tall shy English youth and a fellow wearing the Argyll kilt. The former was straight from an officers' training battalion, but the gent in the kilt filled us with wonder.

101

I suppose he did hail from Bonnie Scotland, but he was the tamest of the breed that I had ever met.

His Glengarry was worn not at a rakish angle, but square on the head, and pulled down so far that the small red button on the crown stood out like an angry boil. His kilt hung with a decided tail. He walked with his posterior pushed well to the rear, and his head hanging forward. He wore a large ginger-coloured moustache, did not swear, drink or smoke, and apologized for himself whenever he spoke. He looked like an emu, had the voice of a child, and was always sucking air through his teeth. His favourite expression 'Wind up' aptly described his whole outlook on life.[5] He was perpetually writing to our colonel extraordinary ruses for use against the German army, including one fantastic scheme for flooding Germany with the North Sea. The fact was that Jock was not keen on going across to France as a combatant, and we came to the conclusion that he wanted to establish insanity as a reason for his being kept out of harm's way.

To No. 12 Platoon came also several New Zealanders, and it became the strongest in Colonials of the company. They were wonderful fellows, those New Zealanders. On the whole, of all the nationalities that made up the British Army of the Great War I would rank the average New Zealander as the outstanding best. They were all fighters second to none, good sports, great comrades. They were far more English than the Australians, had a higher discipline (measured by the old army standard), and as shock troops they were the equal of any on the Western Front. I once heard an English officer giving a lecture at the 4th Army School at Flexicourt, in which he declared that the New Zealand Division was rated by the High Command as one of three best divisions in the British Expeditionary Force.

Five of the New Zealanders attached to No. 12 I will describe in passing. Bill Cotterill, a C.S.M. approaching middle age, big, with dark face and clipped moustache, had the reputation from his unit of being a parade-ground martinet. But he joined in all our horse-play with the youngest of us. A ginger headed fellow named Street had seen a lot of line service and played football with the zest of a man engaged in mortal combat. Another was Snowy Monro, a fine-looking, smart young fellow who wore his yellow hair brushed straight back, and he was the dandy dresser of the crowd. He was well educated, unassuming, played a great game on the wing of our rugby team, and ran like a hare. Long Saunderson stood about six feet, and was as broad as a stream of pump water. I became very friendly with him, and he ably seconded Bert Matthews in the reformation of our queer Jock. A thick-set, dark-haired chap named Forgie, completed the New Zealand bunch, a likeable fellow and a very smart boxer.

Attached to No. 9 Platoon was another New Zealander, Phil Bennett. Thick-set, fair-haired Phil was one of the cleanest-living men whom I met in the army. He held the rank of company sergeant-major, was a 1914 man, and (it was said) was the first New Zealander to be awarded the D.C.M. on Gallipoli, where he had been badly wounded. He was brave to the point of foolhardiness. Many were the tales told by other New Zealanders of his wild escapades and forays in the line, but Phil himself seemed to regard the war as a great opportunity to walk about in the face of the enemy as though he belonged to the swagmen's union.

He loved to tell of the time he had done three weeks in the clink at Abbassia, Egypt, under an Irish sergeant-major who used to kick the prisoners' packs about the sleeping hut because they were not aligned to his liking, the while he bellowed that he had tamed lions in his time and would break the hearts of men who had done ditto to their mothers. Phil was an educated man, and although he was only the same age as most of us he soon took over the self-imposed duty of leader, adviser, and consoler of the Colonials in the company. I never heard Phil swear, and he did not smoke or drink, but he was sport mad, the driving force that organized the rugby team and gave a helping hand to anything for the amusement of the members of the company.

Our company commander was a Regular, Captain King, tall and fair, and as handsome as a cigarette advertisement. He had been wounded in 1914, and carried a crocked arm as a memento of the early days of the war. He was a real type of the pre-war Regular officer of the British army, a gentleman, impartial, and before the course ended was liked and respected by us all. Second in command was Captain Proctor of the Border Regiment, another Regular officer who knew his profession thoroughly. A couple of subalterns who taught trench-warfare and gas were hardly up to date in their subjects.

After looking over Cambridge we realized why the Army authorities were using the colleges as training schools. Conscription had left them without scholars, the town depended largely upon the money of the students, and so the government, to keep these colleges open until the return of the days of peace, sent soldiers here to go through a training course for commissions. The only students in the colleges were a few Hindus and Burmese. There was another cadet battalion in the town, one company of which was just completing its course.

In this were a pal of Archie's and a sergeant from my battalion. These two instructed us in the way we should deport ourselves while at the college. Sport was the key to success. Organized games were thought so much of that inter-company and battalion contests were going on all the time. Company officers fostered the spirit of competition, and if a man played a good game of football, hockey, pulled a good oar, or could box, and kept away from pubs and women, he could enjoy the term in peace. A.I.F. Headquarters (they said) thought so little of the military knowledge

103

gained that if a man failed in his final examination he lost only one day's seniority. Since the A.I.F. followed the system of selecting war-experienced men for commissions it was making no great mistake.

Our friends also told us that the good townsfolk of Cambridge had protested strongly about Australian and New Zealand troops being allowed in the colleges, and that the first cadet officers from these overseas troops were drafted out of the platoons for separate training as though they were suffering from some contagious disease. Finally a Tommy officer who had been a middle-weight boxer volunteered to take over a platoon composed only of Australians and New Zealanders. He paraded them and explained how matters stood, that they had been sent to the college against the wishes of the townsfolk and the officers of the cadet battalion, but that he personally would not condemn them without first giving them a trial. He then put them on their honour to conduct themselves properly.

The Anzacs appreciated the manly manner in which this officer spoke to them, and took a keen delight in showing how well they could behave. At the end of the course, after they had won the company competition for drill, and had come out on top in the sports, the colonel of the battalion paraded them and said that henceforth he would be glad to welcome any New Zealander or Australian to his battalion. This happened some months before, and many Anzacs passed through Cambridge without any citizen having been garrotted, murdered, or served up for a cannibal feast by Anzacs in the market-square. The dear, smug provincials of England loved to be frightened with the bogey of wild Colonial troops, held to be socially no-class, but 'hellish stout fellahs, what?' when there was a strong point to be stormed or a line that wanted holding against massed German attack.

One of the social-superiors among the conscripts whom we met at Cambridge was surely the queerest bird on which the British Army ever wasted its good money. W——— came to Cambridge from an artillery officers' course at St John's Wood, where he had failed hopelessly. He had been in France for three months in an A.S.C. base sixteen miles out of Paris. His only interest in the army was to shirk even the duty of sweeping out his bedroom. He avoided anything that might injure his small effeminate person. He was the uncrowned king of lead swingers in the British Army.

While the rest of the platoon was hurrying to parade, he would remain calmly brushing his eyebrows before the mirror. Then just before the company moved off he would sneak through the gateway and take up a position in the rear rank. His stand to attention should have been copyrighted, all the weight on the right foot, with the left knee having a distinct bow to the front, his rifle at his side doing duty as a leaning-post.

To see a young man such a deliberate malingerer used to make us want to lay violent hands upon him. A week before our course finished, the C.S.M. called him out to move the platoon across the parade ground, and in spite of twelve months' training in officers' schools he could not give the necessary word of command. When asked to name the unit to which he wished to be sent, he chose the Ordnance Corps. He roomed with the ginger-headed Street, who confided to us that he never felt so much like murdering a man in his life. On the day Street passed his final examination he raced upstairs, threw W———— on to a bed, tore his breeches down, and blackened his backside with boot-polish.

In contrast was the treatment of an Australian cadet, a first-class N.C.O. One morning our company was specially paraded for the colonel, who, after we had been drawn up for him, stood before us and said: 'In my first address to this company, I laid stress on the fact that cadets must, on and off parade, conduct themselves as officers and gentlemen. Especially did I mention that I would not tolerate any cadets under my command associating with the town women of reputed easy virtue. Unfortunately, a member of this company was seen last night. My police spoke to him, and now I call upon that cadet to step out and take the consequences. I will give him five minutes.'

It did not take five seconds for a voice to call 'Sir,' spring to attention, slope arms, step out smartly, and to bring his hand in a resounding smack to the small of his rifle-butt in the salute. We nearly dropped in our tracks to see that it was an Australian. 'Go to my office,' said the colonel, and then 'Captain King, march your company away.'

We Colonials felt very sore over this incident. No doubt the colonel had to demand exemplary conduct from cadets, but here was a sergeant with a good line record, a soldier who knew his work, turned down as a cadet officer, while the system could tolerate malingerers like W——. Of course, Horseferry Road had to return the sergeant to his unit, but his colonel seconded him as an Instructor to the Australian Corps School, and they sent no duds there to that work.

One day, in compliment to the company, Bert Matthews and Phil Bennett were asked to take tea with Captain and Mrs King. Bert was inclined to funk the appointment. 'They picked you and Bennett as the two roughest diamonds in the company,' I told him. 'Be sure, there are no beer stains on your D.C.M. ribbon, and don't tell them about the time you scaled King George.'

Nevertheless, I believe Bert did, for the story was one of his favourites. He had been sent across along with other heroes to be decorated with the D.C.M. by His Majesty. Bert arrived in London with his pocket full of money and a determination to celebrate his return to civilization. In consequence he was semi-conscious in some bar when he should have been pushing out his manly chest to have his medal pinned on by royalty. Bert came back from Mrs King's tea party with his big good-humoured face wreathed in smiles.

105

It appears that Mrs King had put them both at their ease as soon as they were ushered in, and then egged them on to tell of their experiences. They readily did so, and Bert said that Mrs King laughed till the tears ran down her face. From what I could gather, it developed into a competition between Bert and Phil to see who could tell the best tale. Phil started to talk about the Maoris and Bert of his life in the wilds of Australia. I do not think he was ever farther west of Sydney than Parramatta. But he described scenes of the dense and fearsome bush, its snakes and wild animals, and a thrilling fight for life with a horde of naked savages, crazed through eating their boomerangs. He declared that both Captain and Mrs King were wonderful sports. They must have thought him and the noble Phil a pair of wonderful liars.

A typical field day – the sky overcast and a keen wind blowing. From company parade we marched across to the dining-hall, filed through past a long table, and each received a paper bag containing a cold pie, a healthy lump of cheese, and two slices of brown bread cut an inch thick. We paraded on the gravelled path and marched through the town at the slope. Once on the country road we marched at ease, and led by Bert Matthews the company kept step to the ribald song of 'Barnacle Bill the Sailor.' Long Saunderson started it by calling out – 'All is lost!' The foghorn voice of Bert Matthews would reply – 'All is not lost!' Then another – 'Who can save us?' Bert again – 'I can.' Then – 'Who are you?' to be answered by an ear-splitting yell of 'Barnacle Bill the Sailor.' Cheers from the ranks, and then voices uplifted in a spasm of the classical song. Phil Bennett always marched with a football tied to his haversack. Most of us believed that Phil took the thing to bed with him.

The scheme for the first part of the day was company in attack. Several cadets were issued with queer wooden rattles, which, swung on a wooden shaft, created an awful din. These were to represent machine-guns in today's tactical scheme. Our company commander for the day was a tall anaemic looking young fellow from an O.T.C., with a big Hebrew as second-in-command.

Arrived at the chosen field the company commander detailed the scheme, posted the 'enemy' (cadets with rattles), and then proceeded to deploy for the attack. Between him and the big Hebrew they tied the company into as many knots as a kite's tail. They finished up by having the platoons so mixed up that Captain Proctor had to sort the company out again and deploy them afresh.

This over, we lunched on a pie, cheese, and bread. Phil Bennett walked about as he ate, picking two sides for a game of rugby. This proved such a willing affair, and the officers so interested, that we had an extended lunch-hour. The afternoon was devoted to occupying a series of trenches dug in white chalk formation. Under assumed night-conditions sentries were posted, a listening-post pushed out, and a patrol detailed.

Rowe of the 54th Battalion bombed the post occupied by Bert Matthews, Saunderson, Street, and myself, with dried cow manure. That acted as a signal. Up and down the trench swayed attack and counter-attack, and the fun was fast and furious until interrupted by Captain Proctor. Then we marched home singing and whistling like a lot of children returning from a picnic.

Those of us who were from France lived in two worlds at once – that of the friends we made in the training school, enjoying while it lasted the good free manly life in their company, and that of our real home in the line battalions, which was never long absent from our thoughts. By October letters from France, full of news of the stern fighting in the Ypres salient, brought us back to the grim seriousness of life, while reinforcing in us, convinced fatalists, the personal luck of this respite in scenes of peace.

The savour temporarily went out of rugby and raging under the influence of those letters from surviving friends describing the fierce fighting at Polygon Wood and Menin Road, and the death in action of many closer to us than brothers, fallen, perhaps, in our own places in the attack, and carrying with them out of life vivid and irreplaceable parts of ourselves. It had happened before; it was always happening while the war lasted. But it made a deep emotional difference that it should happen while we, fit and proud in our fitness and away from all danger, took no part in the gamble and the sacrifice to which we had sworn ourselves with those unforgettable comrades.

The 56th Battalion shared fully in the great victory at Polygon Wood, and in the losses it entailed. The gallant Colonel Scott, the adjutant, the doctor, two company commanders, and several lieutenants were among the dead. Scott was a man for every soldier to mourn. He stood six feet, of a lithe, sinewy build, on great athletic legs in tight-fitting breeches; his waist was small enough for a girl's, and he had long powerful arms, blue eyes, rosy cheeks, white teeth, rather a bashful manner of speaking off parade, but on parade a voice like a foghorn. We used sometimes to think that he ruled us with too much iron, but he made of his battalion a disciplined fighting unit equal to any in the line.[6] He was shot by a sniper while showing an English colonel around the sector after the battle. The sniper's bullet ricocheted from some private's steel helmet and killed both Scott and the English colonel.

While the campaign in France rose to its climax – or anti-climax – at Passchendaele and Cambrai, our training course drew to its conclusion in strenuous football, boxing, and rowing competitions. With blackened eye, burst lips, and lumps like eggs behind the ears, I, for one, sat for the final exams, and Cambridge soon became one of the things of the past.

After the exams we were each asked to state to which unit we wished to be posted as an officer. All the Australians named their own battalions; those few who belonged to other arms usually asked to be posted to a battalion in their Division. Queer Jock went to some gas brigade. His stay among men had broadened him somewhat, but he should have been sent to France in charge of Second Lieutenant Bert Matthews just to finish his education.

I wonder if the student who now occupies Room 03, Whewell's Court, is ever disturbed by visions of Phil Bennett and those others packing a football scrum in his domicile? Or ever hears Long Saunderson raise his huge voice to sing: 'On the right side of Bond Street, I met Mary McGee!'

Probably not, though in my own eyes and ears they are still real enough.

On the last night we were guests of the college at dinner in the dining hall of Trinity. At the end of the room a long table ran across at which were seated the Dean, dons of the college, and the battalion officers. At three long tables, spread like wings towards the main entrance, were the cadets of the two companies. It was a sumptuous repast with much wine. We had been teetotallers for months, and we felt in festive mood.

To conclude the evening a huge loving-cup filled with Trinity's famous black beer was passed round. It was the size of a bucket. We all stood up. With great ceremony the senior don present drank, and the cup was then passed to arrive eventually at the tables occupied by the cadets. A waiter with a large jug followed it in case it wanted replenishing. Bert Matthews confided in a stage whisper to Archie and me that when he had had his turn at the loving-cup the reserve beer would have to be called up. He drank at it like a famished draught-horse, and when he had drained it he turned to the waiter and said: 'Fill her up again, there are some chaps farther along who are really dry.'

It must have been great stuff, that beer. Inside of five minutes Bert said to me: 'I am going outside. Look after my hat.' I was still minding his hat when Archie and I drifted out among the last to leave. Outside the ground was covered with snow, which was still falling. We were almost sober when we left the dining-hall, but before we reached the main gate we required our identification disks to be sure which was the other.

I do not know how we parted, but I found myself upstairs in Mason's eating-house, still searching for Bert to give him his hat. I decided to return to college, and in the darkness and the snow walked past the main gate three times without recognizing it. Somebody directed me and I reached Phil Bennett's room, where the King of the Colonials was standing in front of a huge fire, stone sober, the centre of a collection of Aussies and Kiwis in the talking stage of drunkenness.

While I was explaining to Phil that I wanted to find Bert to give him his hat, the noise was heard of tramping feet on the stairs and much puffing as under heavy burden. The door opened to admit Archie, Saunderson, and Bill Cotterill, with the unthawed person of Cadet (and next week 2/Lieut.) Bert Matthews. Snow was thick in his hair. He had been found, stiff with cold, spread out on the sacred lawns of Trinity College and fast asleep in crocodile formation. Phil Bennett sprang into action, and shooed out of his room several men who were lying across his bed arguing. Bert was put on the bed, his tunic stripped off, and Phil set to work to restore circulation in him. When Bert could sit up and blink his eyes, he admitted that he knew nothing of what had happened after he had taken two steps outside the dining-hall.

The completion of myself as an officer was performed at Horseferry Road on 19 December, where I received two black stars for my shoulder straps, and a brand new Sam Browne Belt. Archie Forbes and I then departed for Glasgow for a few days' leave with the Duncans. On Boxing Day we left their hospitable home.

Our long picnic ended in England on 29 December, a black, cold, rainy day, and at the end of it (spent mostly smoking in bed before a roaring fire) Archie, Bert Matthews and I took train for Warminster on Salisbury Plain. Here in the most cheerless military camp, we believed, in the British Empire, we spent several days with a large number of Australian officers and other ranks awaiting draft to France.

In accordance with the Army habit we were inoculated again. Ugliness, old age, and lack of money were now about the only three dreaded diseases that I had not been made proof against by means of a needle. To this date I had been vaccinated against smallpox six times, and as for inoculations, it used to take me some little while to add up the list duly recorded in the back of my pay book. Inoculation was about the only incident in a period of some days' sitting in a little group around the stove in our hut, stone sober, and nearly blinded with smoke from the blackfellows' fire that smouldered in the stove. We welcomed the orders to leave for France on 7 January.

Our large draft proceeded to Southampton for embarkation. South-ampton we found to be the usual provincial English town. One interesting feature was the Bar Gate, a wall built across a main thoroughfare with passage ways for footpaths and traffic. A statue of somebody in armour was in a niche over the main thoroughfare, a link with the days when knights were bold and maidens were reputed to be shy and virtuous. But me doubts if any of those said maidens ever put their shoulders to the wheel when King and Country called as did the women of wartime England in 1914–18.

They were magnificent all of them – the perky girls in breeches, coats, and caps, who, as bus-conductors, kept the crowd back with biting sarcasm while giving rigid preference to wounded soldiers; the women from good homes who worked like slaves around the hospital wards; the pretty ones that drove ambulances; the peaches that drove staff cars and R.F.C. limbers; the women who turned to all over the country to carry on heavy farm work; and the W.A.A.C.s who worked as orderlies and domestic servants in the clubs and canteens of the bases in France. They earned the deep admiration of all soldiers who, like them, did not require conscription to force them to do their bit.

A vile crossing and a snow-storm at Le Havre re-introduced us to the theatre of war.[7] At Harfleur Base Camp Archie and I were posted for our battalions that night, and in a railway-carriage minus one door and any lights, with not a window that could be closed, we crawled away towards the front at that troop-train pace which a snail affected with stringhalt would laugh at.

We fished out from our packs those candle ends without which no soldier in France ever moved, blocked one of the open windows with the back of a seat, and there, while the candle-grease coursed down the sides of the carriage and the snow beat in, we sat and dozed fitfully with collars turned up to our ears and hands buried deep in pockets.

It took us two days and nights, with long stoppages en route at Rouen and Étaples, to reach Boulogne, in the neighbourhood of which (at Samer) we heard (to our amazement) that our division was resting. There Archie left me with: 'Good-bye, old boy; keep your head down till we meet again,' and with that abrupt farewell, hiding a world of emotion, I knew I was really back in the army – at war.

Note

1. A furphy, also commonly spelled furfie, is Australian slang for a rumour, or an erroneous or improbable story. Some accounts state that the term was derived from the water carts made by J. Furphy & Sons of Shepparton, Victoria. Large numbers of the Furphy water carts were used by Australian forces during the First World War, and, with 'J. Furphy & Sons' written on their tanks, they became popular as gathering places where soldiers could exchange gossip.

2. The name Polygon Wood was derived from the shape of a plantation forest that lay along the axis of the Australian advance on 26 September 1917. The British and Australian attack was part of the second phase of the Battle of Passchendaele. General Herbert Plumer introduced a series of small attacks with limited objectives, which he termed his 'Bite and Hold Plan' to replace the general assaults that had previously been employed. Following a preliminary artillery bombardment, lines of skirmishers, followed by small infantry groups, led the attack – as was the case at Polygon Wood. Plumer's intention was to outflank the German divisions rather than execute a main frontal assault. Each advance would stop after it had moved forward between 1,000 and 1,500 yards. Preparations were then made to fending off any German counterattack. The Allied forces succeeded in securing the wooded area after heavy fighting – though shelling had reduced the wood to little more than stumps and broken timber.

3. The A.I.F. Headquarters had been established at 130 Horseferry Road in London. Colonel R.M. McC. Anderson, a businessman, was appointed as its commandant.

4. As the war progressed, the demands on the officer training system forced dramatic changes. Consequently, in February 1916, a new system of training for officers was introduced – the Officer Cadet Units. Those selected to attend the units had to be 18½-years-old or more and to have served in the ranks or to have previously been with an OTC. The training course lasted four and a half months. Initially, the Officer Cadet Battalions had an establishment of 400 cadets at any time, though this was raised in 1917 in the case of those units that could deal with greater numbers. By the end of the war, more than 73,000 men gained infantry commissions after being trained in the Officer Cadet Battalions.

5. One contemporary account describes the term 'Wind up' as referring to fear – but is not to be confused with 'cold feet'. It is said that to 'have the wind up' implies no disgrace, and that it could be mentioned in conversation, though usually in the past tense.

6. A veteran of the Battle of Lone Pine and Fromelles, the Australian War Memorial website contains the following detail on the death of 27-year-old Lieutenant Colonel Alan Humphrey Scott DSO: 'When the 56th Battalion was relieved at Broodseinde, Belgium, a fortnight before the attack on nearby Passchendaele, he characteristically opted to remain behind to help the incoming unit. On 1 October he and a British officer, to whom he was explaining the defence of Polygon Wood, were shot dead by a sniper whose location, though known to Intelligence, had not been passed on to Scott. In 1917 he was mentioned in dispatches three times.' Both Scott and the officer he was guiding, 25-year-old Lieutenant Colonel Dudley Ralph Turnbull DSO, attached to 20th Battalion Manchester Regiment, are buried in Buttes New British Cemetery near Zonnebeke.

7. During the First World War, Le Havre was one of the ports at which the British Expeditionary Force disembarked in August 1914. Except for a short interval during the German advance in 1914 it remained No. 1 Base throughout the war.

111

Chapter 12

Gas Warfare

Gas warfare – Into the line at Wytschaete – The pillbox country –
Battalion life in the new winter line – Am made Battalion Patrol Officer.
(January to February 1918)

In that quaint way in which the military powers switched about the life of
the individual serving soldier, I was ordered off to a week's course at the
Australian Corps Gas School at Bailleul before I had had time to do more
than hunt up old friends in 'A' Company. A number of officers from other
battalions with the division were, I found, booked for the same course.
With me came my batman, a young, thickset, sunny-natured lad named
Collier, commonly called 'Nugget'.[1] He looked after my belongings with
the watchful eye of a terrier. He was my batman from the time I rejoined as
an officer until fate in the shape of death and wounds rang down the
curtain for both of us, when the battalion was decimated in the bloody
fighting around Péronne and Mont St Quentin in September 1918.

At one station where we halted we were interested to see a battalion of
American infantry detraining. They formed up by companies in the station
yard. They wore khaki uniform little different in colour from the British,
but their tunics seemed too short at the rear for smart appearance. Instead
of puttees they wore light coloured canvas leggings. Their equipment was
similar in design to ours, but instead of our square pack theirs was circular
and was worn more into the small of the back. On a long march it must
have been hard to carry, as the drag on the shoulders appeared to be more
severe than with ours, which was bad enough.

We were surprised to see them wearing British steel helmets and armed
with the Lee-Enfield rifle. The fact was that the Americans drew upon the
British Army for equipment. Even their food was in great part supplied by
Britain and France. So was their artillery, and this remained so until the
end of the war. The American airmen were either absorbed by the British
and French squadrons or else their flying units were equipped with British
'planes. Certainly the Americans created a huge reserve of troops in
France, thus allowing the Allies late in 1918 to attack incessantly and so
force the Germans to sue for peace.

Physically, this American battalion looked a great body of men, all young and well setup. They resembled the Australians more than any other troops but had not the Australians' hard, fierce-looking faces. Our fellows with their sun-bronzed skins, sunken eyes, and lined features often looked like birds of prey beside other troops.

Arrived at Bailleul we were met by an N.C.O. from the gas school with the information that we had arrived a day before the commencement of the course and that no accommodation was ready for the officers at the school. Under a senior lieutenant from an 8th Brigade battalion we went into the town in search of the town major to obtain billets for the night.

The war created many little tin gods – notably assistant provost marshals and town majors.[2] The officer and temporary gentlemen before whom we now stood ran true to form. After listening to our story he point-blank refused to allow us to stay in the town overnight. Of course, the place was under military control, and no civilian dare take in a soldier for the night without a permit from the town major. He was not even courteous. But he met his match in our spokesman, who, after some argument, told him that we certainly were not going to walk the streets all night, and that either we must be given billets or we would enter an hotel, take possession of sleeping accommodation, and the town major could try his hand at turning us out.

The autocrat backed down, and, wheeling about, instructed an N.C.O. to issue us with permits. The lodging proved to be a fancy goods shop, shuttered and in darkness. We returned to the town major's office, the N.C.O. made out another permit for a hotel in the main square of the town, and here, after a meal of eggs and chips, we retired to bed.

We found the school staffed by officers and N.C.O.s who were right up to the last detail in training. Our course was for only a few days, but every hour of working time was instructive, with helmet drill, lectures, and demonstrations. For some time the Allies had undoubtedly gained supremacy in this form of warfare.[3] The Germans had initiated the use of gas, but in the last two years of the war their troops must have often cursed the introduction of this new weapon of warfare.

The intense blockade of the Central Powers no doubt hampered their research in the endeavour to keep up with the new inventions of the Allies. Chlorine gas discharged from cylinders was the first used. Tear, phosgene, and mustard gas were in turn developed by the Germans, but the Allies generally countered with something more deadly. By early 1918 it was generally believed that the gas-helmet used by the German troops quickly deteriorated under the effect of our new gases into poor protection to the wearer. A device had been perfected on our side by which, at the pressing of an electric button, hundreds of cylinders of gas could be discharged from mortars dug into the ground, and set on a compass-bearing.

113

One of the demonstrations at the school was of a *flammenwerfer* (or flame-thrower) as used by the Germans in attack. This device consisted of a metal container, somewhat like a milk can, with a hose arrangement attached. The container was filled with petroleum. When this was turned on through the hose and a match applied, with a roar the red, vicious flame would shoot out for many yards from the nozzle of the hose. No doubt this was an awe-inspiring device, but troops against which it was used soon learned that the further the flame was projected the higher it rose from the ground. It could not do much damage against troops in a trench below the level of the bearer.

These *flammenwerfers* were generally used by German raiding-parties, and their terror had long since passed. The bearer was made a target for rifle-fire, and usually departed this life as a human torch. So unpopular had they become among the German infantry, that it was the custom to detail as carrier a soldier who had been found guilty of some military offence. It was another war horror which recoiled against its inventors.

The course ended and while we were in Bailleul awaiting our train I saw an advance party of the 34th Battalion moving through the town, and was told that the unit was marching into the line around Messines. I learned that my friend, Ben Brodie, was now a captain and a company commander. Shortly afterwards I saw Ben coming along at the head of his commando. I fell in beside him and talked as we marched for some little distance. That was the last I ever saw of this sterling friend. A few weeks later he was killed at the head of a raiding-party.[4]

I returned to the battalion and orders came to move up to the line at Wytschaete. We were under the impression that we were going into a quiet sector to perform for the winter months the usual routine of the forward area. Little did we imagine that the battalion as a unit, excepting for a few days, would not again be withdrawn from the line until the whole German front broke down before the Allies' incessant attacks.

Day was breaking on 29 January as the battalion entered the station yards at Samer. We spent most of the day in the train, but at length left it, and just before dark marched into the village of Kemmel. Here we were billeted in Nissen huts with a raised duckboard track forming a walk in front of them. Behind the village was Mount Kemmel, one of the highest points in the surrounding district. I had turned into my valise for the night when I was ordered to report immediately to battalion headquarters, go forward that night, and learn the dispositions of the troops whom we were to relieve in the line. These were one company in the front line, another to the rear in a deep gully known as 'the Ravine', the support company at Rose Trench to the right rear of the Ravine, and the reserve company at Denny's Wood.

114

My company was for the reserve position on marching in, a line of pill-boxes, across the main duck-board track running forward. The whole position was held in depth by a series of strong points based on captured pillboxes, or short trenches, well equipped with Lewis-guns; in rear several strongly manned, distinct lines of resistance, with a Vickers-gun post well hidden, to be used only in case of an attack. The pillboxes were individual fortresses of reinforced concrete and sunk partly below ground level, and bristling with machine-guns. Shells from ordinary field guns were as harmless to them as a stone from a catapult. The Germans had sprinkled the countryside with these pillboxes for the defence of their Ypres positions and the Messines Ridge. Great numbers of them were now in our hands – though with their open entrances, it is true, facing in the wrong direction.

Winter spent in a pillbox was far more comfortable than in the open, rain-drenched, crumbling trenches. But perhaps that very comfort may have been the key to the German failure. It was well known, and proved over and over again during the Somme fighting, that troops made accustomed to deep dugouts, immune from shell fire, often lost their nerve in the open under heavy bombardment, and were tempted to cower in their shelters when they should have been manning their parapets. This sapping the courage of men was a queer thing. Put men out into holes in the ground where they could see the shells bursting around them and could hear plainly the rattle of the machine-guns, inure them to exposure of weather and battle, and they would fight whenever occasion arose.

Take those same men and put them in a dugout (even if composed of only a sheet or two of galvanized iron and a waterproof sheet), and let them stew in their fears for several days, and they would soon get windy. In that condition every shell fired, every machine-gun that uttered its chattering speech, seemed to the individual to be directed against him-self and his shelter. In the midst of danger and death the man who will force himself to look the unpleasantness straight in the face will retain his courage, but he who tries to cover up his eyes will probably become a gibbering coward. Nothing in war is so cruel, so terrible, so ghastly, as shattered nerves working on the imagination.

I spent the night with the officers of this company of the 3rd Battalion, and next morning one of them took me around the position. All the com-pany was housed in some ten pillboxes. That used by the signallers went underground to a depth of about eight feet. The portion above ground-level was about another eight feet high, with a flat top. Many of the pillboxes bore marks of direct hits from shells, but all were habitable. Entrances to them were of various sizes, some so small that one had to crouch on hands and knees to enter.

115

The 'wood' that surrounded the position consisted of gaunt, limbless trunks or stumps, all of a blasted dead appearance. The ground was churned into innumerable shell-holes, filled with discoloured water, or coated with a thin layer of ice. To venture off the duckboards that ran through and around the wood was to sink knee-deep in mud. The very air reeked of war, gas-fumes, the acrid smell of high explosive shells, and the cloying odour of dead bodies.

To the right of company headquarters was erected a large strong post of sand-bags, hurdles, and the trunks of trees, and containing fire-steps and duck-boards, reminiscent of the old Armentières sector. This was the reserve company's battle position in case of an attack from the right front. The strong post was supplied with the usual reserve stores and was camouflaged with the branches of trees.

There was also a battle position against a frontal attack farther into the wood. The left front position was a waterlogged trench perhaps three feet deep. To the right rear, several hundred yards away, was a bomb and ammunition dump, housed in a strong pillbox. The structure used for company headquarters had a spring of water in one corner. This caused such seepage that it had to be constantly pumped out.

The company commander told me of an officer of the battalion that had taken out a patrol. He had crawled forward to investigate a pillbox. It was unoccupied, but while he was nosing about a party of six Germans came down the steps, threw off their packs, and prepared to spend the night there.

The Australian officer hid under some debris in a dark corner. All night long he lay there while the Germans talked, smoked, and took turns at post on top. When they withdrew and the Australian crept up the steps, he was horrified to see that it was a clear bright morning. There was nothing to do but sit tight and wait until darkness fell. He managed to reach our lines before the German party moved in again for the next night.

Our company came in to relieve about 8 p.m. Its commander was Major Roberts, and the second-in-command was Lieutenant C————. At Kemmel we had been joined by a new officer who had come across from Australia in charge of reinforcements. For months he had been on the staff of instructors at the training battalion in England, and this was to be his first introduction to the line. I was the junior officer of the company in rank, but had seen more line service than either of the other two subalterns. The major ordered me to live with him at company headquarters, and the other two officers were to sleep in a pillbox near their platoons, messing at company headquarters.

I could see that the little second-in-command did not like this arrangement. The new arrival, Lieutenant B————, was a fine upstanding type of a man. But it was plain that he would not be popular unless he quit

116

talking of 'wanting to be with the boys and to do his bit'. The surest way to 'get in bad' in the A.I.F. was to express in words your eagerness to be a real fighting soldier. When you spoke of the war as an individual the correct form was either to laugh at it, or curse the army, the mud, the chats, and the bully-beef stew.

Major Roberts was a tall, gaunt man, always on the fidget as though he had ants in his boots. He had seen service on Gallipoli, was a good officer to serve under, and was known throughout our unit as 'Chunda Loo'.

Our cook, a full-blooded Australian aboriginal, was a likeable fellow. His round face always wore a grin, and he would sit over the fire (which smoked vilely) and sing to himself, 'I'm going back to the shack where the black-eyed Susan's grow' in a tuneless unending strain until the major would roar: 'For God's sake, stop that noise!'

He was not exactly an oil-painting of what the army cooking schools aspired to turn out. He usually looked as though he had spent the morning up the flue of the chimney. Nature made him black, but the wet wood of his fire had smoked him a hue that would be very fashionable on the hobs of Hades. His eyes were red-rimmed, an army cardigan jacket had formed an alliance with his shirt, and both had withdrawn several inches up his body away from the trousers, exposing about the waistband of his breeches a roll of dark flesh. His breeches hung low, and there were spacious rooms to let in the backside. Puttees had been discarded, perhaps for freedom in his culinary tasks. From his belt hung the large issue knife that contained almost every useful article except a mouth-organ and a tooth-pick. He somehow did not give the impression that he was on very good terms with a wash. Still, he could produce a decent meal.

We often growled at the army food. Certainly there was not much variety, and very often one felt so hungry that he could almost have eaten the platoon's issue, but the health and well-nourished look of the men said a lot for the scientists who evolved the diet of the British Army. It taught us how much the majority of us over-eat in civilian life. Here were men living under the most rigorous conditions, sometimes working as hard as navvies, yet thriving on an amount of food that would look like a starvation diet (as to quantity) to most civilians.

Let me describe one evening 'at home' in the forward reserve line, when we had been working and digging all day, protected from observation by endless fog and drizzling rain.

It is after tea and we four officers sit around the table. The cloth is a Sydney newspaper, spread so as to feast our eyes with pictures of actresses of the day. The major and Lieutenant C——— are playing army bridge, using a dummy hand; the former is just beginning to learn the fine points of the game. B——— is trying to be interested in a magazine dated shortly after the Ark grounded on Mount Ararat. The pages are so badly dog-

117

eared that the publication has to be placed on the table and the reader to employ both hands in holding it open. I am writing a letter to a girl in London.

The cook, fat as a parish priest, is sitting by a smoking fire, in company with Nugget and another batman with fair hair and an impudent look on his young face. They are holding a sort of community sing-song, not raising their voices too loud for fear of distracting the major. The singers render: 'Take me back to dear old Aussie' with much feeling, and think so much of their effort that they encore themselves. Then 'Mademoiselle from Armentières' has the tale of her amours chanted, to be followed by that well-known classic, 'The O'Reilly's Daughter'. This affects the cook so much that he beats time with an old bayonet employed as a poker on the fire hobs. The air is thick with tobacco and the smoke of the fire. Outside an adjacent battery is firing by single guns, and away to the right, a couple of machine-guns can be heard tick-tacking as they traverse. After some time on my letter I envy the cook and the two 'Dingbats' their hilarity.

A runner comes down the steps with a waterproof sheet tied around his shoulders, from which the rain drips as he gives a written message to the major. The latter puts his cards down, reads, dismisses the runner into the rain and darkness, and enlightens us upon details of a working-party ordered for the morrow.

Working-parties to improve the defences were the chief duties of the moment, for the Allies expected in the coming weeks, at one or more points on the Western Front, a German offensive delivered with all the force provided by the extra divisions of the German Army now being released from the Russian front. The British Army's new system of field defence was organization in depth – in order to economize in loss of men under preliminary bombardment, assist in breaking up the line of an attack, and facilitate local counter-attacks. The new system permitted also better use of sited machine-gun batteries in the harassing of a hostile advance.

In the Wytschaete sector, for instance, our front line could easily have been blotted out of existence by the enemy. Compared with the front line organization of the Somme days it could never have beaten back a strong infantry assault under cover of a heavy barrage. But under the system of defence in depth it was not meant to do so. Rather the front line garrison was intended to disorder the attack to the utmost of its power, sacrificing itself if necessary in the effort; and the real resistance would be encountered by the enemy later. No wonder patrols were active during hours of darkness. Besides, our active patrols each strong-post would also push out listening-posts.

Already short bitter fights had taken place around these small posts when the enemy sent out foraging parties against them. In every case he had been sharply repulsed, sometimes leaving his dead and wounded. The whole British line was on the alert for the first signs of the German offensive.

While I was occupied with my party in the work of improving the defences, my attention was attracted to a spot near our task in the Ravine. This was the remains of a German 5.9 battery position which had been blotted out under the British bombardment during the Messines battle. It was awe inspiring to gaze upon the havoc wrought by the British heavy guns. A concrete pillbox had been shattered and its iron girders twisted like lines of candle-grease. The road and the ravine were pitted and churned with shell-holes, until the whole looked like a rough sea. The four guns of the 5.9 battery had been in pits, with strong overhead coverings. The whole had been simply swamped in a storm of metal and high explosive. Wheel-less gun carriages were mere heaps of twisted iron. Ammunition in cane baskets had been scattered like corn. The remains of the crews that had served the guns were still lying about the place – here and there a dismembered limb or skull, but generally in mounds of corruption. The barrel of one gun was intact and was prettily stamped with German eagles and a crest.

Of other pillboxes romantic stories were handed on from one battalion to another till they became legendary. One was said to contain the dead body of a woman with blonde hair. I did not inspect the place myself, nor can I recall anyone in the company who did. But all the men firmly believed it. Another pillbox was supposed to have been occupied by Prince Rupprecht of Bavaria, and was described by those Australians who occupied it as of palatial grandeur, with glass doors and a bathroom.

Our company's turn came to relieve the front line in the battalion's orderly rotation, and on the evening of 11 February we moved up. I was in charge of the strong posts of the right sector, with two platoons as my garrison. The other two platoons were on the left under Lieutenant C———, who had B——— with him to acquire front-line experience.

Once we are in, the active night-life of a trench garrison begins. Sentries are posted and visited every hour. Listening-posts depart into the darkness, and finally reappear. The major comes along the line, stops for questions and exchanges, and proceeds. Fritz's flares shoot up at frequent intervals. Vickers-guns fire occasional bursts. Our 18-pounders bark intermittently like sleepless dogs. The German dogs reply.

Rations, water, and rum appear with a carrying-party. Then a fatigue squad, laden with angle-irons and coils of barbed wire on their shoulders, pass along to the left sector to do some wiring, one of the worst jobs in the army. A runner comes with details of patrols to be sent out by the battalions on the right and left, their hours of departure, approximate time of return, area of patrol, and strength; the artillery will shoot at such and such an hour on such and such a target. Such is the general routine of orders sent along to a platoon officer in the line. Anything in them of special significance I jot down in my field message-book, initial the order, and the runner departs for the left sector.

The night drags on with such traffic and occupation. Every hour I tour my posts and yarn with the N.C.O. in charge. About 3 a.m. the Germans shell my sector with whizz-bangs. Two men are slightly wounded. They are given first aid, and, the shelling over, are sent to the rear accompanied by two bearers. They are walking wounded, and their mates offer them francs to the value of thousands for their 'blighties'.[5]

An hour before daybreak we stand to. Sentries crouch low, peering into No Man's Land. The usual early morning hate is indulged in by the guns of both sides. The major does his rounds again. Daylight comes. The men stand down. Day sentries are posted. A rum issue is handed out. Everybody turns to eat; those not on post crawl into the dugouts and sleep. Having seen all this come to pass as in duty bound, I trudge back the hundred yards or so to the company headquarters, tired and dirty beyond words. After a nip of rum undiluted, I eat the bacon, bread, and jam, like one famished, shave, roll myself in a blanket, and lying on the floor, fall into a sleep that lasts until late afternoon.

My batman awakens me to biscuits, cheese, and a cup of tea. Then I put on my equipment, move up to my post, stand to before dusk, and thus begin the night again. Soon our ration party comes up, laden with containers of hot stew and tea, also the usual bread, jam, and cheese, and the grand old S.R.D.[6] with a sand-bag encircling its jar.

All except the sentries eat, and they are soon relieved to have their share. In the A.I.F. officers in the line ate from the company's general dish. Taught by the experience of the Somme where no cook's fire could be lighted in the forward area, the A.I.F. had invented a container made from petrol tins, and planned on the thermos system. Food in this was carried many miles and was hot when received by the troops in the front line.

Four days of this and, the rotation rotating according to precedent, our company was relieved and took over in turn the immediate support position in the defences – Rose Trench, to the right of the Ravine. This was a rather good defence work about a lone pillbox. The platoons were housed in trenches, containing a number of dugouts in which men off post slept. Our position was on the extremity of a spur that jutted out over a valley running toward the old German front line. A belt of timber, Denny's Wood, ran from our posts to the left.

In so exposed a position no fires of any size could be lighted; all movement during the hours of clear daylight was forbidden. The lone pillbox, erected on the extreme lip of the spur, was very strongly built, sunk into the ground to a depth of perhaps twelve or fifteen feet. A few steps down was a ledge where was installed the company's field telephone. The signallers managed to eat, sleep, and work on this ledge; day and night a figure with a blanket around its legs crouched with the ear-phones on its head, a message-pad at hand, and three lighted candles stuck around. He looked like some uncouth deity in a shrine. Continuing down the steps one came to the officers' sleeping-quarters. In a space of perhaps 6 ft. by 6 ft. were erected four bunks, with wire bottoms. So short were they that it was impossible to stretch out on them, and one slept curled up like a dog. The lowest of the tier was mine. In the centre was a large hole, through which, though I plugged it with a groundsheet, a large part of my anatomy sagged.

The floor was covered with seepage water to a depth of some two feet, and we entered or left by aid of three piers, made of benzene tins sunk to provide a footing, with just their tops visible. The roof and sides of this apartment dripped water. It was as cold as an ice-cellar, and our illumination was a solitary candle stuck precariously on the edge of the top bunk.

We went to bed and arose by turns, and I often thought what a pantomime it would be if we ever tried a movement of 'All up together'. Seeds of rheumatism, lumbago, whooping-cough, influenza, must have been plentiful in that water-logged chamber. Still, we felt no ill-effect; life in the army was a wonderfully hardening process. Our meals we ate in a rude structure of timber and galvanized iron, leaning against the outside of the pillbox, with a table and (for seats) two planks resting on ammunition boxes.

Company orders in this position were that one officer must be on duty during hours of darkness, and we three subalterns arrange a roster to share the duty. About midnight C———, who had gone out first, comes down to our cellar and awakens me. Waiting until C——— has vacated the stepping-tins, I make my way upstairs. The night has the bitter, chilling cold of the wet Flanders country.

A tour of the posts completed, I sit on a fire-step near a Lewis-gun post, and smoke a pipe while listening to the N.C.O. in charge telling of the time he was a boxer on the northern coalfields of New South Wales. He is thickset, with a strong jaw, and a nose bent and twisted. Boxing had permanently altered the contours of his face, but had given him a great fund of rough humour, and he amuses me greatly with his stories. My allotted number of hours completed, I go down, wake B———, and when he comes up I have a cup of hot *cafe-au-lait* ready, made over a brazier. B——— seems very tired; his tour in the front line has made him feel that he wants to sleep for many hours to recuperate. I tell him he will soon get used to short sleep. But the real trouble with him is C———'s constant nagging at him, for some obscure reason, and it is not only making B———'s life miserable, but upsetting the mess.

121

Morning. Fog gone, and a wintry sun shines weakly over a forlorn landscape. A German 'plane comes across to have a look at us, flying low down. Vickers-guns on the left open fire at him, and soon gun after gun, Vickers and Lewis, join the vicious chorus as the German coolly approaches. Just as we were wondering what mascot the pilot carried to preserve him from the streams of bullets concentrated upon him, a shell from one of our 18-pounders scores a direct hit. A burst of white smoke under the wings, and the graceful deadly war bird crumples in the air like a child's kite. It drops steeply into a twisted wreck, from dugouts and possies emerge men, who, having cheered the disaster a moment ago, now race across the mud of the shattered wood to succour the airman. All that can be done is to pull his mangled body from the wreckage and establish his identification.

Soon they are racing away again even faster. In the language of the trenches, the fallen 'plane 'draws the crabs'.[7] A report from behind the enemy's line, a rushing through the air, and the first 5.9 shell arrives. Whenever the Germans observe one of their 'planes to crash in our territory they invariably try to destroy it with shell fire. As a rule, the 'plane was barely on the ground before his artillery began ranging upon it.

On 18 February word came through that I was to be made patrol officer for the battalion, and had to report with kit and batman to battalion headquarters. Really, I was glad to get away from the company, so unpleasant was C——— making things with his animosity towards B———. I could not help contrasting the difference of atmosphere in this company mess from the wonderful comradeship that existed among the senior N.C.O.s of my old company, before I left for a commission.

At battalion headquarters I was paraded before the C.O. Major Simpson. The major chatted to me for some little while, with the friendliness that he showed to every man in his battalion who happened to be brought in contact with him. He was commanding officer and godfather to us all. An original Anzac, he served with the 4th Battalion on Gallipoli. After the death in action of Lieutenant Colonel Scott, he took command of our battalion.[8]

On my way out to some brief special patrol training at Kemmel village, I met coming along the road in a detachment my old friend Peter Hughes, now with the 1st Division signallers. He brought back a flood of memories. After a few minutes' conversation, he expectorated loudly and remarked upon the dryness of his throat. I deliberately ignored the suggestion, and went on talking. At last Peter said – 'Being an officer now, I suppose you know where a rum issue is to be found for an old pal?' I told him that I had not seen the semblance of rum since I came back from the line. He could not believe this, and again stressed how dry marching made one's throat. I told him to wait for me, and went to a Tommy canteen where I purchased him four small bottles of Guinness. These I shoved into his pack, and then watched the man who had given me more laughs than any other in the A.I.F. set off after his detachment.

Note

1. Private 5352 Ernest Walter Collier from Sydney, New South Wales.
2. Also known as a Town Major, or T.M., these were officers permanently stationed in a town or village with the responsibility of billeting passing parties of troops.
3. For an excellent account of the Allies' development of gas warfare, it is suggested that the reader refers to: Major-General C. H. Foulkes, C.B., C.M.G., D.S.O., *'Gas!' The Story of the Special Brigade* (W. Blackwood & Sons, London and Edinburgh, 1934).
4. Born at Parramatta, New South Wales, and the husband of Mary Brodie, of 105, Pitt St., Sydney, 33-year-old Captain Benjamin Greenup Brodie was killed in action on 5 March 1918. Leading a raid on the German trenches, Brodie was seen standing on the parapet urging his men on when a burst from a machine-gun hit him in the side and chest. He fell to his knees, but continued to issue commands. By the time Brodie had been brought back to the Australian trench by the stretcher-bearers, he had died. He was buried in Berks Cemetery Extension at Comines-Warneton, Hainaut.
5. 'Blighty' was soldiers' slang for the United Kingdom and/or home. To those serving on the Western Front, a 'Blighty' wound was one that generally secured a return across the English Channel.
6. The exact meaning of the term S.R.D. appears to have been lost in the mists of time. Possibilities include Service Ration Department, Service Reserve Depot, Service Ration Depot, or, as frequently stated, Special Rum Distribution.
7. A term used by front line troops which means 'to attract enemy artillery fire'.
8. Major Adam James Goldie Simpson was the temporary Commanding Officer of the 56th Battalion until 3 March 1918.

Chapter 13

The German Offensive

The great attack – Feint move in the north –
Australians ordered south again – Their splendid moral –
Staying the German advance –
Recapture of Villers-Bretonneux in night attack.
(March to April 1918)

March and an early spring found us still working at strengthening the defence system of our sector of the Wytschaete-Messines Ridge and myself training my battalion patrol, with two N.C.O.s selected by myself from the battalion. Our location was at Piccadilly Farm, behind St Eloi, with a half-company of the battalion in charge of Lieutenant C————.

There was increased activity of the artillery on both sides. Previously most of the shelling had been done by our guns, but now the Germans were becoming aggressive again. Not only would their artillery reply with new spirit to our guns, but without any apparent provocation during the day or night they would suddenly open upon some point behind our lines and deluge it with shells. It was plain to all of us that behind the mist the Germans had in the last few weeks been massing artillery – the forecast of a coming storm.

It was now confidently expected throughout the British Army that heavily reinforced German armies would shortly be hurled against the Allied line. Our present positions guarded the way to the Channel ports, and what more tempting goal could there be for a big German offensive? At least, that was how we figured it out.

Further evidence of enterprise contemplated by the enemy was the occasional drifting over our lines, in a favourable wind, of a number of small gaily-coloured balloons, not much larger than toys. These carriers would deposit for the edification of civilians behind the lines papers printed in French and English setting out in sensational cartoons and letterpress the 'shameless conduct of perfidious England towards the black races,' or the 'horrors of the prison compounds which English troops established to herd, starve, and let be ravaged by disease, the men, women and children of the late Boer Republics in South Africa.' It was propaganda of the most childish kind, and one wondered at the working of the German mind that used it among French civilians, our allies.

Army intelligence was intrigued with the novel working of these balloons. The Allies had a hardworking propaganda department of their own.

The events for which we had been waiting began on 21 March.[1] During the night preceding the Germans did not shell us as usual. But while it was still dark, towards morning, a shell landed near our dugout behind the Ridge. I was awake immediately. Soon there came the familiar sound of a gas-shell, followed quickly by others. I arose, pulled on my boots, and went out. The shells were landing around an adjacent battery position.

Reaching the first sentry post, I could see the white mist of the gas-cloud rising from the ground. I warned the N.C.O.s of our half-company to have their men ready to come up from the deep dugout in battle order at a moment's notice, and took two men up to the entrance. Here we opened the reserve boxes of ammunition and bombs. I told off men to remain at each entrance and in case of alarm to issue an extra bandolier of cartridges and two bombs to each man as he came up from below. The shelling had increased. The gun positions were being pasted with gas and high explosive. A bombardment of our front line was in progress.

I returned to the hut and found C———— and A———— still curled up in their blankets. I ventured the opinion that the day had dawned of the long talked of German attack. They disagreed with this, and advised me to get back to bed. Instead, I ate some army biscuits and jam, lit my pipe, and went out to look round. Many of our batteries had now come into action, but the 18-pounders directly in front of us had their position enveloped in a thick cloud of gas, and were not firing.

Our big dugout and the two adjacent strong points were being shelled with high explosive. One shell just skimmed the roof of our tin shack and burst to the rear. Up the line machine-guns could be heard firing – not the usual short bursts, but belt after belt on a barrage line, like the roll of a great drum.

Everything indicated an attack. I climbed on to the roof of our shack to see further forward. The first streaks of dawn were in the sky, a dawn that was to usher in for the British Empire a period of danger and tension so acute that to equal it the pages of history must be turned back, perhaps to the day when the mighty Armada of Spain was sighted off the coast of England.

I stood on the roof gazing forward, wondering when the front line would call for assistance. The machine-gun fire was now at its heaviest, and the noise of the barrage to left and right was like the sound of a mighty organ that made the earth tremble under its detonations.

125

Presently over the front line shot up the 'red over green over red' of our S.O.S. rocket. The round balls of colours hung for an appreciable time in the air. Away to the left soared another S.O.S. I scrambled down, rushed into the hut with the news that the S.O.S. was up, and then hurried across and gave orders for the two platoons to scramble under cover of the sunken road. Within a few minutes the half-company was in position. We had been there perhaps ten minutes when a company runner came with orders to be ready to move at a moment's notice. Gradually the shelling eased off, and the sun was up when a further order was received to stand down. Later we learned that the Germans had attacked the Australian Division on our left, but had been repulsed. On our own division front a large enemy raiding-party was easily beaten off. The effort was a feint in accompaniment of the real attack that morning in the south against the 3rd and 5th British Armies.

Our patrols during the next two nights found the enemy front lines intensely active and watchful. But by 23 March we had, when off duty, lost interest in our present sector. At meals, in dugouts, and along the duck-boards, wherever little groups gathered, discussion was of the one topic – the battle down on the old Somme fields. The conviction bred itself that we should soon be drawn into the conflict.

On Monday, 25 March, all rumours were confirmed. The Australian Corps was marked down for the fight; the 3rd Australian Division was reported to be already on the move, and our division was to prepare for relief by the 1st Australian Division.

In the attenuation of the front of the British 5th Army, now overwhelmed by the massed German onslaught, were to be seen surely the evil fruits of the prolonged Passchendaele fighting during the latter months of 1917. Lives of good troops were squandered there lavishly. The shattered divisions had been reinforced with drafts in many cases composed of mere youths. Besides, there were not enough of them to resist such a blow as the enemy delivered. It was no new story in war.

The great Napoleon, when fighting his rearguard action through Germany, after his disastrous retreat from Moscow, appealing for rein-forcements said: 'Do not send me lads of eighteen years of age; the rigours of the campaign causes such to drop by the wayside, or clutter the hospitals. War demands seasoned men.'

Mr Lloyd George has been blamed for denying to the British Commander-in-Chief troops held in reserve in Great Britain. Whether this be true or not, the fact remained that the British Army had suffered a crushing defeat for want of reserves, and its right wing was in retreat. The darkest days since Mons or the first Battle of Ypres had now come upon the Allies.

126

The spirit of the men of our battalion in this crisis was magnificent. They knew that probably within a few days they would be thrown into a battle in which they would have to fight desperately against a mighty army flushed with success. Their manner would almost have led one to believe that they were about to participate in a sports meeting. The thought that the Australian Corps might be smashed or routed had no place in their minds. Was it personal vanity? A sight of them would surely have been a wonderful tonic to faint-hearted croakers in Blighty who seemed to think that the Germans were going to fold up the British front and drive it into the sea.

After-events were to prove that the confidence and ability of the men of the 56th Battalion to do any task allotted to them was general throughout the whole Australian Corps. The British Army had other good divisions which had not yet been engaged, besides the Australians, and these the Germans were to find tough fighters.

On 28 March the 5th Division was concentrated behind Ypres. I had been for some days suffering from the effects of gas, and on this day completely lost my voice. The doctor said I should be evacuated, but I told him that I did not want to leave my battalion at such a time. At midnight we paraded, marched to the little station of Hopoutre, and entrained. Lewis-guns were mounted throughout the train against hostile aircraft. Never before upon any of our main train journeys had this been done, and the precaution made us realize what a mess the British front must be in.

Daylight of 29 March found us moving at a pace much faster than that usual with troop trains. Once, before sun-up, our train stopped in a deep cutting. We could hear the hum of three 'planes overhead. Fortunately the Germans did not see us, and when they had gone their way our journey was continued. At St Pol, during the afternoon, we saw a large fatigue party feverishly clearing a line of several trucks that had been struck a few hours previously by a long-range shell from which the 58th Battalion had suffered many casualties.

Doullens we found a hive of activity. This town had been the detraining point of the other brigades of our division, and also of the 3rd Division. We went five miles farther along and commenced to detrain at Mondicourt. Whilst this was in progress I saw Captain Smythe (who was now on brigade staff) and asked him: 'Where is Fritz?'

'That is what a lot of people would like to know,' he replied. 'You have to march until you find him.'

Soon the battalion was on the move with companies in artillery formation. A drizzling rain fell as we marched off. Presently we were on a good road and met surely the saddest procession in the civilized world. Old men, women, and children, with their movable possessions in carts, handbarrows, and other conveyances, were fleeing from their homes, and intermingled with them were stragglers from British units without arms or equipment, many of them evidently from Labour Battalions and all apparently very windy. Flying Corps tenders passed with aeroplanes in tow. We Australians alone seemed to be marching towards the enemy.

As I tramped at the head of my platoon, the rain driving into our faces and dripping from our steel-helmets and greatcoats, I saw the crowds of fugitives hurrying past, and from the little band of my command heard whistling, laughter, and jokes. I was vastly proud of being an Australian soldier. These same men had been cooped up in crowded trucks for nearly twenty-four hours; at one of our halts, when a group of middle-aged Tommies from a Labour battalion asked for cigarettes and said in awe-inspired voices that it was impossible to stop the Boches as 'they were coming over in swarms', I overheard one of my platoon remark to his pal: 'Struth, Bill, we'll get some souvenirs now!' The more Germans, the more prisoners to 'fan' for postcards, watches, perhaps a pistol. Could any person who did not know the sang-froid of the Australian infantryman credit such a remark at such a time and place?

The raw recruits of Egyptian training days were going forward in the spirit of veterans to meet an enemy exulting in victory. Even if they had not stuck out the bitterest winter for fifty years in the wastes of the Somme, whipped the picked German rearguards in the open, held Bullecourt, swept Polygon Wood in irresistible waves, held Broodseinde Ridge under continuous bombardment – even if they had done none of these things, their moral on that march forward to meet a victorious enemy would have marked them as first-class troops.

We marched all the afternoon, and dusk was coming down when we entered, wet and tired, the village of Louvencourt, near Albert. Here we found the civilian population all ready, with their belongings loaded on to conveyances, to evacuate the village. Their joy at our arrival was most flattering. Old men and womenfolk, they all pressed around telling us that now the 'Bon Australiens' had arrived they would not 'depart.' Never was our popularity so high. In our billet Madame bustled around and told us that she and her daughter would vacate the house so that we could have more room. She even unlocked her cellar and offered us her store of potatoes and fuel. We did not use the good lady's potatoes.

The 15th Brigade had already established an outpost line in advance of Louvencourt. We were behind the right of the 3rd British Army, which had withstood the German attacks more successfully than had Gough's 5th Army. Just before entering the village we saw some Canadian troops. They also had been hurried south, but we learned that they were returning with all speed to their familiar sector, around Arras, where a German offensive was expected.

We stripped our sodden greatcoats, puttees, and boots, and sat around the welcome heat of a great fire, with the steam rising from us in clouds.

We were ravenously hungry and very tired. After being cooped up in crowded troop-trains for many hours, we had marched about ten miles through the rain with no food since the previous afternoon save a little army biscuit and bully-beef.

We learned that by the night of 27 March – two days earlier – both the 3rd and 4th Australian Divisions had pushed brigades into the line. Within the next few days these bore the brunt of severe fighting, and, to their glory and to the honour of their far away Australia, the German massed attacks were repulsed again and again and never gained a yard of ground from the Australian Divisions. It was not simply the exhaustion of the German attack that halted the enemy's advance at the point where the Australians stood.

Meanwhile, on the Albert front which our brigade was supporting, the immediate tension had eased. For several days I had been resisting evacuation on account of gas-sickness. On 1 April I was spitting blood, and the doctor declared my right lung affected as well as my throat, and I was ordered away by ambulance to hospital.[2] The Canadian hospital at Doullens passed me on to Wimereux, and this in turn to a hospital at D'Hardelot, somewhere near Abbeville. The last was said at Wimereux to be a gas-hospital, but on arrival I was informed that it specialized in treatment of boils, scabies, and carbuncles. However, such was often the way of the army.

At D'Hardelot hospital I was greeted in a most friendly fashion by an Australian nursing sister, one of those evacuated from the Australian hospital at Abbeville when the German offensive was at its height. My name conveyed nothing to the friendly sister, but no doubt she would have been surprised to learn that our respective fathers had been the bitterest of enemies many years ago in a small township of New South Wales. She was the youngest of her family, and I the eldest of mine, so she probably did not know what I did of that story.

Here I was put to bed in a small room in the upper story of the villa. From the window I could see the large tented expanse of the hospital – and beyond it the seashore. A gale howled round the building; rain beat against the windows. I lay in the little room utterly depressed and longed to be back with the battalion. My voice was almost normal next morning and the coughing was much easier. The gale still howled. I felt I was in solitary confinement, and that if I lay here much longer I should go mad. I made up my mind to get out of hospital with the utmost speed.

When the medical officer came in I told him I had quite recovered and wanted to be discharged that day. He said he would let me get out of bed on the morrow, which I duly did. I felt weak enough on going for a walk, but got my discharge next day, 7 April, and orders to report to the base camp at Le Havre. The doctor warned me that the authorities would take severe action against any officer who failed to report to his base. 'This

129

specially applies to Australians,' he added, 'as you chaps have been in the habit immediately you are discharged of boarding a train and rejoining your units.'

After a few days at Le Havre, where I met my old pal Jimmy Sowter again as a newly commissioned officer returning from England, a large party of us entrained for the line. A journey of wonderful circumlocution, lasting some forty hours, landed us at Vignacourt on 14 April, and I found the nucleus of the 56th Battalion nearby at Gorenflos, a small village mostly deserted, with one muddy street.

Some stirring events had happened during the fortnight I had been away. The 3rd and 4th Australian Divisions had halted the German advance between Albert and Villers-Bretonneux, their line running across the valleys of the Ancre and the Somme. Villers-Bretonneux on the high ground south of the Somme was recognized by the British High Command as the key to Amiens, nine miles away to the rear. Amiens was the principal town of Picardy, but, what was more important, through it ran the railway connection between the British and French fronts. To lose Villers-Bretonneux was to deny Amiens and the railway to the Army Supply services, and the consequence must soon have been either the separation of the Allied armies or the abandonment by the British of the Calais coast.

On 4 and 5 April the Australians withstood strenuous efforts of the enemy to force the entrance into Amiens – on 4 April at Villers-Bretonneux and next day at Albert. Each assault was beaten to a standstill by the determined resistance of Australian brigades. Hardly had this fighting died down when a fresh German offensive began in Flanders between Armentières and La Bassée.

Their blow fell on a Portuguese division which was holding portion of the line near the latter place. The Portuguese bolted like startled fowls, and the Germans poured troops into the gap. Fleurbaix, Estaires, Merville, which we had known nearly two years previously, quickly fell. The 1st Australian Division, which had only just reached the Somme, was hurriedly re-entrained for the north, and with other British reinforcements it stayed the German advance short of Hazebrouck. But the Messines Ridge, Bailleul, Kemmel, and a great area of the Ypres battleground were overrun by the German advance before it was finally arrested.

The Germans made one last bid for Amiens on 24 April. Up to a few days before, the 5th Australian Division had been holding Villers-Bretonneux and the high bare downland to the north of it towards the Somme. On 20 April, the 8th British Division took over the defence of Villers-Bretonneux. The 14th and 8th Brigades of our division then held the line on the north flank, down to and beyond the Somme, with the 15th Brigade in reserve.

Early in the morning of 24 April the Germans, under cover of a terrific bombardment, launched an attack here along a front of several miles. On the Australian front the enemy was repulsed decisively, but the British were driven out of Villers-Bretonneux, and the 56th Battalion, the reserve of the 14th Brigade, had to be deployed to protect the right flanks. It is interesting to note, and I may appropriately mention it here, that a German map captured shortly afterwards showed Villers-Bretonneux about 200 yards out of its true map position. It was considered that this error probably saved the 56th Battalion many casualties on 24 April.

That night, 24–25 April, Villers-Bretonneux was recaptured with the bayonet in a brilliant night attack by the 13th and 15th Australian Brigades operating on either side of the town. The operation was planned as a surprise and was, therefore, conducted without artillery preparation. Early in the silent advance of the 15th Brigade a large party of Germans were found erecting wire entanglements. Upon these unsuspecting toilers of the night the Australians fell with a deadly rush. Not a shot was fired by the attackers, but the Germans were bayoneted left and right.

As deeper the attacking waves advanced, they encountered strong opposition. Rifle and machine-gun fire poured into them. German flares lit the scene as a general order to charge was shouted by the senior officer of the attacking waves. Here was enacted over again one of the many bayonet charges practised by the battalions over the sands of the desert of Egypt. With bayonet at the 'engage' the leading waves rushed the German trenches. They wielded the weapon with awful effect. Strong point after strong point was swamped in that rush, and isolated German garrisons were annihilated in succession. The enemy obligingly denoted his position time after time by throwing up flares, which vastly assisted the attackers in thorough performance of their work.

By 3 a.m. the 15th Brigade had reached its objective beyond Villers-Bretonneux; during the day the 13th Brigade from the other side of the town joined up with them. The Germans within the town were mopped up by the 57th Battalion and British troops.

The recapture of Villers-Bretonneux was an achievement fit to rank among the most brilliant of the victories gained by the Australian Imperial Force. The plan undoubtedly was 'Pompey' Elliott's,[3] and that his brigade and the 13th carried this night attack to such a brilliant conclusion proved to what a high standard of battle discipline and initiative Australia's volunteer soldiers had attained.

Notes

1. The series of German attacks known as the Spring Offensive, *Kaiserschlacht* (Kaiser's Battle), or the Ludendorff Offensive, began on this date. There were four separate German attacks, codenamed *Michael*, *Georgette*, *Gneisenau* and *Blücher-Yorck*, launched in that order. *Michael* was the main attack, which was intended to break through the Allied lines,

outflank the British forces which held the front from the Somme river to the English Channel and defeat the British. Once this was achieved, it was hoped that the French would seek armistice terms. The other offensives were subordinate to *Michael,* and were designed to divert Allied forces from the main offensive on the Somme. The attacks marked the deepest advances by either side since 1914.

2. Williams was admitted to No. 5 British Red Cross Hospital (Lady Hadfield's Hospital) at Wimereux on 1 April 1918. Three days later he was transferred to 25 General Hospital at Boulogne. These establishments were large base hospitals with 250, 500 or 1,000 beds.

3. Brigadier-General Harold Edward 'Pompey' Elliott.

Chapter 14

New Somme Battlefield

The Australians hold the enemy's advance –
A new line in clean country – General Monash's achievements –
Patrol fights – Our superiority over the enemy.
(May to July 1918)

On 12 May I left the brigade nucleus camp at Pernois to rejoin the battalion. I was glad to go. All the household of my billet turned out to see me off the premises. Monsieur came in especially from the field to shake me by the hand and wish me *bonne chance*. Madame kissed me on both cheeks, tears in her eyes, and told me that if ever I came back to Pernois there was a billet waiting for me. Old Auntie hobbled out with her stick, and in her shrill voice told me to kill all the Boches and then return to drink champagne at her expense. Mlle Alice cried for me and her absent French artilleryman together, and told me that she would pray for me. These kindly folk had treated me while I was recuperating like one of their own sons. I was one of quite a number of officers for the brigade; we filled a large lorry. Bert Matthews was also one of the party.

On arrival at battalion headquarters, a chalk-pit beyond Corbie, I was posted again to 'C' Company, now commanded by Lieutenant Pitt. In 'A' Company's trench I was greeted again by my old pals, Grimmy and Shepherd.

As darkness came down we moved into the front line. Our position ran in a series of strong posts roughly following the crest of a rise; in front the ground sloped away to a road, beyond which rose steeply a bank about fifteen feet high, and then a series of terraces. Immediately in front was Vaire Wood, which in one part ran right to the crest of the high bank above the road. This end of the wood, a small plantation, jutted out from the main part, and was held by an advanced post of the Germans. The enemy also occupied strong posts along the terraced ground.

'C' Company held the left of the battalion frontage, and joined the 54th Battalion, whose right post occupied ground somewhat higher than ours. 'A' Company was on our right. Villers-Bretonneux lay away to the right, covered by the 4th Australian Division, joining our own right near the main Vermand-Amiens road, which ran straight as an arrow through our line. Away to our rear over undulating ground lay the town of Corbie.

Our present policy was defensive. The Germans had failed to reap the full fruits of their advance in March. They had been driven out of Villers-Bretonneux with heavy losses. The battle in the north round Hazebrouck showed them material gains in territory, but the fighting had died down to trench warfare once again. The enemy had still large reserves, and was expected to attack again. Our policy was to push on with all speed with the strengthening of local defences barring the way to Amiens.

We had hardly settled down in our posts when our batteries opened a tornado of shell-fire upon Vaire Wood. The high bursting shrapnel above and the savage orange-coloured flame of the high explosive on the ground soon wrapped an acrid cloud of smoke over the German positions. The screaming shells overhead, the earth-shaking concussion of their explosions, the showers of sparks and flame made a scene of awe-inspiring grandeur. From our immediate rear Vickers-guns joined in the devil's orchestra. We gazed over the parapet at the hurricane of destruction visited upon the German positions. Then Fritz's batteries retaliated. We caught some of the strafe, but mostly the Germans searched our battery positions.

The bombardment ceased as suddenly as it had begun, and the garrison began the night's business. A patrol went out and returned. Another from the 54th Battalion next door fell foul of a German post away on the left. We could hear the reports of the German stick bombs and the vicious whining replies of the Mills grenades. An enemy attack was expected in the morning, and before dawn another heavy artillery shoot was carried out on No Man's Land and the German front line posts. We stood to arms for the expected enemy; but he did not come.

Daylight burst upon us with the suddenness of a lifted curtain. The dawn was a beautiful thing to behold. High up in the sky the larks sang, the morning air had a freshness as if the dew of the night had washed it, and made it so clean that it was a delight to inhale. In that first light the countryside showed up the attractiveness of France during the summer months.

Our trenches were situated in surroundings which the ugliness of war had not yet spoilt. Here the earth was unraped by bombardment; the trees still wore their green leaves. A crop of wheat, knee-high and vividly green, ran from our line out into No Man's Land. Everywhere the grass sparkled in the early sun, laden with crystal dew, and away on the ridges behind and in front could be seen patches of wild flowers in carpets through the grass.

Even more cheerful than the beauty of the countryside was the absence of old trench smells. That penetrating, cloying smell of dead bodies,

134

latrines, chloride of lime, dugouts noisome from constant occupation by verminous unwashed men, mud made foul with death and refuse, the hideous litter of broken wire hanging from bent and twisted angle-irons, the pathetic little white crosses among all the filth and ugliness – the depressing features of the old Somme line – were here conspicuous by their absence. After stand down we ate our breakfast; sentries posted, we stretched out in the bottom of the trench and went gratefully to sleep in the sun.

In the afternoon I awoke, and was writing a letter when suddenly an outburst from German machine-guns interrupted all local occupations. Looking over the parapet, we saw one of our observation 'planes low down and heading towards our line from the direction of Hamel. Flying lower and lower, it came over the left of Vaire Wood and turned up the gully that ran parallel with our line, with a host of German machine-guns concentrating fire upon it. The 'plane was evidently in trouble, and soon crashed in No Man's Land beyond the Amiens Road, some distance out from a 4th Division post.

Hardly had it come to earth when the ground around it arose in puffs of dust as German machine-gun fire fell upon it. Suddenly two men from the 4th Division post leaped over and raced through the bullets to the 'plane. The gods who guard brave men looked well after these for a time. We saw them in the midst of the hail drag two wounded men from the 'plane and into the shelter of a shell hole. The machine-guns ceased. Then one of the infantrymen again risked death. Jumping from the shell-hole, he raced across and set fire to the 'plane. The machine-guns were on him in a twinkling, and as he raced back to his shell-hole we saw him crumple and fall.

His companion then displayed a heroism wonderful to behold. Out from the shell-hole, with his arms around one of the stricken airmen, and with the infantryman on his back as though swimming, he dragged towards the trench. The machine-guns opened up again. Snipers from the cover trenches fired, and, as we watched, the brave fellow rolled on one side and lay still. But the drama was not yet finished.

A white flag was waved from the Australian strong post. And then the waver stood fully exposed upon the parapet and a stretcher party came out. Another stretcher appeared and the soldier with the white flag stood over the wounded men, waving the flag while the bearers lifted the stricken men on to the stretchers. Then both parties shouldered their burdens to the trench. Two trips were made into No Man's Land; after the wounded had been given first aid in the trench they were taken out again under the cover of the white flag. And the Germans fired not one shot at them. It was a revelation to us to see this respect for the rescuers, but the

135

sheer bravery of the spectacle probably dominated the enemy's feelings of the moment as well as our own.

Our nightly patrols did not always return unscathed. That night my old friend, Sergeant Shepherd of 'A' Company, was killed in a fighting patrol sent out to secure a prisoner for identification purposes.[1] He was lured by an enemy party into a machine-gun ambush. Another patrol brought his body in without loss, a ticklish job.

In the following night I took a party along the company front. We lay just behind the barrage line when our guns opened their early morning bombardment, and then, as the first streaks of dawn became visible, started to work slowly back towards our line. We were still two hundred yards or more away from it when daylight broke with extraordinary suddenness. Watchful Germans saw us and made targets of us as we got up and raced for our trenches.

On 16 May, after dark, I was ordered to have a patrol of one N.C.O. and six men ready to escort the division intelligence officer in a search of the terraced ground on the other side of the road. I took him along the line, and he listened while I made sure that each post knew the details of the patrol, the point where it was going out, the number of men, approximate route, length of time they were expected to be out, and probable place of return to our line. Under a waterproof curtain by the light of a candle I showed him on a patrol-map our route, and again out of the trench pointed out to him the salient features of the ground occupied by the Germans.

Outside our line the patrol got into the usual diamond formation. I asked the captain to occupy the centre, just in rear of myself and the corporal. A dependable soldier took the position of 'tailer'. The night was dark and overcast. Through the wet standing crop we worked, and I could not help thinking what a job the captain's batman would have next morning in cleaning his smart breeches with their white knee rubs.

Past the crop we worked towards the plantation. I intended to try to enter this copse, and if possible work up close to the strong post which I knew was in it. We were crawling along and had almost reached the road, when my eyes caught an object on the ground. At a pre-arranged signal my patrol halted as if frozen to the ground. A whisper to my corporal and he edged over to me. Yes, we could make, out several men lying in pairs from twenty-five to fifty yards away. Slowly the corporal and I wormed our way forward some yards; then, peering into the darkness, we could make out about twenty men lying out in crescent formation.

Inch by inch we worked our way back to our patrol. I whispered to the captain that we had almost crawled into the left horn of a crescent of men set out as a trap. While I was saying this, my 'tailer' came forward on his belly like a snake, with the information that a party of men had moved around and were now entering the crop in our left rear. Let them get into position and we would be caught in a nice trap. The Germans had at least thirty, perhaps forty, men on the job; we numbered nine, and were not constituted as a fighting patrol.

We had to slip out, fighting only as a last resort. To lose prisoners or men killed and so enable the Germans to secure identification would have landed me in trouble. I did some furious thinking for a few seconds, then passed the word back to the patrol to crawl sideways, slowly and quietly, still keeping our diamond formation and our face towards the Germans. The 'tailer' was to keep a sharp look-out for the party towards our rear. Inches at a time we edged away, gambling on our proficiency in the art of crawling on our elbows to get us out of close contact with the crescent before the German flanking party could work through the crop behind us.

Minutes were drawn out to incredible length as we edged away, but at last I could see the right horn of the crescent and knew that we were almost out of the mess. A few more yards, and we rose to our feet under cover of a fold in the ground. We could not distinguish the men in the crescent, and knew that they were unable to see us. I was curious to see what the party in the crop would do, and presently we saw them emerge creeping forward in extended order. We counted sixteen of them and, as we watched, they moved forward to fall, as they expected, upon the rear of my patrol. Our new hopes that they might fall foul of each other came to nothing.

We then patrolled away to the right of the company sector. Before returning home we investigated the gully for signs of the enemy's party, but they had been withdrawn. We regained our line without further excitement. The captain from division was thrilled to the finger-tips with the experiences of the night.

The battalion was relieved on 17 May and went into support position behind the ridge of Hill 104 on the northern flank of Villers-Bretonneux. Here our duty was the digging of support defences against the renewed German attack that was still expected.

The news of immediate interest was the departure of General Birdwood from the Australian Corps to take command of the British 5th Army, which after its defeat in March had been withdrawn from the line, reorganized, and was now in Flanders. The command of the Australian Corps passed to General Sir John Monash, a citizen soldier with the organizing brain of a military genius. Monash was soon to plan attacks which were recognized by G.H.Q. as models of organization and attention to detail. Under him the corps smashed its way through every defensive position in its path, and by its exploits contributed largely to the termination of the war before the end of 1918. Yet, his task finished, he returned to his own land unsung, practically unnoticed, and ignored on important public occasions by the Government of Australia and its professional soldiers.

General Monash had sailed from Australia with the 4th Infantry Brigade, with which he served at Gallipoli. After the evacuation he was sent to the 3rd Australian Division, and brought it across from England when it made its appearance on the Western Front. Under him this division had taken part in the signal victory of Messines and in the bloody fighting during the Passchendaele offensive. But Monash's great chance came when it fell to the lot of his, the youngest Australian division, to be the first to reach the sorely-pressed remnants of the British 5th Army in March 1918. The situation around Villers-Bretonneux was then desperate in the extreme, and it was the 9th Brigade of Monash's Division, thrown with great daring across the Somme, which saved the situation. By their tenacity and fighting pluck they won out in an action that the British Corps to which they were temporarily attached had fully expected to be the commencement of another retirement.

When the civilian population fled from Villers-Bretonneux on the approach of the Germans in March, they took with them only so much as they could carry or pack into a few small carts. In spite of frequent shelling, troops in the early days of the occupation of this sector used to wander into the town and inspect the houses. In many of these madames and ma'mselles had left behind intimate articles of attire. Some of the troops who had been strangers to a bath and a change of underclothing for many weeks promptly discarded their verminous undergarments and decked themselves out in feminine finery. A few of these men, garbed underneath their uniforms in the daintiest of lingerie, became casualties, and great was the astonishment and amusement of nurses in the casualty clearing-station upon undressing them.

One of our little group told of a man belonging to our battalion who had wandered into the town, sampled many wines, and under that mellowing influence had conceived a desire to see himself again in civilian clothes. He donned the dark Sunday-best suit of some monsieur, and a hard felt hat. He bethought himself to take back some liquor for his comrades, commandeered a baby's perambulator, and loaded into it one of those large wicker-bound flagons of wine which abounded in village cellars.

Arrayed in his civilian suit, he sedately pushed the pram down the straight white road from Villers-Bretonneux to where his company lay in reserve. The spectacle soon attracted curious gazers, but unfortunately, one of the earliest was his company commander, whose memory for faces, even in disguise, was no weak faculty. The adventurer was promptly placed under arrest, and his guard walked him back up the road, still pushing the pram, to the house where his uniform had been abandoned. Into this he changed, and later in the Orderly Room he found that the escapade cost him 28 days' loss of pay.

A more amazing story of the early days around Villers-Bretonneux was that of a battalion headquarters signaller named (let us say) Lucas. This man when sober was quiet, even tame; but with a few drinks taken he arose to heights of valour and self-assertion. On a certain night our battalion was to be relieved in the front line, and, following the usual custom, the incoming battalion sent in its signallers some hours before the actual relief. While Lucas had been in the line crouched over the switchboard with earphones on his head, or in hours off duty, he had carved a plaque of an Australian coat-of-arms from a piece of white trench-chalk. So pleased was he with his handiwork that he had promised it to the commanding officer as a souvenir of the sector. Proudly he exhibited the finished masterpiece to the relieving signallers. In their admiration they invited him to share some rum. Lucas did so.

Soon he was no longer a humble soldier of the Australian Army, but a Michelangelo reincarnated. He talked sculpture, carving, and plaques, until his listeners, to change the subject, suggested another rum. Upon leaving, he was given yet another to cheer him on his way. He set out laden with his kit and the precious plaque. Unfortunately, on the way he tripped over some wire and smashed his work of art. He was prostrated with grief. Would not the colonel be disappointed of the promised souvenir? Lucas there and then decided that the colonel should have a real live souvenir in substitute – one that would clean his boots, hold his horse, and do a goose-step. In short, Lucas decided that he would go back to the line, advance upon the enemy, and pluck from their midst one of their number.

This amazing fellow turned about and walked through our outpost line and then into the German position until he came upon a large dugout. Standing boldly at the entrance, he called out for the occupants to come up and surrender or be blown to pieces in their lair. Eight Germans came sheepishly up the steps with their hands above their heads. Lucas lined them up, entertained them with a wild demonstration of bayonet-lunging, called out to an imaginary patrol behind him to keep down behind the parapet, and then beckoning a young Fritz to his side, chased the others below with threats that if they came up again they would be cut to pieces. With his prisoner he returned through both the German and our own lines of posts without being halted.

In festive mood, and having conceived a liking for the young German, Lucas decided that a holiday in the back areas would do them both an immense amount of good. So, crossing the Somme at Corbie, he and his prisoner became for five days and nights lost to the ken of men. Meanwhile Lucas was reported missing by his battalion, and was thought to have been blown to pieces by a shell on his way back from the line.

On the sixth day a strange pair walked into the battalion horse-lines at Corbie – a young German carrying the web equipment of an Australian

139

soldier and a boltless Lee-Enfield rifle on his shoulder and, beside him, flourishing a walking-stick with the air of a showman parading a rare exhibit, the mourned signaller Lucas. Lucas was, of course, placed under arrest. His story was not believed at first, but the German when examined confirmed it. Lucas would, no doubt, have received a decoration but for the reward in the shape of a holiday jaunt which he took unto himself.

We regarded as signs of an approaching attack the fact that our duties in reserve position included carrying up to the front line great quantities of heavy trench-mortar shells and barbed wire. The wire was in coils, and these were carried by the men on the fixed bayonets of their rifles.

Another sign seized upon was the earnest engagement of the machine-gunners for many days in sorting small-arms ammunition. Much of this was of American manufacture and varied greatly. For use in rifles it was not so bad, but for machine-guns it had to be of correct size or it would cause a gun to jam. I suppose the rush of orders in American factories was so great that proper supervision was not given to examination of the munitions manufactured there. But nothing short of deliberate robbery could account for the core of many bullets being made of paper, instead of lead, inside the nickel envelopes.

The artillery had even worse to contend with in some of the American-manufactured shells. Many of these blew back in the breech of the guns, with disastrous results to the crew, or gave short bursts perilous to our own infantry. There must have been some easy money made in Yankee-land out of munitions contracts.

On 26 May I was ordered to take out a patrol, penetrate the small plantation that jutted out from the main part of Vaire Wood to the high bank above the road, and reconnoitre the strength of the enemy post there, and the nature of its defences. This was to be preliminary to a raid upon the position.

With my party I moved out after midnight. The moon was a great yellow ball in the heavens, and moving objects could be seen for hundreds of yards. If the Germans maintained any sort of an alert look-out we should need some magic cloak to get into the plantation without being seen. In the line company a pal of mine (Courtney), the lieutenant in charge, told me that the Germans had, since we were relieved, dug a new strong post underneath the high bank near the plantation. Courtney decided to come out with my patrol.

We entered No Man's Land and moved through the standing crop as conspicuous as a wart on a man's nose. The Germans must have known all about us before we had crawled fifty yards. We could already distinguish the mounds of earth that marked the position of the new strong point, and we manoeuvred to approach it from a flank. The night was very still, and we listened at intervals to catch any sounds from the post. The position of this new trench rather puzzled me, as its garrison would have at their backs a bank at least fifteen feet high, and if it were attacked none of the other German posts could support it with their fire because of the dead ground. It seemed to me that if ever a post were held out as bait to a fighting patrol, this one was.

The patrol got to within perhaps a hundred yards of the strong point. We could hear no sound, so Lieutenant Courtney and myself wormed our way across the road towards it, while our patrol remained ready to rush to our assistance if we were attacked. We found the post unoccupied. Then we scaled the high bank, hanging on by the long tufts of grass that grew on its face. I came up under the shelter of a low bush, and could see a German post fifty yards ahead. The moonbeams shone on the steel helmets of its garrison, who were lining the parapet as if waiting for an attack. As our two heads appeared over the bank in the bright moonlight, a party of six or eight Germans, as though by signal, ran from the plantation and entered the post.

Lieutenant Courtney and I whispered together and decided that we would try and work to the plantation about twenty yards on our left. We agreed that the Germans had been watching us since we moved out from our line, and that our boldness in crawling up on to the bank with the moon behind us had temporarily perplexed them.

With revolvers ready in hand, we edged towards the plantation. We had not moved far when a shower of broomstick bombs exploded in quick succession. So close were some that the dirt was thrown into our faces, and we were only saved by the fact that our heads were lower than the place where the bombs exploded.

The suddenness and closeness of the explosion caused us to fall from our perches on the bank. We scrambled to our feet, and stood waiting for a rush from the trench. When no enemy appeared we backed away from the bank. Crawling across the road on our stomachs we must have been very conspicuous, and we fully expected a machine-gun to open on us, but none did. It was useless to seek to enter the plantation on so bright a night; so we rejoined our patrol and went back to our lines.

I reported the post in the plantation and the one on the terraces strongly held, and that their garrisons had a system of mutual support in event of an attack and were very much on the alert. On the following night, when 'A' and 'C' Companies relieved the front line, I took out another patrol and managed to get the information required with regard to the wiring of the post in the plantation. This night was overcast and we met with no excitement. The Germans must have been carrying out a relief, so quiet was their line.

Next afternoon the enemy ranged on 'A' Company's advanced strong post with an 8-inch or heavier howitzer. In 'C' Company on the flank of this bombardment we could not understand the use of such heavy artillery against one small infantry post, and as soon as dusk came I set about investigation. The enemy's sixth shell had landed fairly in a post to the rear, and that satisfied the gunners. The crater made by each of these howitzer shells was at least ten feet deep and as big as an ordinary cottage room.

From Lieutenant Davies, of 'A' Company, I heard the full story. At daylight he had been surprised to see a working-party of about 200 Germans spaced out and digging a communication trench from the main part of Vaire Wood towards the plantation. Evidently they had arrived on the task just before daylight, and were digging furiously to get under cover. They presented an ideal target for a machine-gun. Although we always had Lewis-guns mounted in the front line, orders were that they were to be used only in case of an attack. On such an occasion as this the prescribed duty was to report the target to company headquarters for the artillery to engage. Davies accordingly reported, but no response from the artillery ensued.

Time passed, and the Germans had dug down to a depth of a couple of feet. The No. 1 of the Lewis-gun team was beside himself with irritation. Here was a target made for a machine-gun, and he had to stand and watch it sinking itself into the ground and safety. Time after time the Lewis-gunner asked Davies to let him have a go at the Germans. At length, as the artillery barrage did not materialize, Davies gave orders for the Lewis-gun to open fire. Its crew instantly did so.

At the first discharge many in the German working-party crumpled up and went down. As burst succeeded burst with the replacing of panniers on the gun, the execution among the Germans was terrible. They made a perfect target. Those who broke for cover of the woods were sprayed with bullets as they ran. Others cowered into the shallow trench, but, as parts of this could be enfiladed by the Lewis-gun, some of these also were killed as they pressed themselves into the earth. The Germans evidently decided to take their revenge by blowing out a post in our line which they considered responsible, and that accounted for the heavy howitzer's effort.

On 1 June the division was relieved in the line by the 4th Division, and we moved back to a rest area near Querrieu. Here for a fortnight we idled in pleasant enough surroundings; the chief incident was a great sports meeting with swimming and horse races, to which latter came entrants from far and wide.

When, after a fortnight of rest, the division was ordered into the line again – north of the Somme, on the Morlan-Court Ridge – I found my name among those detailed to remain behind in division nucleus at Pernois. Every division on going into the line left a nucleus in rear areas for various

142

reasons, not least the preservation of its entity in the event of the worst emergency. Officers remained behind in this nucleus in turn.

I endeavoured in this case to have the arrangement altered, not because I was a fire eater, but because I discovered that my evacuation to hospital with gas on the previous occasion was held not to have counted in the rotation observed by our battalion, and under the unwritten laws could not regard the circumstances were of no effect. Later my soldier's conscience was appeased; when next it came for someone to be left behind I might have missed the great events of the advance in August.

With other officers of the division nucleus I was ordered to a course of training in Lewis-gun tactics at the Australian Corps School at Le Crotoy, near the mouth of the Somme River. On return to Pernois on 29 July we moved at once to rejoin the battalion at Poulainville.

Note
1. Twenty-one-year-old Sergeant Herbert James Shepherd, the son of Alexander and Susan Shepherd, of 19, Lawson Street, Hamilton, Newcastle, New South Wales, killed on 14 May 1918, was buried in Aubigny British Cemetery.

Chapter 15

Preparing the Return Blow

Battle of Hamel – Monash's new methods – Plans for a big attack –
Australians and Canadians together – The Assembly.
(July to August 1918)

Meanwhile, the Battle of Hamel was fought on 4 July, in which three brigades (one each from the 2nd, 3rd, and 4th Divisions) under direction of the 4th Division staff, overran a considerable section of the German positions immediately south of the Somme. This was the sector in which I have already described our battalion's activities. The Battle of Hamel illustrated both the marked superiority of the Australians over the enemy and the astonishing success of General Monash's methods of reintroducing surprise into the strategy of frontal attack. His scheme for the use of tanks, avoiding preliminary (and tell-tale) artillery bombardments, and using aircraft and gas (plus smoke) discharges to deceive the Germans and cover essential preparations under the very noses of the German front-line garrisons, opened the eyes of the British High Command to the possibilities at hand.

Hamel was the experiment upon which the great attack of 8 August was decided and planned. It was noteworthy also for the employment for the first time of small detachments of new American troops (seeded in among the Australians) in offensive action with British units.[1]

Following the Battle of Hamel on 4 July, French and American divisions under Foch on 18 July counterattacked the last German advance on the Marne and obliged the enemy to abandon hastily his final bid to break the Allied line and reach Paris. The great climax of the war was now at hand, and the appreciation of it (though for a little time subconscious in many of us) came upon us with dramatic suddenness.

It was more with a notion that we were being given an insight into the methods by which the battle of Hamel was won than with any premonition of something shortly to come, that on 31 July we studied a demonstration of tactics by the new tanks. Trenches had been dug, wire defences set up, and obstacles devised such as tanks would meet in advancing over ground strongly held. Detachments of infantry were deployed into attack formation, the tanks were manoeuvred into position, and then the demonstration was opened. We had a grandstand view from the sides of a field.

The attacking waves came on, and at prearranged signals the tanks would diverge from their course to deal with a supposed strong point holding up the advance. These monsters moved with surprising speed. Reaching the strong point, the tank would straddle the trench, swing around on its tractors, and obliterate the post by simply crushing it into the ground. These manoeuvres were a revelation to us, and we could fully appreciate what a wonderful asset they must have been to the infantry in the attack on Hamel.

The show was repeated several times with fresh detachments of infantry. Then the tanks halted, and we were told that they were for our inspection. Soon men were clambering over and into them. Lieutenant Musgrave and I entered one, and were shown the armament of the monster. A gun firing a small shell protruded from the front; the sides bristled with machine-guns, housed in turrets, and capable of being swung over a wide field of fire. The machine-guns were Vickers and Colt guns. These latter were a type that had been discarded some years before by the British Army on account of lack of cooling apparatus, and the water-cooled Vickers superseded them for infantry use.

Then we were taken for a ride in this land battleship. It was a queer sensation. Coming to a bank the machine reared upwards and clawed its way forward, even knocking down small trees in its path. Standing in the field was an old captured German tank. Its height dwarfed the new British models that we had just seen in manoeuvres, but it was cumbersome in appearance and had been as slow as a lame duck. Now it stood with its Iron Crosses on its sides and the names of many soldiers scrawled around them. I suppose it was here for purposes of comparison. Whether or not for lack of material, the tank as a weapon of offence was not extensively used by the Germans.

These demonstrations were propaganda work instigated by Sir John Monash to break down a prejudice of the Australian infantry against tanks which dated from Bullecourt days. Our men had seen so much fighting that they could judge almost instinctively whether a departure from accustomed methods of attack was likely to be a success.

On 3 August all battalion officers were warned to attend a conference in the village school at Poulainville. We went expecting to arrange final details of a sports meeting, plans for which had been tentatively drawn up at a meeting on the previous day. The colonel duly appeared, and after the usual procedure we were told to make ourselves comfortable at the children's desks. He said that he had called us together to give us details of an attack that was to be launched within the course of a few days, and in which the Australian Army Corps was to play a major role. The Canadian

Corps of four divisions was to be brought from Vimy and placed on the right of the Australians.

For the first time in the war the five Australian divisions were to co-operate in attack, and for this purpose the 1st Division would be brought south from the Lys front, where it had been holding a sector against the German drive for the Channel ports. In addition the British III Corps was to attack on the left of the Australians, also, if our attack made headway, some French divisions on the right of the Canadians. The attack was approximately on an eleven-mile front, from Morlancourt to Hangard.

The unique feature of the battle plans was that every mechanical aid was to be used. It was Monash's theory that the infantry should not bear the full brunt of breaking the enemy's resistance, and that tanks, artillery, aeroplanes, and armoured cars should be used to the utmost to smash and disorganize the German defences to a depth well forward of the infantry advance intended.

The attack was to be in three distinct phases. The 2nd Australian Division on the right and the 3rd on the left were to open it under cover of a creeping barrage, and with the aid of many tanks were to press forward for about two miles. Then the 5th Australian Division on the right and the 4th on the left were to pass through, and in open warfare formations carry on the advance to a map line drawn some 6,000 yards ahead. The 1st Division was to be Corps reserves. In a third phase the attack was to be exploited by fast tanks, filled with machine-gun crews from the reserve battalions, who, when the tanks had dealt with any German resistance, would form an outpost line. Armoured cars and cavalry had also their tasks in this stage of the action.

Secrecy, it was enforced upon us, was still of the utmost importance. There was to be no preliminary bombardment, but a creeping barrage was to assist the tanks and infantry in the capture of the first objective. The artillery was forbidden even to register on the enemy lest the doomed garrisons should be made suspicious. Some batteries were especially detailed to combat German guns. Here, again, cunning was used. German batteries that had recently shifted their positions were left strictly alone in their new quarters, and their old vacant ones were before the attack religiously shelled periodically by our artillery. The German gunners must have laughed at our apparent ignorance. But their new positions were well known from aerial observation.

The 5th Australian Division was to employ in the attack the 8th Brigade on the left and the 15th Brigade on the right, on a two-battalion front. Much to our disgust the 14th Brigade was to be in reserve and from its battalions were to be drawn the machine-gun crews to go forward later in the tanks. Our battalion was to be the 14th Brigade's reserve, so that if things worked out to plan we should be for the greater part onlookers.

146

It took some time for the colonel to outline the plans to us. Then he mentioned a more delicate matter which had been discussed at the Army Conference. The Australians had been holding the line practically since January. The men had every right to expect a rest. But our colonel said that the opinion had been general at the conference that the Australians would forget their line weariness if detailed to take part in a grand scheme of attack in which all five divisions were employed, especially if the Canadian Corps were to operate with them. Whoever so summed up our feelings must have known us well. The officers of our battalion unanimously agreed that the men could be trusted to hold their tongues; so we were told to inform our commands that an attack was coming, and to warn them not to discuss the matter in the *estaminets,* but only to mention the arrival of the Canadians to relieve the Australian Corps.

All now became haste and bustle. A nucleus was detailed to be ready to leave for Pernois. Lewis-guns were critically overhauled, and all ammunition inspected. Shortages in iron rations were made good. I was detailed with an officer from each of the other companies to prepare a new billeting area, on the Somme at Daours. Bicycles were furnished us for this purpose, and with darkness we were on the main road for Corbie.

But with the coming of the night this road sprang to amazing life. Rain had fallen recently, my bicycle was a model that dated back many years, and the mud constantly choked the wheels in the forks. But it was the traffic on the road that really retarded our progress. Tanks, guns, army-wagons, horse-drawn limbers, moved along in a solid mass. The tanks were stacked high with boxes of ammunition, bombs, coils of wire, iron pickets, and general engineering material. Big Thornycroft wagons were loaded with shells and more shells, and the transport limbers with quarter-masters' stores.

Mile after mile, this long chain of traffic stretched along the road. We wondered where on earth it had all come from. I was to learn later. Another scheme to make the attack a complete surprise was that these motors, tanks, and transport travelled during the hours of darkness only, and orders were that when daylight broke not one of them was to be seen on the roads. They were parked in woods, under banks, or, if in the open, covered with camouflage netting. Daily our aeroplanes were ordered to report on efficiency of performance in these instructions. The amount of material that was transported under cover of the darkness of the nights preceding the attack was stupendous.

After an all-night struggle to avoid or make progress amid this traffic, we reached the Daours area at daybreak, sweating and exhausted. We reported to Captain Smythe, now of brigade staff, who sent us forthwith back to our units, as 'a change had been made in the plans'. Without having anything to eat, we immediately started on the return journey to

147

Poulainville. Two of the officers, riding good machines, pushed ahead. The fourth, Lieutenant B—, whom I had helped at Wytschaete when he was a new-chum, stayed to keep me company with my crock of a bicycle.

In one village, where we found an Australian unit billeted, we sought and obtained from a quartermaster a square meal of bully beef, bread, butter, jam and tea. When we reached the battalion we found that nobody knew why we should have been turned back from Daours, that Daours was still the battalion's destination, and that we must repeat the journey. The army had a habit of doing things like this. So we rode to Daours again, were given billeting areas along the river-bank, and here at evening, into holes cut out of the high bank of the river, the battalion eventually crept out of the rain to await the advance.

Details of the plan of attack and the formation in which we were to move forward at zero hour were made known to all ranks on 7 August. On the same day General Monash's historic order was read by each platoon commander to his men:

TO THE SOLDIERS OF THE AUSTRALIAN ARMY CORPS

For the first time in the history of this corps all five Australian divisions will tomorrow engage in the largest and most important battle operation ever undertaken by the corps. They will be supported by an exceptionally powerful artillery, and by tanks and aeroplanes on a scale never previously attempted. The full resources of our sister dominion, the Canadian Corps, will operate on our right, while two British divisions will guard our left flank.

The many successful offensives which the brigades and battalions of this corps have so brilliantly executed during the past four months have been the prelude to, and the preparation for, this greatest and culminating effort. Because of the completeness of our plans and dispositions, of the magnitude of the operations, of the number of troops employed, and the depth to which we intend to overrun the enemy's positions, this battle will be one of the most important of the whole war, and there can be no doubt that, by capturing our objectives, we shall inflict blows upon the enemy which will make him stagger, and will bring the end appreciably nearer.

I entertain no sort of doubt that every Australian soldier will worthily rise to so great an occasion, and that every man, imbued with the spirit of victory, will, in spite of every difficulty that may confront him, be animated by no other resolve than a grim determination to see through to a clean finish whatever his task may be.

The work to be done tomorrow will perhaps make heavy demands upon the endurance and staying powers of many of you, but I am confident that in spite of excitement, fatigue, and physical strain, every man will carry on to the utmost of his powers, until his goal is won, for the sake of Australia, the Empire, and our Cause.

I earnestly wish every soldier of the corps the best of good fortune, and a glorious and decisive victory, the story of which will re-echo throughout the world, and will live forever in the history of our homeland.

John Monash,
Lieut. General Commanding Australian Corps.

In the short time during which he had commanded the corps Sir John Monash had so thoroughly proved his organizing ability that he stood high in the esteem of all ranks. They were certain of one thing – that the corps was not being launched into any half-baked scheme of attack that would fail on account of incompetent staff-work.

But for all the care in planning there were moments of anxiety. One or two prisoners had been captured on the front by the enemy – they might give the secret away! But they did not. Late in the afternoon of 7 August a German shell set alight to a tank park, hidden in an orchard near Villers-Bretonneux. These tanks were laden with supplies of ammunition and petrol, and soon a great fire was blazing just behind our front line. Had the Germans identified the tanks? But again luck was on our side; it was only a chance shell, and the resultant fire was evidently supposed by the Germans to be in an ammunition dump.

As night came on the troops ate their meal, and then in all the little dugouts, honeycombing the bank like birds' nests, candle-lights appeared, and men about them lifted up their voices in song. The way in which they passed the hours before an attack always intrigued me.

From the battle of Hastings in 1066 to 7 August 1918, this old world had seen many changes. But one thing time, environment, civilization, or climatic conditions has evidently not altered, and that is the manner in which men of the Anglo-Saxon race pass the hours before battle. History relates that the army of Harold, the last of the Saxon kings, awaiting the dawn to engage the invading Norman hosts in battle, spent the hours of darkness in drinking and singing. Tonight, in a river bank in France, and near enough to the old Normandy, was gathered an army of descendants of the race that gave battle to the Normans nearly nine centuries ago, awaiting battle in the same fashion. Drinking they were not, for water was the only liquid refreshment to be had, but certainly singing as though a battle meant anything but death and wounds.

I shared a dugout with three other young officers. Laughter and merry talk was the atmosphere of this cramped shelter. For weeks I had had the premonition that I was to be wounded, and this was a topic which in army fashion was greeted as a great joke. To look back and remember how

149

confident I felt that I was going to be knocked, and how I talked about it in the most light-hearted manner, makes me realize what fatalists the war had made of us all. A wound was something that got you a rest in a clean bed. The pain or the thought that the wound perhaps would mean disablement for life never seemed to enter our heads. I was fully aware that the time was close at hand for me to prove my claim to be called a member of the British Empire, by the right which the Tommy sergeant-majors in Egypt used to tell us was the only recognizable one – namely, that of a man's having spilt his blood for it.

Note

1. Planned and commanded by Lieutenant General John Monash, the Battle of Hamel was undertaken by Australian troops and several American units against German positions in and around the town of Hamel. The battle was a success, with all objectives being achieved only three minutes over the planned battle time of ninety minutes. The battle was notable because it was the first time in the war that American troops participated in an offensive action and it was the first time that American troops served under non-American command. Four American companies participated with Australian troops under Australian command (although three of the companies were recalled before the battle). There were 1,062 Australian casualties (including 800 dead), as well as 176 American casualties (almost 100 dead), while there were probably 2,000 Germans killed and 1,600 captured, along with the loss of much of their equipment.

Chapter 16

The Battle of Amiens

The stirring advance – German lines shattered – Ludendorff's Black Day.
(8 and 9 August 1918)

We were aroused at 3 a.m., and ate a hot meal at the cookers by the light of flickering candles. Cigarettes glowed in a few brief puffs before the whistle went for fall-in. We paraded upon the flat ground above the top of the bank, platoons were checked, and we stood under our equipment waiting for the battle to begin. A heavy ground mist hung low. Low-flying 'planes droned heavily in the distance; they were purposely disguising the noise made by the tanks getting into position at the front line. Darkness and ground mist were hiding the movement into attack positions of an array of over 100,000 infantry, and the gun-crews around the battery positions, with guns loaded and run out, and ranges checked, waited for their watches to crawl round to the fatal hour 4.20 a.m.

At zero hour the bombardment fell in one mighty blast. The mist was stabbed with flashes. The rush of the shells through the air sounded like express trains passing. The earth appeared to tremble with the concussion, and when the order to move was given the officers and N.C.O.s had to roar at the top of their voices. Company after company, platoon after platoon, moved forward into the bank of mist.

Up in front the barrage sounded like strokes on a mighty drum. We knew that at the first descent of this curtain of shells the men of the 2nd and 3rd Australian Divisions, the Tommies on our left, and the Canadians on our right would, in their battle formations, advance behind that moving wall of death, to assault the front line of German trenches. The rat-tat-tat of machine-guns firing continuously, belt after belt, told us that the fight was on. Through the fog we could hear the movements of many men – up the valley towards Villers-Bretonneux were marching in compact formations the whole of the infantry of the 5th Division.

Day broke as we started on the ascent near the town. Now we saw the batteries working as though their crews were driven by the devil. The blasts from the guns made our steel helmets jump on our heads; the acrid smell of the cordite burnt our nostrils. Soon we saw the first casualties of

151

the fight. A German 'plane flying low had dropped bombs on some gun-teams waiting for the barrage to lift. Approaching the front line of a few hours earlier we saw the first signs of victory – a large batch of German prisoners hurrying along, shepherded by an Australian infantryman with a blood-stained bandage on his head. Soon we saw other prisoner parties, some of them carrying our wounded upon stretchers. But already we were struck by the few wounded that were coming back. We halted on the line of trenches from which the 2nd Australian Division had an hour ago attacked.

The sun broke through the pall of smoke, dust, and mist. The 'sun of Austerlitz' had been an omen of victory to Napoleon; I thought of it this day. I went forward with Lieutenant Pitt to the first objective upon which the 2nd Division was about to consolidate. Crossing what was yesterday No Man's Land, we saw a few of our dead who had fallen in the advance to the German front line. This position had been badly strafed by our barrage, and many dead Germans lay in the trenches. Beyond these we moved over undulating field ground. Here again were many German dead, and apparently they had been shot down in hurried retreat. Behind what was yesterday the German front line stood in places crops of grain. This had been harvested by the Germans, and I saw a farm wagon loaded with stocks, with the horses lying dead in the shafts, as though a fatigue party had been at work harvesting when the storm of attack broke upon them.

German battery positions had been overrun and many gunners lay round their pieces. Every gun had been chalked with the name of the battalion that had captured it. One battery had dug-in its guns in cunning fashion in a gully to the right of Warfusee-Abancourt. The guns were covered with bomb-proof roofing, and fired from openings just above the ground-level. A tank had passed over the coverings of each gun, and the gunners were now either shapeless masses of flesh in the debris or were lying outside the position shot by rifle bullets. One of them had been run over by a tank, and his body lay pressed as flat as a wafer and to a surprising length.

We found the infantry of the 2nd Australian Division consolidating a trench system. One officer told us that the Germans were caught by the suddenness of the attack and showed very little fight. He also said that although the fog helped to cover the initial stages of the advance, after the front line had been taken direction was hard to maintain. He was of the opinion that very few of the German infantry had escaped, and this was borne out by the many prisoners we had seen passing to the rear.

We returned through the village of Warfusee-Abancourt, in the shattered precincts of which a large dressing-station was already established. From this village the road went straight as an arrow rearwards to Villers-Bretonneux. During the years of war many roads in France had at different periods presented strange appearances. But never had there been seen within a few hours such a transformation as we now witnessed. Along this road no wheels had turned for many months, as it ran through German and Australian front lines. But now the scene in the bright morning sunshine made us rub eyes that surely deceived us.

Coming along with all haste were motor lorries, loaded with ammunition, stores, and tools, horse-drawn limbers, cookers, water-carts, dispatch-riders on motor bicycles, heavy guns, here and there an armoured car; mounted men regulated the traffic; and only a mile or so forward could still be heard the spasmodic rattle of machine-guns. The traffic along the road so close to the moving battle was possible only because all the German batteries which yesterday supported their front-line infantry had been captured in the advance.

Monash's clear vision had foreseen all this when he planned the attack. To overrun and destroy the German infantry in the front line trenches had been done during previous advances. But to overrun and destroy in addition the German artillery swung open wide the gateway to a great victory. In former attacks wherein the German infantry defences alone were destroyed, the attackers were always heavily shelled by the enemy's artillery during the work of consolidation, and in this phase generally lost more casualties than in the assault. Monash's scheme did away with this danger. The very magnitude of his plans of battle were doubted by some seasoned soldiers, so used had they become to the old type of attack set with a very limited objective.

Now the cavalry were moving up. The long-desired break-through had come, and the cavalry's opportunity was to be put to the test. What a glorious sight they presented! The sun shone on their well-groomed horses, their burnished harness and the oiled tin-hats of the riders. The troopers' smart fitting uniforms looked brand-new beside the stained clothing of the infantry, and their long sabres, bucketed rifles and bandoliers made a most warlike equipment. In long lines they came on through the brown stubble of crops, and then deployed into wave after wave to harry the German rear-guards.

The sky swarmed with low-flying 'planes. Some of these as they passed overhead sounded klaxons and the pilots waved to us with an air of abandon. The British aeroplanes harried the retreat of the German troops by machine-gunning them, along with their transport, and one 'plane dropped a bomb on a railway line and prevented the withdrawal of a large railway gun. But the day's fighting cost the British Army about fifty 'planes; many were shot down from the ground.

Soon our battalion was moving forward in artillery formation. Already detachments of pioneers were busy burying the dead, remaking roads, and bridging trenches. As we advanced the battle seemed to be over. Only an occasional machine-gun chattered in the distance. A long-range German gun dropped some shells. This was one of the variety known to the troops as 'rubber-heeled' on account of its shell's noiseless approach.

We halted in the gully across the line of advance from Warfusee-Abancourt. Here we learned that on our divisional front all objectives had been gained on time. German units had been surprised by the rapidity of the advance. A field officer and his staff had been captured in their head-quarters, and I overheard an Australian complaining, after shooting a German officer who had tried to escape, that his beautiful boots were two sizes too small.

From the gully we moved forward and dug in along a road running from the village of Harbonnières to the railway. The Germans had tried to make a stand here, but Harbonnières had been stormed out of hand by the infantry. Near the line which we were now digging stood a building which had been used as a quartermaster's store, in which were many blankets trussed up in bales. The German storeman had evidently not been in the habit of rising early and on this fateful morning his bad habit of sleeping-in had been the end of him. Our fellows helped themselves freely to the blankets.

Near the store lay one of our fighting 'planes, shot down by machine-gun fire. The 'plane was one of our latest type of fighters and I was interested to see the manner in which it mounted no less than four machine-guns and a Lewis-gun placed so that it could fire perpendicularly overhead.

The war on this sector had moved forward to a depth of seven miles. The attack on the whole front had succeeded with the exception of that part of the operation entrusted to the two British divisions on the left of the Somme. Their advance had been hampered by great difficulty and this had affected the progress of the leftmost units of the 3rd and 4th Australian Divisions. The 3rd Division had been forced to throw its reserve brigade across the river in face of heavy fire to enable the left of the Australian attack to make headway.

In justice to the Tommies, it should be stated that their difficulties were enormous. The bend of the Somme at Chipilly, the marshes on one side, and the almost unscalable heights on Fritz's, heights covered with field-guns, made their task a terrible one.

As evening came on we watched many 'planes coming back, and one of them caused some consternation. During the day observation balloons had followed close upon the forward movement. Now one of these was in the sky in advance of Harbonnières. We had remarked this during the after-noon, and took it as an indication that the enemy's airmen had been driven from the sky. One of the returning British 'planes evidently took this balloon for a German, so far forward was it, and suddenly he broke from

154

his formation and shot down the balloon. Men cursed at the top of their voices. Then Lewis-gunners rushed to their guns, and trained them on to the 'plane, thinking that perhaps he was some daring enemy. But as he flew overhead, we saw the familiar red-white-blue rings on its wings. He probably received a rare old strafe when he reported back to his aerodrome.

Night came without any signs of a German counterattack. We ate a meal of bully-beef and biscuits, posted our sentries, crawled into our burrow-like shelters, and went to sleep in German blankets. Sleep was soon interrupted by the unmistakable drone of the German bombing 'planes. Nearer they came – and then the swish of the descending aerial bombs, followed by the crash of their explosions.

Bomb after bomb was dropped between our position and Harbonnières, and pandemonium reigned in the packed horse-lines just to the rear of the village. We could hear the horses kicking and plunging at their tethers, some neighing, and one poor brute screaming. Their drivers were out trying to quieten the maddened animals. The deadly night-birds had it all their own way. No searchlights or anti-aircraft batteries were in position, so they coolly emptied their loads of missiles, and flew back home.

Several times during the night they repeated the performance. They caused considerable damage in the horse-lines. Personally, I would far rather be shelled than bombed from the air. The near explosion of an aerial bomb of any size seemed to tie one's intestines into knots, and the fragment of the missiles searched a wide area.

We were waiting early next morning for orders when there appeared a sight which broke up all small groups of gossipers. Coming along a rail-road track from the direction of the front line was an engine drawing a huge gun mounted on a platform, and a number of trucks were painted in grotesque camouflage. The gun-carriage bore a large sign painted on it, 'Captured by the 31st Battalion'. Lieutenant Burrows of the 14th Field Company Engineers, with some sappers of the 8th Field Company, had got steam up and were now bringing back this prize. After the war this trophy was brought to Australia, and for many months stood at the Central Railway Station in Sydney before being moved to Canberra.[1]

Meanwhile the 8th and 15th Brigades of our division renewed the advance on the right to conform with the Canadians. The tanks of yesterday had suffered some loss, and were not available to assist; the German machine-gunners fought well, and the advance had not the momentum of yesterday. Our brigades gained their objectives by about 2 p.m., and then the 1st Australian Division which had moved up through us during the morning took over their line. This ended the part played by the 5th Division in the Battle of Amiens. Late in the afternoon we were moved back to trenches near Villers-Bretonneux.

155

The Battle of Amiens on 8 August definitely marked the turn of the tide of victory for the Allies. So far-reaching was the success, and so smashing the blow, that Ludendorff in his memoirs wrote: 'After the severe defeat of 8 August I gave up the last vestige of hope'. And again: '8 August was a black day in the history of the German Army'.[2]

The German army lost thousands of prisoners, many guns, and gigantic quantities, of war stores and transport.[3] On a front of eleven miles, the attack had been driven home to a depth of seven miles, and the Germans who had occupied this sector ceased to exist as fighting troops. To the genius of an Australian general who planned the attack, and to the fighting prowess of his troops, must be given the credit for this victory; it was a defeat from which the German Army never recovered. The material gains in territory, guns, and material had not previously been approached in any effort of the British Army.

The victory was gained at a cost which compared with some of the battles of the past four years, was light in the extreme. Our division lost one-sixth of the toll it paid at Fromelles, and even the success of Polygon Wood cost the 5th Division almost four times as many men as fell on 8 and 9 August.

Notes

1. This is the so-called Amiens Gun. A 28cm SK L/40 'Bruno' gun, it had originally been a naval weapon until it was adapted for land service after its ship was disarmed in 1916. During the advance on 8 August, the train and gun were bombed by a RAF Sopwith Camel, causing the German crew to abandon them. Although RAF aircraft and British cavalry were the first to engage the gun, it was then quickly claimed by the advancing Australian infantry. Corporal John Palmer, 8th Field Company, recalled: 'We had been sent with a quantity of Amanol [sic] to blow up the large gun ... however Les Strahan one of our sappers in the party had been a driver in the Western Australian railways, and he found there was still a head of steam, he asked for a fair go, instead of blowing the gun up he got the engine going, we were told then to try to get it back if possible into a cutting so it could be camouflaged.' The gun was later exhibited in Paris before it was sent to the UK for onward transportation to Australia as a war trophy. While the gun's carriage was eventually destroyed, the barrel remains intact, and is on display outdoors at the Australian War Memorial. Lieutenant George Burrows M.C. & Bar, 31st Battalion A.I.F., was subsequently decorated for his gallantry in connection with the capture of the gun.
2. The British war correspondent Philip Gibbs also noted the effect that the Battle of Amiens had on the tempo of the First World War. On 27 August he wrote that 'the enemy ... is on the defensive' and 'the initiative of attack is so completely in our hands that we are able to strike him at many different places'. Gibbs also credits Amiens with a shift in troop morale, saying 'the change has been greater in the minds of men than in the taking of territory. On our side the army seems to be buoyed up with the enormous hope of getting on with this business quickly' and that 'there is a change also in the enemy's mind. They no longer have even a dim hope of victory on this western front. All they hope for now is to defend themselves long enough to gain peace by negotiation.'

156

Chapter 17

Consolidating the Victory

Preparing the advance – Chaulnes – Switched to the Somme flank –
Relieving a British battalion – Six days under bombardment –
Battle of Bray – Our attack countermanded –
Attack by 1st Australian Division – The souvenir-hunters –
The dead Anzacs.
(11–23 August 1918)

While we were waiting in the position near Villers-Bretonneux, I spoke with an Australian who had been wounded and taken prisoner by the Germans in April. He with others had been in a compound near Péronne. With the overrunning of their position on 8 August, the confusion behind the German lines spread as far back as Péronne. Sensing that a break-through had occurred, this chap and two other Australians had quickly decided to try to reach our outpost line.

They left the compound, struck the main road after a detour, and with this as their guide had entered our outpost line under cover of darkness. They said that the area right up to Péronne was denuded of German troops on the afternoon of 8 August and that we could have overrun the whole of it without opposition. As a matter of fact, armoured cars penetrated much farther than the outpost line where the advance halted according to the battle plan, and did much execution. They had cruised as far as Proyart and Chugnolles, and in one of those villages they machine-gunned a number of German officers sitting at lunch in a hotel. No doubt the con-sternation caused by these cars facilitated the escape of the Australian captives from Péronne.

At dusk Lieutenant Threlkeld and myself were detailed with a large fatigue party to bury a number of dead horses, which offended the atmo-sphere surrounding Brigade Headquarters. The job was so formidable that we procured horses and tackle from our transport lines. Local shell holes large enough to take the carcass of a horse soon came to an end, so we buried the remainder in part of the 'corps line' trenches. We judge that the corps would not again be called upon to man this system of trenches.

157

Anyhow, we removed the noxious odours that were troubling the sensitive nostrils of the brigade staff.

Lieutenant Threlkeld and I lived in a hole in the ground with a rude covering for a roof. Our bed consisted of hay which we had pulled from a crop of ripened wheat; this and a lone waterproof sheet each made our beds. Since we were in battle-order such a thing as a greatcoat or a blanket was absent.

On 13 August 1918, the battalion moved forward to take part in an attack on Chaulnes, on the left front of the sector held by the Canadian Corps. It was a very hot day, and at one halt during the morning some of us stripped and swam in a miniature lake in the grounds of what had been a beautiful château. Its ornamental gardens were now overgrown with weeds, the statues in the grounds had been broken from their pedestals, and the roof of the chateau had been partly destroyed by shell-fire. It was a pathetic ghost of happier days, but we enjoyed the swim and lay in the grass until our bodies were dry.

We marched through many villages still with German signs across the streets. The doors of the houses stood open. Not a living soul was in any one of them. The whole region had been swept of human life.

During the afternoon we at last came to signs of military activities. The road now wound through parts that had high steep banks on the left, and open flat country on the right. In some of these bends we came upon transport lines, and knew that we were approaching the forward area. About 4 p.m. our companies turned to the right from the road, and we found ourselves on a flat terrain which rose steeply from the dusty road. Here were well constructed trench systems, with comfortable dugouts, into which our platoons were guided.

Lieutenant Threlkeld and I took up our quarters in a short tunnel that ran from one part of the trench to another system. The position was one of considerable strength, and had been intended to house troops in comfort on their probable battle-line; the tunnel would allow free passage of troops from one point to another in perfect safety.

Without blankets or greatcoats we passed a very comfortless night in this tunnel. A chilly blast blew through it, and the ground was wet. I put my steel helmet on the ground, fitted my hip into the crown, and draped a *Bulletin* across my loins. Bodily tiredness and military habit at first enabled me to sleep, but before dawn I awoke frozen to the marrow. I resolved to see if I could find a greatcoat on some of the German corpses outside. On top of the tunnel I met Threlkeld walking up and down, beating his chest with his hands.

'Passed a pleasant night?' said I. 'Yes, a pleasant bastard of a night,' snapped Threlkeld.

I unfolded my scheme about finding a dead Fritz with an overcoat.

'You are too late,' said Threlkeld. 'I have already looked them over. None of them has an overcoat.'

So to warm ourselves we went for a walk. The sun was just up when our attention was drawn towards the front line by the rattle of machine-guns. An enemy 'plane was low down in the sky, and as we looked it burst into flames. The pilot then gave a wonderful exhibition. He shot his 'plane straight up and came down in a series of loop over loops. This appeared to keep the flames away from himself, and as we watched we saw him bring his 'plane down still under control. We admired his exploit and wished him a happy rescue.

The army was always full of surprises. We had been marched up eleven miles from Villers-Bretonneux to carry out an attack. For two days we had been studying maps and learning by heart the battle plan; and then suddenly we were told that the attack would not take place, and that we were to march under cover of darkness to a position just south of the Somme to relieve a British division which had suffered many gas casualties.

By what we could gather, Australian Corps Headquarters seemed to be very anxious that relief should be hurried to this division. It was well after midnight when we reached the great timber dump at La Plaque simultaneously with a squadron of German bombing 'planes. However, the bombs missed our column. Here we halted for the rest of the night in some trenches manned by Tommies. We found them to be of a battalion of the Duke of Wellington's Regiment.

Next night our 'C' and 'D' companies relieved the front line. The policy of the battalion while in the line was to be what was known as peaceful penetration, meaning that our line was to be moved forward by means of vigorous patrol work and the pinching out of German posts.

Evidently our intelligence people were of the opinion that the Germans were preparing for a retirement. At dusk we moved forward with guides. Soon we came to the front line. The guide for my platoon entered the trench (which was full of men ready to move out) and pointing to a sap that ran forward said: 'No. 10 Platoon's post is just along there, sir.' The trench appeared to have been an old communication trench which had done service during 1916–17. Its sides had fallen in and grass grew on the bottom.

At length in a T-shaped head we came upon a number of men lying on the bottom of the trench with two sentries peering over the top. I asked for the officer in charge of the post, and was told that he was not present. To my further query a young lance-corporal said he was in charge.

'Where is your officer?' I asked.

To my astonishment the lad replied: 'We have not seen him since we came into the line three nights ago.'

159

I asked the lad where his reserve ammunition and bombs were. There were no reserves. He knew that the German line was across the road about two hundred yards away, but had only a vague idea of where the right post of his own company was situated.

I told the lance-corporal that he could now lead his platoon out. They had occupied for three nights a trench only four feet deep and as wide as a room; no attempt had been made to deepen the trench or repair the ravages of time and weather. Posting my sentries and leaving my sergeant in charge, I started back to the main trench to find the officer who was such a good line soldier that he left his platoon for three nights and days in a forward post without visiting them.

Being directed to company headquarters I asked for the officer in charge of No. 10 Platoon. A young man wearing the two stars of a full lieutenant came forward, and said that he commanded it. I asked him why the hell he had not been in the post to hand over. He made some lame excuse, and I told him that it was rather bad trench manners to leave a lance-corporal to hand over a post. I requested him to come forward and point out the dispositions. No, he could not do that; he did not know whether his post had been wired, had not the vaguest idea of where the right post of his company was situated, or of the proximity of the Germans, or whether any reserve ammunition or bombs were in the trench.

I had determined that this Tommy officer should come forward with me, but my own company commander, Lieutenant Pitt, said in an undertone: 'Don't delay them; I want them out of the trench as quickly as possible.'

They went. They were the poorest line soldiers that I ever came in contact with in France, and the fault obviously lay with the officers. Men who would put their platoons into posts and remain away from them all the while they were holding a front line were not fit to be officers.

My first job was to take out a patrol and actually hunt for our right company post. This I found situated at a cross-roads, occupying the site of a house which had been mined and blown up. The place was a small fortress with two machine-guns mounted on it, and so close to a German post that only the width of the tree-lined road separated them.

The Tommy guide who was leading the headquarters of our 'D' Company led them across his own line, and but for the fact that Major Roberts had memorized the map of the position well and recognized in the darkness that they had gone too far, they would have been led into the German line. So incompetency did not end with 'C' Company of this Duke of Wellington's Battalion. We no longer wondered that we had been hurried across to take over this sector.

Patrols from our own battalion and the 55th established that the Germans were holding their line very strongly. The 55th Battalion rushed but failed to carry a German post, and lost three men. This informed the

Germans that the Australians were in the line – a clear warning of an attack to come. The Germans were not slow in summing up the position; their artillery gave us a torrid time. Fortunately our first work had been to deepen the trench and cut a fire-step in the parapet.

I was lying asleep during the following afternoon when Nugget, my batman, awoke me to say that there was a lot of equipment in an old trench just to the left of my post. Crawling on our stomachs we wormed through the grass and gained this trench.

Like the one we were occupying, this had been a line during 1916–17, now fallen in and grass-covered. It had been occupied during the battle on 9 August 1918, casualties had occurred among its garrison, and several sets of equipments and rifles were lying around. There were haversacks full of souvenirs, German coins, postcards, knives and watches. I did not doubt that the men who had worn the equipment were Australians.

Looking over the trench I saw two Germans creeping along the low embankment of the tree-lined road. Evidently they were going to an adjacent post. I picked up one of the discarded rifles and fired at one of the Germans. He rolled over; the other dived for shelter. The sound of the shot caused men in my post to jump on to the fire-step, and heads appeared over the German parapet. This started a rifle-duel.

My batman and I moved along the old trench, and had to make a rush to regain our post. This we managed safely, and found several of our fellows on the fire-step, sniping at every head that appeared in the German post. They silenced their opponents, and I told them to get down. One chap, in the hope of getting another shot, was slow in obeying, and was wounded from a post on our left. The bullet struck the swivel of his rifle and ricocheted on to his hand, cleaving it as if it had been struck with a chopper. He sat with a cigarette hanging from his lips and watched us bind up the awful looking wound. When this was finished he said: 'Oh well, a man will get a trip to Blighty out of this.'

Before midnight the Germans put a box-barrage around my post. This meant that we were hemmed in with bursting shells in front, flanks, and rear. This was generally done when a post was to be raided. All hands manned the fire-step and stood close into the parapet, while the shells fell thickly around us. Machine-guns traversed our front, and the freshly-dug earth spouted where the bullets struck. I straddled the trench, revolver in hand, just in the rear of the T-head, and peered into the cloud of smoke and dust for the raiders whom I expected.

One shell landed on the edge of our trench, wounding two men, and above the din I told them to lie on the bottom of the trench, as we could not help them until the bombardment ceased. The shelling lasted for perhaps ten minutes, and then ceased suddenly. We stood on post until the smoke cleared; when we could not see any signs of a raiding-party we attended to the wounded.

Hardly an hour had elapsed before two coloured rockets from the German position soared into the sky. Once again a heavy bombardment came down; it searched the ground to the rear of my post, and crept down upon the main trench. The Germans strafed us savagely for half an hour before they ceased. The persistence of the enemy in this intense bombardment of our position at intervals plainly showed that he expected us to be concentrating troops for a set attack. His artillery fire was intended to make such concentration as costly and as difficult as possible.

To the men in the front line the fire was harassing in the extreme, and the nerve-strain was increased by the denial of all rest. Our patrols were unable to penetrate the German line in our sector; the reports of all patrol-leaders were to the effect that the Germans were holding their line very strongly and that advance would be possible only by infantry attack under an artillery barrage. This information had of course been sent back to division headquarters.

The outcome of these reports was that an attack was planned for 20 August, to be carried out by 'C' Company, following a three minutes' barrage. I was to be in charge of the attacking waves. From the forming-up line behind our main trench we should have to advance over three or four hundred yards. The shortness of the barrage appeared absurd to me, knowing the apparent strength with which the Germans were holding their line. An Australian battalion on our right was to carry out a somewhat similar attack with one company twenty-four hours ahead of us, under only a machine-gun barrage.

After another night of enemy bombardment, assisted by trench-mortars, we heard the machine-gun barrage go down for this attack by the Australians on our right. The German artillery awoke and rained shells along the whole front. Evidently he thought it was a general attack. The operation was a failure. One German post was captured and the Australians, after suffering rather heavily, had to evacuate it under cover of darkness.

At the end of the day I explained the plans for our own small operation to my platoon. Rations came up, and we were eating our meal when the German trench-mortar opened fire again. The first shell landed just in rear of our post, and almost in the communication trench. But one of our own medium trench-mortars had been instructed to engage this gentleman, and we were still cursing the German for throwing clods of earth in our tea when we saw our own mortar open and its shell explode among the German posts. Our gun fired three shots before Fritz sent over his second; it pumped over twelve shells in rapid succession, and the enemy fired no more. But he soon set a field-gun searching for our trench-mortar position.

As the night advanced I was instructed, to my great relief, that the forlorn hope for the morning had been cancelled, and that in substitution for it the 1st Australian Division and 32nd British Division would shortly attack through our present position with tanks and an artillery barrage. Evidently the failure of the company on our right that morning had at last convinced the Intelligence Staff that the Germans were holding the front in force.

Early in the morning of 22 August the 3rd Australian Division on the higher ground north of the Somme on our left advanced to the accompaniment of a great drum-fire. On our front both the Germans and ourselves gazed over the parapets to watch the show across the river. We were sure from the movement of the barrage that the attack was making headway, and it was.

The large village of Bray was overrun in the assault, and the line north of the river was carried well forward of that along which we stood on the south. It was invigorating to be able to see the moving battle succeed, and the movement was transmitted promptly to our own side of the Somme. We were warned to be ready to withdraw before dawn through the 1st Australian Division, whose 2nd Brigade was forming up in our rear for the attack. The withdrawal had to be made with the greatest caution and by driblets from one post at a time in order not to arouse the enemy's suspicions.

The Germans were uneasy; they shelled the whole area spasmodically throughout the afternoon. At night their fire increased in volume, and all our platoons suffered casualties. But at the set intervals our company vacated its posts noiselessly. As we moved, we came upon the 5th Battalion, already lying out in extended order along the jumping-off tapes, and we bent down to wish them luck as we passed through.

A group of us stood outside 'A' Company's dugout to watch the barrage go down. We had not long to wait. To our rear a roar of many guns spoke in one mighty voice. The half-light of breaking day was stabbed with flame from the muzzles of a host of batteries, and the shells screamed over our heads.

The sky danced and quivered in the weird flashes of the guns; the earth trembled under the concussion; the air was filled with smoke. Then tanks which had been hiding in the shelter of the great dump, nosed their way forward like the creatures of a nightmare. German S.O.S. rockets soared into the air ahead, to bring down the answering barrage, and a new chug-chug of machine-guns hit our ears. As heavier German metal began to fall in our vicinity, we retired to the entrance of the dugout. An officer from 'A' Company with four N.C.O.s came hurrying through the shell-swept zone. These had led the attacking infantry up to the taped jumping-off line, and had not tarried to admire the scenery on their way back.

163

The regular sound of the German machine-guns died away – comforting news to the ear. Day opened, and batches of grey-clad prisoners appeared escorted by slightly-wounded Australians. Our confirmed souvenir-collectors sprang to life. Close by ran the tree-lined main road which bisected the front. In spite of the heavy barrage still falling around us, many men from our companies stood in the poor shelter of these trees and dived among each batch of hurrying prisoners as it appeared.

The souvenir hunters would halt the little prisoner columns to search the Fritze's; the latter, knowing what was expected of them, would empty their pockets in readiness of postcards, scenes of the fatherland or photos of actresses, and hastily push them into waiting hands. The prisoners at least regarded the locality as unhealthy. I noticed one Australian with a freshly-rolled cigarette between his lips halt a small bunch of Germans. One of the latter pulled from his pocket a large bundle of postcards, passed them to the Australian, and hurried on. The receiver was so delighted that he ran a few paces after the German, and thrust into his mouth the freshly-lit cigarette.

Then two groups of German officers arrived. In the rear lot was a tall soldierly looking colonel of infantry. As they came abreast of us an officer in the leading group recognized the colonel, spoke to his companions, and they turned about and stood stiffly to attention while the colonel came forward and shook hands with each. Their pleasure in seeing their commanding officer again moved us all. Later, that colonel said that immediately the Australians were identified by the loss of some wounded on 16 August, the Germans doubled their front line strength. No wonder our patrols could not make headway.

We saw one amusing scene among the prisoners. A number of German artillerymen were recognized by some German infantry, and the latter attacked the gunners with their fists. It developed into a free fight, and was stopped by our 'A' Company commander. One of the German infantrymen told us that they considered that their artillery had not assisted them as well as they might have done. I think that if members of my company who had been shelled in the line so heavily for six days and nights had been asked their opinion, they would have voted the German artillery active in the extreme.

I was having breakfast when I was ordered to go forward to the front line and report on the situation. Taking the cheerful Nugget, I set out. The German front line we found to consist of a number of small, deep posts, arranged to afford the utmost mutual support. The Germans had made a determined stand. Crossing the road, we saw in a steep bank some rather good dugouts. These had been bombed by the attacking infantry and the area was now left entirely to the dead. Soon the ground rose into a line of low hillocks, on the crest of which an occasional German shell was bursting. Beyond this rise we came up with some of the support troops and were directed to the front-line companies. These were consolidating their gains, and were being shelled from a long way back by an occasional gun. The company commander said that his battalion had gained its objective but had had a stiff fight to break through the German defences.

On the way out I looked at some of the Australian dead. There were some people at home whom I wished could see them too. Each of one group of three wore the brass A on their red-and-black colour-patches which denoted that the wearers had served at Anzac on Gallipoli, and above the cuff of their right sleeves were the red chevrons of 1914 service. A sergeant lying prone in a German post had a golden wound stripe on his left sleeve, and one other of the dead wore a similar badge. We covered with their waterproof sheets these three men of the peerless 1st Australian Division, and went on our way with bitter hearts.

Chapter 18

March Up To Péronne

Our concert party bombed – We march up towards Péronne –
Shelled out of trenches – The brigade's crossing of the Somme –
Mont St Quentin and Péronne positions – A road of horrors.
(24–31 August 1918)

The operation of the 1st Australian Division and the 32nd British Division
on 23 August 1918, was another severe blow to the German army on this
front. Its forces suffered great loss, and were driven into a retreat which
halted only on the high ground around Péronne and Mont St Quentin
across the Somme bend. It was during this attack that the 1st Australian
Brigade captured the historic gun near Proyart, said to be the largest piece
that ever fell into British hands on the Western Front. It was one of the
long-ranged guns which had shelled Amiens. It was set in an immense
gun-pit, and had been disabled by its crew before it fell into our hands.

While waiting for a few days near La Flaque we enjoyed the luxury of a
hot bath in a captured German bath-house mounted on wheels. We also
had a hilarious musical evening with aid of a piano discovered in a large
German dugout. A fatigue party having salvaged the instrument and
installed it in the hut occupied by our battalion headquarters at La Flaque
dump, the colonel invited all officers of the unit to forgather after mess for
a concert. Sixteen or twenty of us crowded into the music saloon, a room
measuring perhaps ten feet by twelve. The adjutant was the musician, and
to his accompaniment we howled all the old songs of the army, and the
latest successes from the music halls of London.

The small shack shook to the roar of our more or less musical voices,
whilst the adjutant worked hard on the piano. The scene was illuminated
by many candle-ends, stuck on top of the instrument or from any part of
the shack that projected; the air was thick with tobacco smoke. Our
musician was just pounding out another classic, beginning: 'Columbus
discovered America, Franklin discovered ...'

But before we announced what Franklin's discovery was the musical
evening was rudely interrupted. There was a sudden whirr through the
air, and then the ear-splitting explosion of an aerial bomb very close at

166

hand. Our musician at once nose-dived through the doorway. Before the next bomb shook the shack he was in a prone position outside, and the doorway was jammed with a bunch of officers eager to follow him. Candles were knocked over in the haste to extinguish all lights, and the German bomber laid several more of his deadly bombs to to the consternation. One of the bombs landed only a few yards away from the hut. There was no more music that night. We turned to a game of banker in underground quarters, at which I accomplished a minor miracle by winning ninety francs.

While the vanguard of the Australian Corps was approaching the new German position at Péronne on the tail of the enemy's rearguard, the British 1st Army delivered a heavy blow at the German line about Arras, and the 3rd and 4th British Armies, on the left of the Australian advance, overran the old Somme battlefield from a direction north-west of Bapaume.

An air of expectancy was upon us all. Our own front, the right of the 4th Army, was now feeling for the enemy's strength just north of the Somme, the only practicable approach to the Péronne position. On 27 August 1918, the 8th Brigade, in the van of the 5th Division, drove the Germans out of Foucaucourt, and by 29 August the way, though difficult, was clear for an assault in force. On that date we of the 14th Brigade moved forward to take our part in the coming battle.

All day we marched over ground torn with the fighting of 1916–17, seamed with old trenches, and littered with rusting wire entanglements. We camped in this desolate scene for the night, and on 30 August continued our march in a half left direction. About noon we were met by guides from our advance party and led into a series of trenches sited just below the crest of a hill.

We were told that the place was under distant observation from across the Somme. The map named it the site of the village of Barleux – in fact long since obliterated. Soon the men of 'C' Company, in the unfailing Australian habit, devoted their energies to constructing shelters with material wrenched from some German huts in a small wood beyond a road on our right. Whenever Australian infantry came into a position they would set about making their quarters comfortable, no matter if it were but for one night. Little groups would set to work and toil like beavers to improve shelters even already more or less comfortable.

The company had been indulging this habit here for a couple of hours when the storm broke. A 5.9 shell landed almost on top of one venturesome band; another and another followed in quick succession. Four of the men were down; others rushed across to their aid, among them the battalion doctor. The Germans then proceeded to shell our position unmercifully, using all 5.9s. Their shooting was very accurate, and casualties began to mount. We suffered his bombardment for perhaps an hour, when orders came to evacuate the position and take up another in trenches on the other side of the road, hidden from direct observation. Here we spent the night.

Dawn of 31 August was ushered in with a terrific bombardment, the barrage for the 2nd Australian Division's attack upon Mont St Quentin. We knew that our turn to be launched into the attack was very close at hand.

After breakfast I walked in bright sunshine to a crescent-shaped ridge of which one horn lay a few hundred yards off the road. Looking back I could see the trenches out of which we had been shelled on the previous afternoon. While I looked three limbers emerged from the cutting on the crest of the ridge and travelled at full gallop down the road at intervals of perhaps twenty yards. The second limber was almost abreast of the trench line that ran to the road when I heard the rush of a shell.

It struck almost under the noses of the leaders of the second team. Horses and drivers went down over one another, as I have seen horses fall at a stiff steeple-fence. Willing helpers rushed to their aid. The poor shattered things that a few seconds ago were men were carried away, and the dead horses and the wrecked limber were dragged clear of the road. The other two teams continued their headlong gallop.

Early in the morning our orders came for an instant move. As we crossed the road the German artillery opened upon us. Away to our right we could see the country dotted with little groups, marching at irregular distances, also being sniped at by the German batteries. The whole four battalions of the 14th Brigade were moving on a course parallel with the front line south of the Somme. We had learned from our colonel that the 2nd Australian Division had failed to hold the summit of Mont St Quentin and were renewing the attack. Our brigade was to effect a crossing of the Somme outside our division's sector and to cooperate in the action.

In the afternoon we halted on some rising ground overlooking the Somme at Buscourt. The actual distance we had covered could ordinarily have been traversed in a couple of hours, but so bad was the country over which we had marched that it took us eight hours to reach the river from Barleux. Another Australian brigade had reached this crossing about the time we arrived, and this caused some delay, as passage was by a single pontoon bridge hidden among the tall trees of the bank.

As we waited, the company commander (Lieutenant Bull) pointed across the river in a half-right direction to a hill about three miles away, saying, 'That is Mont St Quentin. The 6th Brigade will attack the Mont, and our job is to 'mop-up' Péronne.'

The buildings of the town could be seen above the trees. 'When does the show start?' I asked.

'This afternoon,' said Bull.

168

'Well, we will need lanterns for the attack, as we cannot get into position before dark,' said I.

'That's what I think,' replied Bull. 'But the 6th Brigade has orders to attack at once, and we have to be in position before they move.'

But to get two infantry brigades across a river on one pontoon bridge takes considerable time, especially when the crossing is being shelled.

All eyes were turned towards Mont St Quentin. This hill dominated the surrounding country, and was the key of the German position. Viewed from a distance, it had a most ominous appearance. Its steep sides were marked with immense wire belts. The summit was crowned with a wood, the trees of which were blasted with shell-fire. The hill showed up black in the evening sun, as though the very earth had been discoloured by the smoke and fumes of bombardment. The 5th Brigade of the 2nd Australian Division, after winning a temporary foothold on its summit, were now holding to some captured German trenches on its lower slope.

The ramparted town of Péronne, centuries old, lay a mile off to the right. The Somme at this point bent almost at right angles from a northerly to a westerly line, and the river opened out into extensive swamps hundreds of yards wide. From the swamps the northern bank rose in a series of high ridges.

Every hour during which the Germans were left in possession of their present line would make it so much the harder and more costly to storm. Thus we of the 14th Brigade were called hurriedly from the 5th Division's reserve to cross into the sector of the 2nd Australian Division and assist the 6th Brigade in a renewed attempt against the Mont St Quentin-Péronne position.

The town of Péronne was a position of immense natural strength. It was flanked on three sides by the river, and its old walls of heavy masonry were now thick with German machine-guns. The approaches to the town were bridges across a wide moat, which could be swept by fire from the ramparts. Even with a heavy artillery bombardment to assist them, infantry would have found it a formidable position to attack. But our advance since 23 August had been so rapid, over country so broken, that only the lightest field-guns had come up with the infantry. There was no time for elaborate planning, such as preceded the battle of 8 August, and no tanks were present. It was going to be what the history books call a 'soldiers' battle'.

At length our turn came to cross the pontoon bridge. Our commanding officer (Lieutenant-Colonel Holland[1]) with the adjutant (Captain Williamson) were standing near the bridge, and as each platoon officer came up he was told to get his men across the bridge as quickly as possible. As we passed the far end two official photographers with a cinema-camera were recording pictures of the crossing in spite of shells that were searching the area. Some of the men called out to them to 'be sure and make them look nice, as their girls would be pleased to see them on the films'. Just in advance of the moving-picture outfit a battery of Australian artillery was firing at top speed.

We debouched into a road flanked on the right by river marshes and on the left by tall banks. The Germans must have been able to look straight down this road. It was truly a road of horrors. Ambulances full of wounded coming from the front impeded the progress of two brigades, and the traffic became severely congested. Enemy shells constantly landed on the highway or to either side of it. Men killed by shell-fire lay about, and the living stepped over their bodies in their march.

As evening came down our march halted and we were told to seek the cover of the high banks. These were already crowded with men from a battalion of the 6th Brigade. We clambered up the bank and sat down like a flock of birds.

The bombardment continued. The shells that went over the bank and landed in the water were greeted with ironical cheers by the huddled mass of men. Everyone had a fag or a pipe in his mouth, and to hear the cheers for the 'overs' (as they were called), which caused waterspouts in the marsh, one would have thought that the packed gallery was watching some entertainment. Some of the crowd even started to sing, 'Take Me Back To Dear Old Aussie', and this became so infectious that the bank roared the ditty to the skies, while the German shells burst in front and behind us. One fellow produced a large tin, drew water from the river, built a fire, and started to make tea. A shell dropped on top of the fire, and killed four men who were clustered around it.

By now it was dark. The 6th Brigade unit filed off along the road, and a little later we also moved. We had not gone far when a guide led 'C' Company into a trench that ran from the left of the road. Several dead Germans were lying in the entrance, and we walked over them. As the company was being spaced out along the trench we passed several more bodies of dead Fritzes. Nobody appeared even to notice them sufficiently to throw them up over the parapet.

A German whizz-bang battery away on the left enfiladed the position. The shells just skimmed the top of our trench. We ate bully beef and biscuits and sought any cranny for a sleeping-place. The night was raw cold and we huddled together for warmth. Tomorrow we were to face a task as stiff as any ever set before the Australian Corps. But tomorrow could wait. Tonight our weary bodies craved sleep.

Note

1. Later Lieutenant Colonel Austin Claude Selwyn Holland, *Légion d'honneur*, Holland had been placed in charge of the 56th Battalion on 4 August 1918.

Chapter 19

The Battle of Péronne

Advance in the rain – Deadly enemy fire –
All day on the Mont St Quentin slopes –
Entrance forced into Péronne by 54th –
6th Brigade carries Mont St Quentin –
Confusion of the battle on the right.
(1 September 1918)

It was still dark when we were aroused from our comfortless resting-places. A drizzling misty rain was falling. The sound of heavy artillery fire came from our left, and this soon brought down a German barrage. The company commander sent a runner along to platoon officers with orders to get their men on the move and to file out of the trench on to the road. I was told to report to him and found him standing at the entrance to the trench. In the noise of the bursting shells and the boom of the guns he had to shout his remarks.

He told me that the 54th Battalion was attacking on our right. They were to clear the ground in front of Péronne, and then attack the town itself. Alongside the 54th, the 53rd Battalion was to carry the line of attack past the right of Mont St Quentin to a trench called Darmstadt Trench, which ran north and south about a mile east of Péronne. The 56th Battalion was to follow in close support of the 53rd, and, when the latter had gained their objective, we were to turn south, and attack the high ground beyond Péronne from the north. In this we were to be assisted by the 55th Battalion. All this was hurriedly communicated as our company filed out of the trench. I was ordered to take charge of the left half company.

The company clear of the trench, we turned off the road to the right and formed up in two waves of half companies. Just before we went forward in this formation a 5.9 landed close by and knocked over the Company Commander and wounded a sergeant and a runner. Bull arose unscathed, but much shaken. A stretcher which picked up the sergeant was struck a little later by a shell, and the N.C.O. and the two bearers were killed.

Our advance started. The rain drove into our faces, and the barrage fell about us. The Germans were using their deadly 5.9s extensively. In front we could hear the ceaseless chatter of many machine-guns, and before we had gone far we were amid the swishing sound of the bullets.

A quarry opened in front of us. The lines of men went down its steep banks, crossed the bottom, and were soon scrambling up the far side. Just as we were emerging a man next but one to me crumpled up. I turned to see him rolling down to the bottom. He appeared to be dead, and I remember wondering whether if he were only wounded he would be found by the bearers. Next we came to a small wood, the trees still wearing green foliage. The machine-gun bullets came through this, and men commenced to drop fast.

Here we found that we were too far to the right, and the waves turned into file, and, skirting the wood, crossed the road. Just on the left of the wood, I saw a company runner lying badly wounded. He was only a lad of about twenty, and with his smiling face and pleasant manner was liked by everyone in the company. He had an ugly wound in his temple, and his left eye seemed to be gone. The blood was streaming down his neck; the breast of his tunic was dyed red. As I came near he recognized me and, half raising himself, caught hold of my leg. I knew that he wanted the stretcher-bearers, and told him that they were following behind my rear platoon. Our instructions were that no men other than the bearers were to fall out or to attend to the wounded; I knew that it would hurt most of the chaps that were following on to step over the sorely-wounded youngster who was so popular.

Once we emerged from the cover of the wood we came under the fire of machine-guns from Mont St Quentin on our left, as well as that directed at the waves of the 53rd Battalion in our front. In Fiorina trench, the jumping-off point for the 53rd Battalion, we saw many dead Germans. Afterwards we learned that before zero hour, when the 53rd Battalion had moved up to this trench, they found it strongly held by the enemy and had to fight for the possession of the starting-point of their attack.

Our 'A' Company was moving in front of us, and, crossing a railway line, I saw a friend of mine, Lieutenant Cory, being attended to by the bearers. He had been struck in the back by a piece of shell, and, with his blood-soaked tunic cut open, he was shivering in the rawness of the morning.

In front the 53rd Battalion was heavily engaged. The German barrage searched the ground over which the advance was being made. But even worse than the German shells was their machine-gun fire. Never before had I experienced such a volume of their fire. It sprayed our ranks from Mont St Quentin and Anvil Wood. The German positions must have swarmed with machine-guns, and Fritz, being a past master in the tactical handling of these, took a heavy toll of the advancing infantry.

172

In front of Anvil Wood were situated several belts of wire of imposing width and height. In wide rusted lines they swept away across the slopes of Mont St Quentin. Many dead of the 53rd Battalion lay in and around these wire belts. The Germans had left openings; but these were death-traps, swept by the machine-gunners. Some of the 53rd Battalion's Lewis-gunners rested their guns on the wire and gave covering fire to their platoons by engaging the enemy's machine-gunners while a passage of the wire was being made. Then Anvil Wood was cleared, but the fire from Mont St Quentin still caused us many casualties.

The rain ceased, but the dust and smoke hid much from us. The 6th Brigade was heavily engaged against Mont St Quentin. As yet we had not seen any prisoners coming back – a sure indication of desperate battle.

Near Anvil Wood our company came to a halt in a sunken road. Here I saw two German machine-gun posts, each with their entire crew lying dead around their guns. In one post were the bodies of sixteen dead Germans, including an officer. They had fought to the last.

We received word that the 53rd Battalion was held up round the cemetery to the left of Péronne, swept by machine-gun fire from the ramparts of the town. These fortifications gave the utmost protection to the machine-gunners, and our artillery was not heavy enough to dislodge them. Some of the 53rd Battalion dug themselves in among the graves of the cemetery. 'A' Company of the 56th Battalion had become involved with the latter phase of the 53rd Battalion's advance, and were now hold-ing a position among some hutments and a railway line near the cemetery.

Word came through that the 54th Battalion had gained a foothold in the town of Péronne. This was achieved only by the utmost heroism. Small parties were rushed across foot bridges raked with machine-gun fire, in which many were killed, but the few who lived to reach the bridgehead attacked the German machine-gunners and cleared a way for other parties to cross the footbridges.

Once a hold was gained on part of the town, it was exploited to the utmost, and the Germans were rooted out of cellars and other cover. Two N.C.O.s of this battalion were afterwards awarded the Victoria Cross for their bravery and example in this fighting. Only the stoutest of troops could have gained an entry in face of the obstacles of ramparts and moat and the determined garrison.

About 11 a.m. I saw the first German prisoners of the fight, a small party in charge of two slightly wounded men of the 54th Battalion. The prisoners were decidedly different from those we had seen during these last weeks. These were all big men in good uniforms, and wearing white shoulder knots on their uniforms. They belonged to the 2nd Prussian Guards Division, and had been kept in reserve by the German High Command to be used only in case of dire necessity.

The intelligence staff of our Corps Headquarters was surprised to find among the few prisoners taken during the fighting at Mont St Quentin and Péronne men from many units of the German Army. It was soon learned that volunteers had been called for to hold these positions against the coming attack of the Australians. It was no wonder, therefore, that the 6th and 14th Brigades had to fight like demons. The German machine-gunners could fairly be ranked with Leonidas's Spartan Three Hundred, as they fought by their guns to the death, and continued firing when all hope for themselves personally had vanished.

Sitting spaced out along the sunken road, we watched the little band of German prisoners pass. Even in defeat they carried themselves with the upright carriage and swagger of a crack regiment. There was no sign of the bewilderment and terror that we had seen on the faces of the prisoners on 8 and 23 August, when the captives showed all the signs of men who had suffered the effects of heavy barrages. These prisoners now passing had had all the odds in their favour; but, although our attack had not yet reached its final goal, it had made headway.

Meanwhile, our 'A' Company had consolidated a position near the cemetery to the left of Péronne, where the advance of the 53rd Battalion had been halted by heavy machine-gun fire. During the morning a runner came back from 'A' Company to ask for support for its left flank, upon which a counterattack was developing. This flank was well 'in the air', being exposed on the side of Mont St Quentin, the summit of which was still in German hands.

Lieutenant Bull told me to take my platoon gun-team forward to assist 'A' Company against the coming attack. Leaving the sunken road, we entered a trench that ran from Anvil Wood. I noticed that 'A' Company was being subjected to heavy bombardment; the runner told me as we moved along that machine-guns from Mont St Quentin were enfilading the length of 'A' Company's position. As a matter of fact, 'A' Company was under fire from front, left flank, and left rear. Each of my gun team, including myself, carried spare Lewis-gun panniers – metal disks, with the cartridges spaced around them. These were slung across our shoulders in khaki covered carriers each containing four panniers.

Passing along the trench we saw some dead of the 53rd Battalion, and among them two sorely wounded men. Soon we had to leave the shelter of the trench, and the runner told me that we would then be the target for machine-guns on Mont St Quentin. I told my gun team that we would cross the open ground (about three hundred yards) by doubling over it in twos, at irregular intervals, and that I would go first.

I got out of the trench, and before I was into my stride, the machine-gun bullets went 'zip-zip' around me. Half-way across I turned to see that my team were following. Suddenly I was bowled over as if a sledge-hammer had struck me.

My tunic was on fire, and the fumes of cordite made me cough and splutter. Some machine-gun bullets had struck the pannier which was over my left breast. The metal of the pannier had turned the bullets, which cut through perhaps eight or ten cartridges that were in the pannier and set fire to them. I beat the fire out by banging the panniers on the ground, and crushed the burning tunic in my hand.

To my surprise I was not wounded. A few more yards and instinct caused me to adopt the prone position; a shell landed so close that its explosion covered my face with earth, and knocked my steel helmet off. Again unscathed, I arose and continued on my way. I halted in a large shell hole, and when my team caught up we had a 'breather'. With the next spurt we reached 'A' Company's line.

Here the company commander told me that his own gun teams had beaten off the half-hearted attack on his flank, that the assistance of my Lewis-gun was not needed, and that I was to report back to my own company. My team had a rest in a shell hole, while I smoked a cigarette with Captain Dalkeith of 'A' Company. His men were occupying shell holes and any depression in the ground that gave cover. They had endured a torrid time from the heavy shelling and the raking machine-gun fire from Mont St Quentin.

While we smoked Dalkeith told me about the performance of shelling Mont St Quentin with a captured field-gun. One of his men, claiming some slight knowledge of the piece, laid the gun, while Dalkeith and another man did the firing. They had the pleasure of seeing bits of the German trenches spout into the air as the shells landed. Of course, it was firing through open sights, as the crest of the Mont was only 800 yards away.

The enemy's artillery appeared to have decided ascendancy over ours, and even while we talked German shells were deluging the position held by 'A' Company and the 53rd Battalion. I went across to my team and started them on the way back to the trench than ran towards Anvil Wood, and told them to wait in this shelter for me. Nugget, my gun corporal, and myself brought up the rear. The machine-guns again sprayed us as we crossed the open. My corporal was bowled over, and we assisted him into the trench and bound up a wound in his upper arm. Nearby were lying two badly wounded men of the 53rd Battalion. We lit cigarettes for them and after reporting to my company commander, I sent bearers to bring them in.

About 1 p.m. we watched a barrage from our guns go down on the crest of Mont St Quentin, and under cover of this the 6th Brigade stormed the summit and drove the Germans from their position – thus crowning with success the bitter fighting that the 5th and 6th Brigades of the 2nd Australian Division had endured for some days.

Sir John Monash, in his book, declares that when he laid before the army commander his plans for the assault of Mont St Quentin, General Rawlinson listened and then remarked: 'Surely you do not expect to capture such a position with three battalions?' Being assured that this was the intention, he replied: 'Well, I do not think that I should stop you making the attempt, so go ahead.' It certainly took the efforts of two brigades finally to capture the famous hill, but when the army head-quarters heard of the success they were at first incredulous.

Some of our men went through the packs of the dead Germans who were lying in a machine-gun post in Anvil Wood. They came back with a bottle of brandy, handfuls of cigars, also some black bread and synthetic jam. Soon all the company were smoking cigars as if they were million-aires, the brandy was doled out, and most of us tried the German bread and jam. The bread was awful stuff, its base appeared to be sawdust, and how men lived on it and did not die of inflamed intestines puzzled most of us.

But the shelling never ceased along our position, and on the gains that the 53rd Battalion were consolidating a ceaseless rain of shells and machine-gun fire was falling. A pall of smoke and dust hung over the scene. Passing along the sunken road were stretcher-parties carrying the badly wounded.

In most cases they had lain out for hours before they could be moved to the Aid Post. They were all in a pitiful condition, drenched with rain, shivering, and with faces pale from loss of blood. But when spoken to each man could summon a wan smile and never a word of complaint was heard from them. There were some ghastly wounds among them. Shells had smashed bones and cut flesh in a manner sickening to behold. One chap had stopped a burst of fire from a machine-gun, which had torn part of his stomach away. How he lived long enough to be carried back to the sunken road was little short of miraculous; still, he lay among us for some time and smoked cigarettes unceasingly, these being fed to him by our fellows.

We had been waiting for some hours expecting the attack to be renewed and the calling up of our companies into the advance. Shortly after the summit of Mont St Quentin fell, our 'A' Company was withdrawn, and passing down the road moved across to the right.

We were next. Our orders were to get into position on the high ground above Péronne, and, linking with the right flank of the 53rd Battalion, attack the village of St Denis. We moved across more or less dead ground on the right of the road, and wound our way up the rise that hid Péronne from our view. Here were several deep trenches, near which were lying some dead Germans and men of the 54th Battalion. On the crest of the rise we passed through a heavy wire system and immediately came under shell fire. The company was halted in extended formation on the Péronne side of the rise, near a small wood.

We lay out on the ground, some in the shelter of shallow excavations that appeared to have had tents erected over them at one time. Bull left me in charge of the company while he went away to attend a conference. From our position we could look across the ramparts of Péronne and realize to the full what a tough proposition the walled town must have been for the 54th Battalion to storm.

The sky was full of fighting 'planes, and to pass the time and keep my mind off the shells that were dropping around us, I counted seventy of these fighters of the skies. The German gunners soon picked up our range, and the company began to suffer casualties. Time went by and still Bull did not return. Some hitch occurred; the 53rd Battalion left their trenches to attempt the advance without knowing that we were still awaiting orders as to our part in the attack. As soon as they attempted to move the 53rd Battalion met such a storm of machine-gun fire that their attack melted away in face of it.

All this time my company was in exposed position and casualties were mounting fast. It appeared to me senseless to keep the men lying out to be shot to pieces when the attack had been mismanaged. I decided to withdraw the company two hundred yards over the crest of the hill, into the shelter of a large trench which I had noticed as we moved up. I told Lieutenant Nancarrow to commence to dribble his platoon back to this position, through the gap in the wire. The NCOs in charge of the other platoons were likewise instructed. In the failing light of the late afternoon this was carried out, Fritz shelling us viciously all the while.

Company Sergeant Major Golding, Sergeant Owens, Nugget, and two others stayed behind with me. We managed to get the wounded into a large shell hole. One of them had a badly shattered leg, and Sergeant Owens bound it up with a puttee. Both he and Golding were as cool as icebergs under the heavy shelling. Sergeant Owens, a 1914 man, was killed the next morning in the attack on St Denis. Lieutenant Nancarrow sent bearers up from the trench, and the wounded were taken back.

Darkness was coming on when, along with my little band, I reached the trench where our company was. Only then did Company Sergeant Major Golding, stripping his tunic off, ask me to put some iodine on a wound in the upper part of his right arm, where a shell splinter had struck him. I told him to go to the Aid Post. He demurred, and only went when he was ordered to do so.

Some hours later I heard his voice in the trench, and asked why he had not gone back to the Aid Post. He replied: 'I did go back to the Aid Post, but when I saw the crowd of wounded lying around awaiting attention,

I could not go in and show my scratch to the doctor.' This cool, game, young Englishman actually went over the top in the attack next morning with his right arm hanging stiffly by his side. He was a 1914 man and was recognized throughout the battalion as one of the best line soldiers that ever wore our green-and-white colour-patches. He survived the war, and returned to Australia respected by everyone and admired for his unassuming manner and a courage that was enough for three men.

It was dark when the company commander returned. He told me that 'A' Company had lost all its officers, that the conference he had attended had waited in vain for instructions for this afternoon's attack to come through, and that the 53rd Battalion had attacked ignorant of the fact that our battalion had not received its orders. Afterwards it was learned that a senior officer had been sent forward from battalion headquarters to take charge of the attack, and was now missing. Two days later he was discovered. He had trodden on a hidden machine-gun shaft and, the top collapsing under his weight, he had fallen into a hole twenty feet deep. Here he lay and would no doubt have died but a curious soldier some days later happened to peer down, and discovered the hapless prisoner.

We were a tired lot of men that night. Our company had suffered rather heavily during the day. The German guns were still shelling, and presently gas shells drenched Anvil Wood and the vicinity of our position. In the moonlight our rations arrived, with the godsend of a rum issue. We had not had a proper meal since two nights before at Barleux. My batman generally did not drink rum, but this night I made him take his issue. Then we stripped the waterproof capes from two dead Germans, and, wrapping ourselves in these, lay in the bottom of the trench to get a few hours' sleep.

Chapter 20

End of the Battle – And Hospital

Our attack on St Denis – Murderous fire – Wounded –
Out of the fight – Cost of victory – Blighty again.
(September to October 1918)

It was still dark on 2 September 1918, when a runner from battalion head-quarters aroused the company commander. I was awake before he flashed his torch to read the order, and was immediately summoned.

Our battalion and two companies of the 55th were to attack to the north of Péronne to win the ground in the vicinity of the Darmstadt Trench. The 59th and 60th Battalions were to follow in rear of the 56th and 55th, and, when our objective was gained, the 59th and 60th were to face south and attack the high ground around Péronne. The plan was really a continuation of that of the previous day with the leading battalions of the 14th Brigade changed round and with the important addition that three battalions of the 15th Brigade would co-operate.

Our dispositions were to attack on a one-company front, and I was instructed to lead up to the jumping-off place just east of the cemetery. Day was breaking as I led 'C' Company out of the trench. At that moment a runner handed me a letter from Blighty. I glanced at the writing, and without opening it put it into my breast pocket, as the thought flashed through my mind: 'I'll read it when I am wounded.'

Already the German barrage was falling in a shower of 5.9s and lighter shells. The smoke from their bursts made it impossible to see far. Crossing the road past the edge of Anvil Wood, our company deployed into waves of attack. Here I sent two connecting files to keep touch with the rear wave of the preceding company. One of these was my batman Nugget; I could see his short, sturdy figure moving through the murk of the shell-smoke. That was the last I ever saw of this faithful, loyal, and happy-go-lucky youngster. During the forenoon he was shockingly wounded by a shell; he died some days later in a casualty clearing station.[1]

Once into our waves, we moved forward at the double to pass through the barrage as quickly as possible. Our battalion was losing men fast, even before we were to reach the jumping-off line. The Germans were using in their barrage incendiary shells. I saw one of these burst and knock over three men. Two arose, beating the flames from their tunics and from the hessian camouflage on their steel helmets. The third lay in the stillness of death, the hessian burning fiercely on his helmet some feet away.

It seemed a marvel that any of us could pass through the barrage and escape unscathed. The din of the bursting shells was terrific; the earth spurted in geysers from the explosions; the ground trembled and shook. Men collapsed in the waves; their comrades hurried past them, with their faces set and the bright steel of their bayonets showing through the murk of the morning of death. None stopped to help those who were stricken down; that was left to the bearers. But any man who went down in this shell-blasted area stood a good chance of being blown to pieces as he lay, so combed was the earth by the density of the German barrage. The excitement in it forced us on.

Panting, we reached the railway line near the cemetery. Here the company halted for a breather. Just in rear was a trench occupied by some men of the 53rd Battalion, and lying round this and along the railway line were the ghastly reminders of the bloody fighting in which the 53rd and 56th had been involved yesterday. The men of the 53rd Battalion who had held this line since yesterday morning must have passed through hell upon earth multiplied tenfold. Now the German protective barrage was upon them again, and they stood close in to their parapet and watched waves halt to regain their breath in the dubious shelter of the low railway embankment.

Added to the shells was now the deadly hail of the machine-guns firing from the buildings of the village of St Denis. The bullets beat in an incessant drumming upon the railway metal. Yesterday the German machine-gun fire had been terrific, but this morning it seemed there must be a stronger word made to fit it.

Halting for a few minutes by the railway line, I spoke to Captain Cotterell of the 55th Battalion. He was a giant of a man with whom I had spent several evenings in a favourite estaminet in Pernois. He commented upon the inadequacy of our artillery fire to keep down the machine-gun fire. He was killed later in the attack.[2]

Our company commander, Lieutenant Bull, stood up on the railway embankment, his back towards the objective, and with the machine-gun bullets striking fire from the ballast at his feet, called on his company to make ready to move. I broke off my conversation with Cotterell and went down the line of men to get them ready.

I had reached the right of our line when two shells landed on the parapet of the trench just in our rear. I felt a painful jar in my left hand and a stinging pain in the upper part of my left thigh. Looking at my hand, I saw that I had been struck at the base of two fingers, which felt as if they were broken. I could feel the blood running down my thigh and, as I looked, the leg of my breeches became saturated red.

A man next to me offered assistance. I asked him to help me off with my equipment, and from my haversack I took such personal things as shaving-gear and maps. These I crammed into one pocket; into the other I put my Webley revolver. I called out to the C.O. that I was wounded but could take myself out. He waved his hand to me, and I turned about to go through the curtain of bursting shells behind us.

At every step the blood squelched out of my boot; the leg of my breeches and puttee was wet and scarlet. Alone in the bursts of the barrage I remained ice-cool by telling myself that I would win through. A special sense made me take a zigzag course; my ears, tuned to abnormal acuteness, told me by the whine whether near shells were passing overhead or likely to burst close. I could see only a few yards ahead in the murk and smoke, but I knew by the lie of the land that I must bear to the left. It seemed an age until I struck the deserted trench from which I had gone forward with my gun team yesterday. I scrambled along it until I sighted the road; I clambered out and reached Anvil Wood.

Arrived at the battalion dugout, I went inside. The works officer, Lieutenant Harvey, bandaged my hip and gave me a drink of rum. I gulped the fiery spirit, and gave the colonel details of the little I had seen of the advance. I told him they wanted artillery to keep down the machine-gun fire from St Denis. Harvey, commonly known as 'Mud', wanted to bandage my hand, but the rum on my empty stomach made me wave this injury aside as insignificant.

I was still talking when Mud advised me to get back to the R.A.P. before my leg stiffened. I set out along the road among other walking wounded. Among them I met two old cronies from 'A' Company, one badly wounded in the thigh, his less seriously wounded pal assisting him. I linked my arm under his other armpit; we stumbled along together, heedless of the shells now. Instinct told me that I had received my issue.

Many years before, when I was a little boy, I walked across the fields to school on a bright sunny spring morning, to find, on my arrival, that there was to be no school for the master was ill. In my selfish boyish mind there rose a great joy for the unexpected holiday to roam the bush in the sunshine. No other school holiday ever felt half so good as this unexpected one. This morning, as I made one of the trio plodding along that battle road, there came on me again the joy that filled my mind on that long ago spring morning.

The premonition of a coming wound had been on me for weeks, and now it had come. Instead of being shockingly wounded like so many, I had been let off with what all the army knew as 'a nice Blighty'. The utter exhaustion of mind and body caused by the strenuous days and sleepless nights since 8 August seemed to vanish in the foretaste of a rest in a clean bed.

We reached the Aid Post, quartered in a large crater to the left of the road. Stretcher cases were lying around and walking wounded sat among them. The doctor put a new bandage on my hip and field-dressing on my hand. He looked very tired; he had worked without halt since the previous morning in a confusion of blood, wounds, and shattered humanity. He told me that I would be sent out on a stretcher. I laughed and replied that I could walk to Amiens. The doctor retorted that when I had cooled down my leg would be as rigid as iron and that I would not walk twenty feet.

I sat outside and waited my turn to be evacuated. As my stretcher was being wheeled to the ambulance, a little knot of battalion transport men called out to me. I told them in army language the extent of my hurts, and they laughed heartily.

In the ambulance I slept the sleep of utter exhaustion. At a forward casualty clearing station in the ruins of a village a doctor came round and gave us all anti-tetanus injections. Presently I was loaded again on to an ambulance, and was again drowned in sleep. Once as the vehicle almost turned over I awoke with a jerk, but relapsed at once. About noon we pulled up at a casualty clearing station near Daours, the village from which we had advanced before the attack on 8 August.[3]

In the large marquees, nurses, pale and weary beyond words, hurried about. That these women worked their long hours among such surroundings without collapsing spoke volumes for their will-power and sense of duty. The place reeked with the odours of blood, antiseptic dressings, and unwashed bodies. The nurses saw war stripped of even the excitement of an attack. The men in battle had long been disillusioned as to any grandeur in modern warfare. But there was still the excited comradeship of their battalions to buoy them up. These women did not have even that antidote. They saw soldiers in their most pitiful state – wounded, blood-stained, dirty, reeking of blood and filth. Worst of all was the staring look in their eyes. There was something subhuman, terrifying, in their petrified faces, drawn and ashen. Gone was all the nonchalance which made the men face danger with gaiety and resolution; now they were pitiful in their quietness and exhaustion.

During heavy fighting, when the conveyances were arriving all the time laden with wounded, the doctors and nurses in the casualty clearing stations worked the clock round. I believe that the staff were specially selected for this work, but the strain was such that it was almost incredible that a woman could stand it and retain her sanity.

The sun was setting as I was loaded on to a hospital train. The stretchers were placed in tiers like ship's bunks. The train appeared to be of immense length and was crowded with wounded. Here I saw again my friend

182

Lieutenant Cory of 'A' Company. I had last seen him when the bearers were dressing his wound in the rain near Fiorina Trench during the early part of the advance on the morning of 1 September. He looked very pale and haggard; he had a bad wound in the back of his shoulder blade. Before the train started we were given a meal of boiled fowl. I enjoyed it.

The battle for Péronne, St Denis, and Flamicourt raged throughout 2 September 1918. So heavy were the casualties of the 55th and 56th Battalions that early in the forenoon of 2 September they were being used as one battalion. The 56th lost all officers of three companies during the initial stages of the advance. Sergeant O'Connor took charge of the remnants of the 56th Battalion and did such excellent service that he was recommended for the Victoria Cross.

On the night of 2 September, the 14th Brigade was relieved by the 15th, and soon the 8th Brigade was also employed. It was not until the morning of 5 September that the position could be said to be won, with the enemy in full retreat. The two days' fighting of 1 and 2 September cost the 14th Brigade half their strength.

In conclusion I may be permitted to quote General Monash on 'the gallant 14th Brigade at Péronne': 'The men of the 14th Brigade that day had their mettle up to a degree which was astonishing', he wrote in his book. 'On the occasion of the great attack on 8 August, and ever since, it had been the fate of this brigade to be in reserve to its division, on every occasion when there was any serious fighting in hand. The brigade felt its position very keenly.'

Of the 5th Division he wrote: 'After four days of arduous pursuit, General Hobbs's troops were called upon to undertake a long and difficult march over most broken country, to be followed by three days of intensive fighting of the most severe character. The 5th Australian Division followed the lead given by their commander, and General Hobbs led them to imperishable fame.'[4]

In Rouen hospital my clothing was stripped off.[5] My breeches had become cemented to my leg, and the process of separation was far from pleasant. In the afternoon an orderly who did duty as a barber came to my bed. He was a big fellow in his early twenties, who had served with a crack British regiment. He lathered my face, stropped his razor on what looked like a piece of a leather surcingle, and then began to shave me. I have had some painful shaves, but never have I experienced such agony at the hands of an alleged barber. The tears coursed down my face, and I had to ask him to give me a rest, during which he solemnly stropped his razor on the remnants of the surcingle.

At Le Havre we were unloaded and carried on to a hospital ship. As I lay waiting my turn, the world seemed a very pleasant place in which to be alive. Had I realized as I was being carried across the wharf that this was my last look at wartime France, that I was turning my back for ever on the life of the army, I should have been sad. I had long ceased to picture any existence outside the army.

As for this France, surely it was the second motherland of every British soldier who knew it on service. It stood for dangers, hardships, but withal a great adventurous freedom in the lives of most of us, and above all for the comradeship of our fellow-men. Thankful to be lying on a stretcher bound for England, if I had realized that this was the end of my days of soldiering with the men whom I knew so well, it would have destroyed much of my gratitude on this sunny morning.

All the Australian wounded from the ship were marked for Wandsworth, 3rd London General Hospital.[6] Pedestrians waved to our ambulances in the crowded streets. At the hospital I was, at request, placed alongside my friend Lieutenant Cory. We found ourselves then in A3 Ward.

Under the Regular Army Sister in charge, was a small, red-haired Irish Sister, efficient in the fullest sense and with a capacity for work so great that she would have made a galley slave report her to his union. The third Sister was a good type of well-bred young Englishwoman serving as a V.A.D.[7] Her name was Groves, and if ever there were a ministering angel on this earth in the shape of a sweet-faced young woman, it was Nurse Groves of A3 Ward, 3rd London General Hospital. She went about her tasks as though her one object in life was to please everybody and sacrifice herself. Needless to say, she was liked by every man in the ward.

In the centre of the ward was a large stove and around this during the evenings congregated the officers who were able to get up. The tales told around that stove of battles, sprees, women, racehorses, and remote places of the Empire made the Arabian Nights seem tame.

During the first days in the ward I was visited by another officer of my battalion, Lieutenant Hughes, wounded by shell fire when we were moving up from Barleux. He told me that there were fifteen officers from our battalion in the Wandsworth Hospital. Counting those killed also, this meant that practically every line officer that went into the Péronne battle had become a casualty. This gives some idea of the losses sustained by the 56th Battalion; the same was true generally of the whole 14th Brigade.

In the theatres of war the curtain began to fall in September. On 12 September American troops had straightened out the St Mihiel salient in Alsace.[8] Allenby's great attack in Palestine opened on 19 September and shattered the Turkish armies. Bulgaria asked for an Armistice the same day, and on 29 September 1918, British and Belgian armies under King Albert advanced from Ypres on a twenty-three mile front. On the whole Western Front the policy was attack and again attack!

At the end of September the British armies ruptured the Hindenburg Line, that long formidable obstacle, and the 4th Army's successful assault of those defences was the last action in which the Australian divisions were engaged in France.

The 5th Australian Division moved back from the battle zone on 3 October.[9] The toll of the heavy and continuous fighting since the Battle of Amiens was revealed in the battle strength of the division's three brigades on the morning of the attack on the Hindenburg Line. The 8th Brigade numbered 1,926 all ranks, the 15th Brigade 1,584, and the 14th Brigade 1,131. The last was not much stronger than a full battalion.

Notes

1. Private Ernest Collier died of his wounds at 20th Casualty Clearing Station at Heilly, near Mericourt-l'Abbe, on 6 September 1918. He is buried in Heilly Station Cemetery.
2. Killed in action on 2 September 1918, 29-year-old Captain Fred James Cotterell MC, the son of James and Jane Cotterell, of 155 Church Hill Road, Handsworth, Birmingham, now lies in Herbecourt British Cemetery.
3. During August and September 1918, the area around Daours was the location for a number of casualty clearing stations, namely the 5th, 37th, 41st, 53rd, 55th and 61st.
4. Later Lieutenant General Sir Joseph John Talbot Hobbs KCB, KCMG, VD. Born in London in 1864, Hobbs emigrated to Australia in 1886, establishing an architectural practice in Perth the following year. He was given command of the 5th Division on 1 January 1917. At the end of the war, Monash was put in charge of the repatriation and demobilization of Australian troops, and Hobbs succeeded him in the command of the Army Corps until this was completed in May 1919.
5. Williams was admitted to the 8th General Hospital at Rouen on 3 September and invalided to the UK the following day.
6. In August 1914 the Royal Victoria Patriotic School in Wandsworth became the 3rd London General Hospital, one of the four Territorial General Hospitals in London. The hospital finally closed in August 1920. During the six years of its existence it had treated 62,708 patients from all over the British Empire. Williams was admitted to this hospital on 5 September 1918.
7. In 1909 the War Office issued the Scheme for the Organisation of Voluntary Aid. Under this scheme, the British Red Cross was given the role of providing supplementary aid to the Territorial Forces Medical Service in the event of war. In order to provide trained personnel for this task, county branches of the Red Cross organised units called Voluntary Aid Detachments. All Voluntary Aid Detachment members (who themselves came to be known simply as 'VADs') were trained in first aid and nursing. Within twelve months of the scheme's launch, they numbered well over 6,000.
8. The Battle of Saint-Mihiel was fought between 12 and 15 September 1918, and involved the American Expeditionary Force and some 48,000 French troops – all under the command of General John J. Pershing.
9. The 56th Battalion fought its last major battle of the war, St Quentin Canal, between 29 September and 2 October 1918. It was resting out of the line when the Armistice was declared on 11 November 1918. Soon after, members of the battalion began to be returned to Australia for discharge. It ceased to exist as a separate entity on 10 April 1919, when the remnants of all of the 14th Brigade's battalions were merged into a single unit.

Chapter 21

Conclusion

Convalescence – Country house guests – How Joe killed the pheasant –
Homeward bound – Breaking of army ties – The A.I.F. spirit –
Its lessons for the new generation.

From hospital I duly appeared before a medical board at Horseferry Road,
and while the war went forward towards the Armistice, Joe H————
(an officer from the 3rd Battalion) and I went off on convalescent leave
in England.

Armed with our papers we went to the offices of the organization
conducted by the Countess of Harrowby, in a street near Hyde Park.[1] Lady
Harrowby received us very graciously, and asked us if we had any particular fancy as to what sort of leave we wished to spend. Whether we
craved gaiety and life, in the shape of house parties, riding or shooting, or
whether we wished to go away to the country and have a rest. We chose
the latter. A huge map of the British Isles was produced for us to scan, and
we saw that throughout the length and breadth of the United Kingdom
moneyed people took into their homes convalescent officers of the
Dominion Forces to be entertained as distinguished guests. To these
generous English people men of the Dominion troops owe a debt which
can never be repaid.

Eventually we decided to go to a place near West Hoathly in Sussex. At
the appointed railway station a car met us and took us to a country house.
Here we found two other convalescent officers, one a Canadian and the
other an Australian from a field engineer company. The Canadian was
leaving that night, for which I was sorry; he looked a good sort of fellow.
The Australian appeared to me to be nursing a hopeless love. Our host was
a tall man of perhaps sixty, of mind as alert as that of many men half his
age. His niece was our hostess; when we arrived she was wearing the
smock and breeches of a land girl, but she appeared at dinner in evening
dress. This young lady during our stay was most hospitable and kind to
Joe and myself.

Time passed very pleasantly. During the fine days we wandered across
the fields, or tramped along the country roads. I found that I could not

186

walk very far in heavy boots, as my leg pained me considerably and made me limp rather badly.

The Australian from the engineers afforded us much amusement. When alone with us he lapsed into silence or buried his nose in a book. But when our hostess joined the group around the fire he came out of his shell. He was a rare type, seldom found in the Australian Army, and never in an infantry battalion. He used to try to impress the young lady with his superior education, and his conversation fairly blinded Joe and myself.

One afternoon we went shooting, our hostess, a male relative of hers, Joe, and myself. Joe and I were given charge of two Purdy guns, of which it was impressed upon us that the value was a hundred guineas each. I soon surrendered mine, as the pheasants were altogether too quick on the wing for me. The Englishman and Joe were now the shooters, and the girl and myself the beaters. Joe shot at everything that rose, cock or hen. The latter were supposed to be immune, and Joe was promptly informed of this fact. But if my pal were the only one that ever tried to shoot these birds, they would all live to die of senile decay. What Joe lacked in skill he made up for in enthusiasm. He banged left and right barrels at impossible shots. Then he staged a star turn.

We two beaters had entered a depression in the ground in which the long grass of summer had bent beneath the weight of the autumn rains, and made excellent cover for birds. We had been beating this with our sticks for some minutes when the sudden rush of whirring wings rewarded our efforts. The Englishman's gun spoke, once, twice, in rapid succession, and a large cock pheasant fell, and again took cover in the long grass.

Excitedly we commenced beating to start the laird again. Joe was jumping about on top of the depression in great excitement. Presently the bird broke cover, and raced away through a fence with one wing dragging. My pal blazed away, and we saw the shot kick the earth up in advance of the fleeing bird. This caused the cock to veer off at a tangent and make away across a cleared field, with Joe in hot pursuit. Again he fired, and again the bird altered its course.

Joe stopped to reload, and in his excitement jammed the gun. But the lust to kill was upon him, so snatching his cap off he started running after it. Joe gained on the bird, but missed with his tackle several times. At last, catching the hundred guinea gun by the barrel, he boomeranged it at the wounded quarry. He missed badly and the gun fell into a small rivulet. Joe paused not, but continued in hot pursuit, and at last managed to kick the fleeing bird high into the air. He was on to it before it reached the ground, and killed it with his hands.

We other three had followed the pursuit at our best pace, and when the kill was finished the girl collapsed on the ground, overcome with laughter.

Joe came back to us with the bird in his hand and a sheepish grin on his honest face. Suddenly he remembered the gun, and had to wade into the small stream and fish the valued piece from the bed. My pal was full of apologies, but our hostess told him not to worry about the gun, which was not seriously damaged, and that the story of how he had killed that pheasant would go around local shooting parties for many years.

On 1 January 1919, I was ordered to report to A.I.F. Headquarters for embarkation to Australia. My transport was the troopship *Berrima* then lying at Plymouth.[2] A taxi took me to Paddington Station upon the first stage of my journey.

Many times during the last three years had I visualized the joy of setting out for home again. During that taxi journey across London I tried to enthuse over the fact that I was homeward bound; to my dismay I utterly failed. I tried to fight down my sorrow at the passing of the army life by telling myself that I was sick, that once the period of idleness was at an end it would pass. But this morning my wretchedness was not to be denied. I reached the ship in darkness. Among those on board I was delighted to recognize several friends, one of them Joe the pheasant killer.

But, on the whole, the voyage was one of the most unpleasant periods of my army life. There were some men on board whose 'active service' had been spent mostly in the clinks in England. The authorities were glad to get rid of these trouble-mongers, but we had to suffer their company. Entering warmer climes I again became ill from the effects of gas. This was general with men on board who had been gassed during the fighting. I lost my voice, spat blood, my face took on the hue of a banana, and the lassitude and depression were extreme. At no ports of call before reaching Australia were we allowed off the ship, because of the pneumonic influenza epidemic then raging in most countries of the world.

We entered Sydney at last, and I met my mother again on 22 February 1919, at the doorway of the home whence, nearly four years before, I had set out on the great adventure.

Many people in Australia have never appreciated how the war menaced them and their freedom or what the service of the A.I.F. meant. The army life in which we served is a thing which the nation seems, in ignorance or suspicion, to have placed apart, as an episode in history not yet capable of being understood.

Through the annals of the races of mankind there are to be observed three great factors that have made men soldiers. In the days of the Crusaders and for some centuries later religion was the incentive to military prowess. But, excepting with the Arabs and some Asiatics, this died out with Cromwell's Ironsides. Patriotism still enables men to surmount the stress of war and makes great soldiers of Frenchmen and

Germans. But with the staider Anglo-Saxon this is not the chief agent making the fighting quality of the soldier.

The British Army's fighting spirit is based on regimental tradition. In every British regiment the glory of its traditions, recalled often (and thus most easily instilled into the recruit) by so small a thing as some detail of dress, readily develops an *esprit de corps* upon which the regiment relies.

What, then, was the inspiration in the Australian Imperial Force? Even the most caustic critics cannot deny the fact that the Australians were first-class fighting men. On what foundations was this battle spirit established? Religion can be discarded. Patriotism? – we were too British for that. Tradition? – what traditions had we? Probably the very lack of tradition made the Australian soldier jealous of the honour of his particular unit. When his battalion or battery had been through the testing furnace of battle, and emerged with general honour and personal pride to the individual, the foundation of his *esprit de corps* was laid. The camaraderie of an Australian battalion was wonderful. The subordinate leaders had mostly risen from the ranks, were trusted by the men they commanded, and were in turn confident of their men. Woe betide a slacker or a schemer; the men themselves dealt with him! The Australians' love of sport, too, taught them team-work, initiative, self-reliance.

Last of all was the Australian's vanity. His vanity made him spend his pay when on leave to buy breeches, tunic, boots, and hat to please his own fastidious eye. This showed the pride that he had in himself. No man, as a rule, who lacks personal pride will make a good soldier. The Australian was full of this qualification; and it stuck to him in many a tight corner. Those who knew him well enough to guess his thoughts were not surprised that they ran: 'What! Let a bloody Fritz lick me!' It was his vanity that made him think thus, and he mostly lived up to it until his last gasp. Sport, camaraderie, and vanity made of the Australian what patriotism did of the French, and tradition of the British soldier.

The German mixture of patriotism, hate, and iron discipline made a wonderful fighter. But individually the German lacked something vital; otherwise they would have won the war before the end of 1915. Was it the teamwork taught by sport that they lacked? The German nation's whole-hearted interest in athletics today suggests an answer.

The war is now a thing of the distant past, and a new generation does not hesitate to express its revulsion of feeling from that great catastrophe. It is the fashion to depict the war solely as ghastly, sordid, even unnecessary. It would be just as unfair to show the 'piping days of peace' in scenes in our hospitals, great city slums, or the lives of debased men and women who live lower than animals in the midst of civilization. The Allies fought against the greatest military machine that ever the world knew to preserve their freedom and their right to work out their destinies in their own way.

Some pacifists, idealists, and politicians ignore this truth. Germany armed and schooled her people for many years towards one end – the conquest of other nations. In self-defence those other nations had to fight.

No one wishes to glorify war; but any man who saw it at first hand for any length of time realized that through all the horror, filth, and suffering there shone something inspiring, stimulating, sacred. This was the heroism, the selflessness of the men who fought for their country, died for their country, taking only what consolation there is in the submerging of self in country. Each soldier who was spared after chancing his all in the gamble with death must feel a deep satisfaction in his heart that he truly *did his bit* – for the honour of his country and his home.

To the youth of Australia, those who were boys when their brothers and fathers fought for this country of ours, there is something I would say in a final word. You may hear on many occasions criticisms that suggest to you that we fought at the bidding of a moneyed clique, or that the men of Australia were sacrificed to help England. The truth is that the Australians who fought during the Great War on Gallipoli, in France, in Palestine, and on the high seas were defending their land from invasion and subjection as surely as if they had fought in trenches round Sydney. A creed of selfishness and materialism has grown up among us. But down through the ages human nature has not changed, and no nation can survive, far less attain to greatness, on a creed that denies self-sacrifice.

The last war did not end war, unfortunately for humanity. Therefore, the young men of this fair land who are proud to be Australians must ignore doctrines of selfishness preached today, and learn rather the lessons which the A.I.F. taught. They will find these lessons teach a noble spirit of self-sacrifice and of duty to our country.

Note

1. The organisation was actually run by the Countess of Harrowby and Lady Frances Ryder from 19 Grosvenor Place, S.W.1. The scale of their work in providing assistance to 'overseas officers' can be seen in a report issued in March 1919 (Department of Documents, Imperial War Museum, reference B.O.4 7.2/2). This states, for example, that on any one day 375 officers were resting or staying at locations throughout the United Kingdom. Between March 1918 and March 1919, the organisation arranged visits for 1,671 Australian officers, 547 Canadians, 611 South Africans, 143 New Zealanders, forty-nine Americans and thirty-eight officers from other Crown Dependencies or Empire nations such as India.

2. The former P&O passenger liner SS *Berrima*, this ship was requisitioned and commissioned into the RAN as the auxiliary cruiser HMAS *Berrima* on the outbreak of war. After one voyage, she returned to Australia and was refitted as a troopship. Despite being badly damaged off Portland, Dorset, on 18 February 1917, HMATT (His Majesty's Australian Troop Transport) *Berrima* continued to serve in this role until March 1920.

Index

192